Gender and Rhetoric in Plato's Political Thought

Gender and Rhetoric in Plato's Political Thought explores the relation between Plato's *Republic* and *Laws* on the set of issues that the *Laws* itself marks out as fundamental to the comparison: the unity of the virtues, the role of women, and the place of the family. Plato aims to persuade men to abandon the views of the good life that Greek cities and their laws inculcate as the only life worth living for those who would be real men and not effeminate weaklings. What we can learn about Plato is the importance for him of understanding the nature of persuasion in order to come to terms with gender justice and the apparent plurality of human goods. What we learn from Plato is that to tackle the issues that arise in our new political community of men and women, we must comprehend the proper bases and limits of persuasion.

Michael S. Kochin is Lecturer and Alon Fellow in the Department of Political Science at Tel Aviv University and formerly Metcalf Fellow at Victoria College and Social Sciences and Humanities Research Council Postdoctoral Fellow in Political Science at the University of Toronto.

T0381937

Gender and Rhetoric in Plato's Political Thought

MICHAEL S. KOCHIN

Tel Aviv University

CAMBRIDGE
UNIVERSITY PRESS

CAMBRIDGE UNIVERSITY PRESS
Cambridge, New York, Melbourne, Madrid, Cape Town, Singapore,
São Paulo, Delhi, Dubai, Tokyo

Cambridge University Press
The Edinburgh Building, Cambridge CB2 8RU, UK

Published in the United States of America by Cambridge University Press, New York

www.cambridge.org
Information on this title: www.cambridge.org/9780521121484

First published 2002
This digitally printed version 2009

A catalogue record for this publication is available from the British Library

Library of Congress Cataloguing in Publication data
Kochin, Michael Shalom, 1970–
Gender and rhetoric in Plato's political thought / Michael Shalom Kochin.
p.   cm.
Includes bibliographical references and index.
ISBN 0-521-80852-9
1. Plato – Contributions in Political science.   2. Sex role – Political aspects.
3. Feminist theory – Political aspects.   4. Political science – Philosophy.   I. Title.
JC71 .K63 2002
320′.01–dc21   2001052480

ISBN 978-0-521-80852-1 Hardback
ISBN 978-0-521-12148-4 Paperback

For Anna

Contents

Acknowledgments

I thank the Social Sciences and Humanities Research Council of Canada for a Postdoctoral Fellowship, Victoria College for a Metcalf Fellowship, the National Science Foundation of the United States for a Graduate Fellowship, the Institute of Humane Studies for a Claude R. Lambe Fellowship, and the United States Department of Education for a Jacob Javits Fellowship. Together with the University of Chicago and Tel Aviv University, these five supported my research and writing.

Material from Chapters 3 and 4 appeared in "War, Class, and Justice in Plato's *Republic*," *The Review of Metaphysics* 53 (December 1999): 403–23. Copyright © 1999 by *The Review of Metaphysics*. Reprinted with permission. Material from Chapters 5 and 6 appeared in "The Unity of Virtue and the Limitations of Magnesia," *History of Political Thought*, 19 (1998): 125–41. Copyright © Imprint Academic, Exeter, UK. Reprinted with permission.

For more intellectual assistance I must thank in the first place Nathan Tarcov, whose scholarship and whose willingness to pursue the argument wherever it may lead I aspire to emulate. I also learned much from the comments of Harvey Mansfield, Clifford Orwin, Thomas Pangle, Eyal Chowers, Bernard Manin, Robert B. Pippin, Ralph Lerner, Elizabeth Asmis, the late Arthur Adkins, Donald Forbes, the late Trevor Saunders, Janet Coleman, William Clohesy, Allen Speight, Arlene W. Saxonhouse, John Seery, Horst Hutter, Carson Holloway, Gabriel Bodard, Anna Kochin, Angela Doll Dworin, and Andrew Patch. Sections of the argument benefited from the questions and remarks of seminar audiences at Chicago, Toronto, Tel Aviv, McGill, and Arizona State, and of panel audiences at the American, Canadian, Midwest, and Northeastern Political Science Associations. Much of what is right herein I must credit to these, my truest friends, but what is wrong must be debited to me alone.

Introduction

The Centrality of Rhetoric and Gender

The germ of this book was a strictly literary concern: to determine the relation between Plato's two long works, the *Republic* and the *Laws*. Both take the form of expositions of regimes that are not actual, but are nonetheless described as somehow superior to actual regimes. The *Laws* itself is very little read today, and we have Plutarch's authority for the claim that it had little appeal even in antiquity (*On the Fortune or the Virtue of Alexander* 328e). Accounts of Plato's political philosophy are generally dominated by the *Republic*, not only because the *Republic* is more elegantly written and apparently more completely revised, but also because of what are taken to be the most elementary facts of Platonic chronology. The *Laws* was Plato's last dialogue, scholars agree, citing the doxographical tradition (Aristotle, *Politics* 1264b; Diogenes Laertius 3.37), while the *Republic* is the work of Plato's maturity, the fullest flowering of his divine genius.

It is strange enough that we do not permit Plato's last word to be his final word. Now the Athenian Stranger, the principal interlocutor of the *Laws*, alludes to other writings on politics and law that may be of use to the guardians of the city for which he is legislating (811e). Our suspicion that the allusion might be to the *Republic* is confirmed when we recall that the regime of the *Laws* is always being compared to a regime where private families and property are abolished and men and women share equally in every task (739c–e). The *Laws* itself demands that we read the *Republic*. I propose here to take Plato's directions for reading the *Laws* seriously, and thus to understand the project of the *Laws* more thoroughly by reading the *Republic* in the light of the *Laws* and its concerns.

The *Laws* presents as its central objective to explain how a regime can become coherent by having as its goal a single end, the realization of a unified conception of human excellence within all of its citizens as far as possible. Yet the *Laws* is not a political program or manifesto, but

1

is directed to the readers of the quiet hour, even if its characters are compelled to act politically. For all of its political content, the *Republic* is itself even further removed from the public world: The argument of that work explains not only why the philosopher is the best ruler, but also why he does not rule actual cities and why he would not rule voluntarily even under the best possible circumstances. We must then try to explain what work these writings aim to do for their readers, if the simplest account of them as political manifestos is inadequate.

Political theory is primarily a theory of what persuades and what ought to persuade. The art of rhetoric is the art of invoking conventional understandings of the good and the just so as to move one's audience. When conventional understandings of justice and happiness are criticized, this criticism must result in new conventions for citizens to use in their political work of persuading one another. Any political theory that has points of application in present conventions, such as Plato's account of justice had in conventional Athenian understandings of virtue and masculinity, has the potential to transform rhetorical practice. Since speeches and arguments are the substance of politics, rhetorical analysis is substantive political theory.

Both the *Republic* and the *Laws* are arguments that contain within them discussions of the art and aims of arguing about political questions. They are both rhetorical examples and, in a way, rhetorical manuals. To be open to their arguments is to be open to a way of arguing that aims at complete self-understanding and self-justification. The very distance between our understanding of rhetoric and the understanding that Plato presents and applies directs us toward a rhetorical understanding of his writings. Such an understanding must itself both describe Plato's rhetoric and assess it as a rhetorical practice.

Plato's rhetorical problem can be put thus: Men and women have distinctive occurrent aspirations and desires, he acknowledges, even though the natural standard for human excellence is the same for both sexes. To persuade their (male) interlocutors to look to the single standard of human excellence, Plato's principal speakers must address these occurrent aspirations and desires. Plato's rhetoric must be gendered because the prior understandings of the addressees whom he wishes to persuade about the virtues and the passions are themselves gendered. Plato finds a gendered rhetoric useful to move the political community toward the single standard of human excellence. As long as human beings understand the standards for men and women to be distinct, Plato proposes to take up and manipulate their understandings of the distinction in order to move them to attenuate it. Plato is thus willing to play on the continued existence of a distinction between male and female virtues in order to move the two standards closer to the single human standard.

The *Laws* directs our attention to the teaching of the *Republic* on the unity of the virtues, the role of women, and the place of the family. For Plato, justice toward women and men must be defended by an argument that appeals to what is good for human beings. Granting to women their just place and keeping men within their just bounds becomes not merely a matter of principle but a rhetorical problem. Plato aims to persuade men to abandon the views of the good life that the regime and laws inculcate as the only life worth living for those who would be real men and not effeminate weaklings. Since we do not think of gender justice as a rhetorical problem, we have few resources to deal with the rhetorical problems that it in fact presents to us, the problems of living together as male and female citizens who deliberate together and share – without legal regard for sex – in ruling and being ruled. We learn from Plato that we must comprehend the proper bases and limits of persuasion to tackle the issues that arise in our new moral community of men and women.

I will explore Plato's principal and longest political dialogues, the *Republic* and the *Laws*, with a view to examining three spheres where his critique of the Greek ideals of masculinity plays a crucial part: in war, in the constitution of the family, and in the regulation of sexuality. Because women do not participate (or ought not participate) in war, the essential activity of the city, women are not usually called citizens in actual cities.[1] The city considers women to possess the martial virtue of courage or manliness (*andreia*) only in a secondary sense. As Aristotle writes, "a man would appear to be a coward if he were only as brave as a brave woman." Courage is the manly virtue simply, and the courage ascribed to women is not thought to be the same thing as the courage ascribed to men (*Politics* 1277b; cf. 1260a). War in actual Greek cities was both the fundamental manly activity and the fundamental political activity, so I assess Plato's transformation of the manly ideal by examining his transformation of military practice.

---

[1] Gould 1980, 40. Female children born to an Athenian man were not presented to the phratry, the first step toward securing due political rights for a boy (Gould 1980, 21). An Athenian man is generally referred to as a *politēs*, a participant in the Athenian regime, while an Athenian woman is merely an *astē*, a "townswoman," a member of the community of families that reside in Athens (Patterson 1986). The Athenians told and reenacted in ritual the story of the first male Athenian, Ericthonius – but they had no tale of the origin of the first Athenian woman. Ericthonius was paired on the Acropolis with Pandora, the first of womankind simply (Loraux 1993, 10). When women set themselves up as a political community at Athens in Aristophanes' *Lysistrata*, they do so as the people of women, divided only by residence among the cities of Greece (*Lysistrata* 29–41; Loraux 1993, 118, 152–3; on a similar point in the *Thesmophoriazusae*, see Vidal-Naquet 1986, 216). "The sole civic function of women," as Vidal-Naquet tells us, "was to give birth to citizens" (1986, 145).

The family is constituted by the laws and customs of the city inasmuch as these laws regulate marriage, prohibit adultery, fix inheritance, and give women and men their tasks in public life. In actual Greek cities, the household or *oikos* was constituted as a space in which the *polis* wielded power only indirectly, for the authority of the city over women and slaves was mediated through the male *kurios*, the legal head of the household.

Sexual matters, "the things of Aphrodite" in Greek euphemism, always encompassed both homosexual and heterosexual relations. The Greek ideals of masculinity influenced a man's choice between these relations insofar as his notion that women are inferior moved him to pick a partner of the superior sex.[2] In addition, the sharp division of gender roles appears to allow friendship to play a greater part in sexual relationships between men than in sexual relationships between men and women. Lovers desire to become friends, sharing to an ever greater extent in each other's lives in every area, but lovers of opposite sexes find that the demands of their individual roles are so different in kind as to seemingly leave little room for joint activity. If the family allowed greater room for collaboration in rearing of children and in its material life, friendship would play a larger role in heterosexual relations. This would require a transformation of the role of the husband from sovereign lord of the household to partner and collaborator.[3] Plato, however, chooses a different route: he argues that the city ought to limit the importance of the family and make men and women collaborators not in family life, but in civic life.

In a city ruled by law, a city's mode of war, its form of family life, and its sexual norms are all creatures of its laws. From gender and politics I move to an exploration of gender and law. Plato emphasizes the political limitations of law and also, perhaps paradoxically, that the law and the speeches it licenses or mandates form the souls of the citizens. The

[2] See, famously, the speech of Pausanias in Plato's *Symposium* (180c–185c), as well as the apologies for pederasty in Plutarch's *Erotic Essay*.

[3] This is, of course, the liberal vision of marriage between equals foreshadowed in Locke's critique of Filmer in the *Two Treatises of Government* (see *First Treatise* secs. 47–8, 61; *Second Treatise* secs. 53, 65, 77–86). This ideal of liberal marriage was brought to full expression in Wollstonecraft's *Vindication of the Rights of Women* and by her marriage to William Godwin, and, more famously, by John Stuart and Harriet Taylor Mill. In Wollstonecraft's writings, this new ideal of marriage is marked in part by an attempt to minimize the importance of sexual relations between husband and wife. As Andrew Sullivan writes, "One of the least celebrated but most important achievements of the increasingly successful battle for women's equality is that it has properly expanded the universe of friendship for both men and women and made marriage more of a setting for friendship than for love" (1999, 207).

limitations of law prove limitations on the power of the city to remedy gender injustice; the psychology of law-abidingness and dissent determines how law's limits produce resistance to the law on the part of the governed.

The problem of masculinity is both political and psychological, and so its diagnosis and treatment are part of Plato's single science of city and soul. Plato asks men to cure themselves of the disease of masculinity by choosing how to live based on a careful examination of their true alternatives. Men can choose for themselves, Plato believes, what is truly good from the ideal of the masculine that their city and its laws have set out for them. Men can make such a choice, Plato says, because they can think of themselves as only contingently male: In the language of the myth of Er, men could choose to be born women next time (*Republic* 618b2, 620b7–c2). In this life, men can choose good features of what their city regards as a woman's character and good features of what it regards as a man's to weave for themselves a truly human and virtuous way of life.

Yet Plato teaches in the *Laws* that the full spectrum of choices that includes the ideal of the philosopher is available to men and women only as individuals. As citizens we come together as members of families, with ties to particular persons that compel us to distinguish sharply between private and public spheres. If our already existing families are ruled by fathers, a regime built from these families must be a *patriarchal* regime. The regime itself will support the authority of fathers and husbands over the persons and bodies of women, and in law and in public life women will be recognized as subordinates. Nonetheless, Plato claims, actual patriarchal politics can be reformed and improved in the light of the ideal of human excellence.

In Chapter 1 I discuss gender relations as a rhetorical problem. Contemporary moral theory and social science have obscured the rhetorical situation, and have left us ill-equipped to handle the challenge of integrating men and women into a rhetorical "we" that can speak and be spoken about. I then explicate the rhetorical problem that Plato confronted in attempting to defend philosophy as the best life against the ordinary Greek conceptions of the manly life. Plato redefines male excellence to cure Greek cities and their male citizens of the psychic diseases that were their conceptions of masculinity. To do so, he must overcome the radical separation of gender roles that Greek cities expressed by distinguishing male from female virtues.

In Chapter 2, I investigate Plato's psychology and its relation to the problem of the unity of the virtues. Plato explains psychic conflict by partitioning the desires, and he presents the virtues as attempts to resolve the conflict by organizing the desires in hierarchies aimed at final goods.

Conflict among the virtues, and in particular the conflict between
courage or manliness and what Arthur Adkins (1960) called the "quiet
virtues" of justice and moderation, implies a plurality of the goods aimed
at by the various virtues. Plato aims to give an account of human excellence that unifies the virtues, that places each good within a consistent
and complete conception of the good of the whole individual. This conception can be implemented by a regime because, Plato claims, law itself
is internalized within the soul as a pull on desires. Yet, while such a
process of the internalization of law empowers the speeches of the law
to turn our soul around to the good, it also, in actual regimes, puts the
law into the soul as it is, with all its existing defects. The excessively masculine ideals that an actual law embodies, Plato implies, are already
present within us as an obstacle to our psychic reformation. Colored by
these manly aspirations, citizens see justice as the good of other men. To
defend justice as the good of one's own soul, Plato's Socrates must challenge his interlocutors' received conceptions of the good and the manly.

In Chapter 3, I consider the critique of manliness in the *Republic* as
a crucial part of the defense of the life of the just man against the life of
the tyrant. I show how Socrates refutes the pretensions of manly tyranny
by providing an account of the soul that completes the partial psy-
chologies implicit in the views of Cephalus, Thrasymachus, Glaucon, and
Adeimantus. I then discuss the critique of the heroic conception of masculinity that emerges in Socrates' description of the education of the
warrior-guardians of *Republic* II–IV.

Chapter 4 elucidates the three waves of *Republic* V as the radical core
of Socrates' defense of justice against the purportedly manly life of the
tyrant. The city described in *Republic* II–IV fails to meet the manly challenges to justice of Thrasymachus, Glaucon, and Adeimantus because
that city's understanding of justice is distorted by the civic conception of
manliness. This second city inculcates self-control in its warriors in order
to make them capable of getting more for the city. The best city of *Republic* V–VII is saved from this civic version of manly injustice because it
incorporates the female within the city and its military life, and because
it engages in war in order to moderate and educate its enemies, not to
subjugate and pillage them.

I then reconstruct Socrates' arguments for the equality of men and
women, and I discuss the connection between his argument for sexual
egalitarianism and his argument for the abolition of the family. Many
scholars have claimed that the communism of the *Republic* denies our
separate selfhood, but Socrates' apology for communism is in fact pred-
icated not on unselfishness but on a radical selfishness that denies the
inherent goodness of family ties. Socrates uses the critique of manliness
he has developed to diagnose the ills of actual cities in *Republic* VIII.

I conclude by discussing how the best city remains relevant for us as an alternative to patriarchal politics that is naturally best if actually unattainable.

Chapter 5 explores the contradiction between Socrates' egalitarianism in the *Republic* and the Athenian Stranger's apparent inegalitarianism in the *Laws*. The Athenian Stranger attacks the regimes of Sparta and Crete for fostering excessive manliness in their men and for not incorporating women into public life and military training, yet his own regime discriminates against women in the allocation of public responsibilities and in its education. The regime of the *Laws* excludes women because it requires the sovereignty of general law, and law must discriminate against talented women because of the general failings of women in a patriarchal regime.

In Chapter 6, I argue that the failure of the regime of the *Laws* to emancipate women is connected to the failure of that regime to reconcile manliness and moderation in a single human excellence. Since the regime of the *Laws* distorts the true human excellence, it requires an ever-vigilant body within it to prevent further distortions, a Nocturnal Council to keep watch over the laws. Yet the Nocturnal Council in the regime has a problematic place in the dramatic context of the dialogue. Because the Nocturnal Council is all-male, women are excluded from philosophy as institutionalized in the second-best city; I will therefore examine the relationship between manliness and the desire for wisdom in Magnesia, and the relation between the gendering of the virtues and the psychology of deviance and impiety Plato supplies in *Laws* X. In the Conclusion, I survey the principal features of Plato's rhetoric of gender justice so as to elucidate our own situation by appreciating what in Plato's rhetoric is most alien to our own norms and aspirations.

1

Gender and the Virtues in the Rhetorical Situation

> Nor is it at all clear that, faced with the problems of our
> own age, we are at a less primitive stage of political think-
> ing than the Greeks were when confronted with the forma-
> tion of the *polis*.
>
> – Christian Meier (1990, 125)

If the political community is a "we," it is only very recently that this
"we" has ceased to mean "we men" and come to mean "we men and
women." Until virtually the present moment in the history of civilization, women could not generally speak for themselves in public debate.
In order to understand how women are and can be included in the new
"we," we must not take their exclusion as a simple and regrettable historical fact but as a cultural and ideological process.[1] In that sense, at
least, we can get some help from the twenty-five-hundred-year history of
political thought and political rhetoric: We can get the most help from
those who discussed the exclusion of women explicitly and assessed its
justifications.

Plato understands the exclusion of women and the female from political life as corrupting the ethical development of men. Unlike contemporary arguments for the inclusion of women under the rubric of "gender
justice," Plato's arguments appeal to what we, the philosophical heirs of
Kant, would call nonmoral or submoral considerations. Plato appeals to
the desires and aspirations of men that, he claims, are frustrated in the
regimes that inculcate and perpetuate women's exclusion. Such an appeal
is in essence rhetorical: Plato creates and deploys a rhetoric of gender
that can aid us in understanding our new "we."

---

[1] As Brian Smith puts it, "You have to stop being what you were when you start paying
attention to the work it takes to maintain your clear distinctions" (quoted by Haraway
1997, 67).

The problem of forging a community out of many disparate elements is hardly new, of course. The classical Greek orators developed a rhetorical art that took as central the plurality of classes within the regime and usually within their audience.[2] We, in our new and unprecedented rhetorical situation, need to develop a rhetorical art that is suited for the new public in which men and women for the first time have the full right (if only formally recognized) to speak and to listen. We need an explicitly gendered art of rhetoric, to take the simplest reason, because we now must make gender issues the subject of collective debate. Such an art must recognize that speeches are always heard with the gender of the speaker in mind, and it must also teach us to craft speeches that take account of the very different experiences of the men and women who listen to them.

1.1 THE ECLIPSE OF THE RHETORICAL SITUATION

Our rhetorical needs are poorly recognized because we all half-believe in features of modern moral theory and contemporary social science that obscure the essential features of the rhetorical situation. The rhetorical situation and the conception of politics that it presumes even appear mythical, a story of a lost Golden Age invented by Philathenian political theorists such as Hannah Arendt and Cornelius Castoriadis. We are used to moral theories that contrast duty with interest, justice with happiness, the right with the good. Morality has its demands, and on the contemporary moral understanding, one of these demands is the demand for the equality of men and women. Like all other demands of morality, according to our semi-Kantian common concept of moral reasoning, the demand for the equality of women and men cannot be impeached in its obligatory character by nonmoral considerations. Compromise on that demand may be humanly necessary, but these compromises are not in themselves morally credible. They are mere concessions to vested interests, or, to use a more Kantian tone, concessions to "man's radical evil." To build a justification of gender justice on the satisfaction or reweighting rather than the simple irrelevance of these interests is to deceive and seduce our reason from moral duty.[3]

These Kantian considerations would constrain our defense of gender justice along with other moral questions; the role of values in

---

[2] The principal recent works on rhetoric and class pluralism in Athens are those of Josiah Ober (1989, 1996). Ober 1999 explores the relation between Plato and other critics of the Athenian democracy, on the one hand, and Athenian political-rhetorical practices, on the other.

[3] See, e.g., *Critique of Judgment* 327; *Groundwork of the Metaphysics of Morals* 410–11 and n.; *Critique of Practical Reason* 84–6, 89–90.

contemporary social science makes discussions of any moral question appear superfluous and inexplicable when such discussions occur.[4] I am not going to discuss the alleged fact–value distinction, but I do want to point to another important consequence of our adopting the language of values. "Everyone has his or her own values" gets translated in the rational-choice models now prevalent in economics, sociology, and political science into "Everyone has his or her own fixed preferences about the structure of society as a whole." Some prefer more liberty, say, and others prefer more equality; some, greater distribution according to contribution, and others, greater distribution according to need. Even among those whose preferences locate them on the left, some prefer a stronger welfare state paid for by high marginal tax rates while allowing less government regulation of the economy. Others prefer lower tax rates, with welfarist results achieved through more regulation and more state ownership of enterprises. To return to gender issues, some prefer a social order that maintains male privileges, others prefer a social order that guarantees equality of all, and perhaps still others prefer a social order that guarantees female privileges.

This pluralism of and about values is itself supposed to be a fact, the most correct description of our present moral condition. Values are multiple, and at the same time, every individual is equipped with a full range of value judgments about the possible circumstances of every other individual. These preferences about individual and collective "states of affairs" are not changed by the political process, our models assume. Values are merely "strategically revealed" by their holders in attempts to deceive others and so to maximize their realization. By the proper design of institutions, social scientists who work within the rational-choice paradigm aim to compel all to express preferences "sincerely."[5]

The result of our Kantian moral theory combined with our post-Kantian recognition of value pluralism is strange. We think that moral argument is easy, and at the same time impossible. Everyone, every "rational being," knows that equality is necessary, and yet everyone who reads the newspaper or watches political talk shows knows that those who deny that, or even those who interpret equality in a different fashion – as substantive equality rather than equality of opportunity, say – cannot

[4] See, e.g., the demonstration by Thomas Pangle and Peter Ahrensdorf that the great weakness of Hans Morgenthau's "realism" is that he did not explain but only condemned the appeal to justice in interstate relations (1999, 218–26, 234–5).

[5] A superior starting point for political analysis is indicated in this comment on the role of feminist civil servants in the Australian welfare state: "There is in Australia a recognition that femocrats [feminist bureaucrats] are actually articulating interests that are by no means pre-given, and which have to be constructed in the context of the machinery of government" (Pringle and Watson 1992, 60).

for practical purposes be convinced.[6] A post-Kantian theory of values and a political science in which individuals are assumed to enter politics with fixed preferences about the policies that affect their interests can understand only a politics of interest groups. Women in the contemporary political scene are simply the largest interest group, a potential "feminist majority."

The rhetorical situation assumes rather different preconditions. It assumes that considerations of justice or of rights are not "trumps" in deliberation, but that compromise with interests and desires is always necessary and can be both morally and prudentially credible. Men and women enter into the rhetorical situation in order to *form* their preferences about collective actions and organize themselves into a body capable of acting collectively, in order to persuade and be persuaded about the existence of a common that includes them and thus of a common good. They do not compose critiques of existing arrangements that are addressed to others, "speaking truth to power" as though confident that the speakers of truth would forever be spared the responsibilities of power. These speakers aim rather to compose their critiques, if critique is what is called for, so as to constitute themselves and their listeners as an audience capable of acting on them.[7]

---

[6] Chantal Mouffe, for example, uses Carl Schmitt's notorious thesis that the concept of the political rests on the distinction between friend and enemy to expound her claim that differences over conception of liberty and equality cannot be reconciled. Mouffe asserts that the political "we," the friend's side, as constructed in the course of political action to elaborate and impose "our" social-democratic, liberal-democratic, feminist, or syndicalist conceptions of liberty and equality (1993, 68–9, 84–5, 114). Mouffe's aim, which she shares with other supposedly "antifoundationalist" Left intellectuals such as Richard Rorty and Stanley Fish, is to relieve her faction of the burden of arguing for her substantive political position. The result, paradoxically, is that Mouffe adheres to a form of foundationalism in which every aspect of her political program is supposed to be self-justifying.

[7] Elizabeth Spelman's *Inessential Woman* (1988) is a sweeping attack on numerous feminist accounts of the "condition of women" as generalizing improperly from the circumstances of a few privileged white middle-class women to the difficulties that all women face, whether oppressed by sexism, racism, or class bias. Yet it seems rhetorically unsophisticated to detach such accounts from their circumstances and critique them on the basis of their descriptive value alone. Spelman generally ignores the fact that all actual statements of the "condition of women" are offered with a view toward constituting an audience that will respond to that condition as so described. Such descriptions must be assessed for their effectiveness in achieving worthwhile goals in the circumstances of their deployment. The expression of such biased generalizations of the sort Spelman and other have described may serve only the interests of white middle-class women (see, e.g., hooks 1984, 6). Yet to assess that charge, one would have to know not only the extent to which feminist rhetoric is exclusive, but also whether more inclusive rhetoric would have better served the interests of white middle-class women.

The rhetorical situation can be democratic if the audience itself is made up of all who are understood to share in the community, and if the audience is empowered to act as a body, but it is itself not egalitarian but agonistic. Few speak, but many listen (and heckle), and these few contend with each other for the adherence of the many.[8] It is not an ideal speech situation à la Habermas: Speakers are known to lie, but speakers who are caught in a lie will find persuasion difficult to achieve. While modern moral consciousness turns our attention toward the subjective, toward what is going on within each of us, in the rhetorical situation our attention turns away from our own consciousness, toward the goods and evils the speeches present to us, but also to the motives and qualities of the speaker.[9] Members of the orator's audience do not ask "What do I really think?" but rather "What is he saying?" and "Why is he saying it? What's in it for him?"

The emancipation of women has coincided with the emergence of a politics and a social science that obscure the rhetorical situation. Nor is the correlation between the entry of women as citizens and the delegitimation of rhetoric accidental. Since the French Revolution, the politics of the class-stratified community has been under continual attack from a politics that aspires to transform the political community into a classless society. In that kind of revolutionary class politics there is no "we" that transcends "we bourgeois," "we workers," or "we aristocrats." Early feminist writers such as Mary Wollstonecraft and John Stuart Mill were themselves important practitioners of the rhetoric that delegitimated the old stratified community. To enlarge the community of citizens required that what had previously been understood as the political community, namely, the body of male citizens, be shown to be no genuine community of interests or judgments. Yet it was not merely the historical community of interests that represented some interests very poorly and others very well, but the very idea of appealing to or constituting a community of initially diverse interests, that came to be discredited.[10]

---

[8] On the tension between the elite qualifications of the principal speakers in the Athenian Assembly and courts, and the democratic character of the norms and procedures in which they participated, see Ober 1989; 1996, chaps. 3 and 7.

[9] The principal part of the art of rhetoric does not lie in the manufacture of apparent goods but rather in their arrangement and presentation as reasons in the speech. Rhetorical invention is the composition of statements that make reasons or facts present to the attention of the audience (see Black 1965, 132–77; Perelman and Olbrechts-Tyteca 1969, 115–20).

[10] In reading Mill, the best-known supporter of the emancipation of women in the canon of political thought, one is surprised to note how many of the most telling points are intended to exploit the class divisions among male voters. How can power over women be granted to every illiterate farmhand and drunken casual laborer, while control of their

Notwithstanding its origin on the Left, this skepticism about the possibility of political community given the diversity of interests has been even more influential on the contemporary Right, and could be fairly said to be the animating sentiment of the economic approaches to law and politics, whether of the public choice, rational choice, or law and economics schools.

These contemporary arguments contend that a political community of the sort that the rhetorical situation characterizes is impossible. One reply to this contention is that it is not the diversity of interests in modern societies per se but the modern expectation that social problems can be addressed through politics that makes the political community unworkable. One could thus argue that such a community of political men and women, if it came into existence, could not respond politically to the most important feminist demands. Hannah Arendt notoriously argued that public life demands the abandonment of private life and its merely economic concerns to a kind of primeval darkness. The tragedy of modern revolutionary politics, she claims, is that the cry for bread drowned out the give-and-take of political debate. For Arendt, one would suppose, comparable worth and sexual harassment ought no more to be political issues than social (as opposed to legal) racism.[11]

Arendt claims to describe political life as realized by the Greeks. Yet as a description of the Athenians, Arendt's claim that the male citizen's roots in the household were politically invisible is far from accurate. We know from many forensic speeches that a politically active Athenian man might have to demonstrate to a jury of 501 his birth from citizen parents, show that his sexual life fit within the appropriate conventions, or expose

property and the franchise are denied to educated women in the middle and upper classes? Mill asks (1988, 85–8). In advocating the emancipation of women, Mill describes men as linked together in a community of interest in dominating women, but he argues that this common interest is outweighed by the class interests that link together educated, middle-class men and women. Mill disparages the community of male citizens as unjust toward women and blind toward class divisions among men. The rhetorical sophistication of Mill's tract has generally been ignored, and his concessions to the prejudices of his readers are taken as showing the limits of his liberal feminism rather than the aspects of his rhetorical situation that he skillfully exploits (see inter alia Pateman 1989).

[11] Arendt 1958, 7; 1965, 64–5. On the controversy provoked by Arendt's opposition to compulsory school desegregation see Young-Bruehl 1982, 312–13; on Arendt's deprecatory use of "social" see also Pitkin 1981, 1998. In her notorious essay "Reflections on Little Rock" (1959), Arendt distinguishes between political reforms of race relations such as the recognition of interracial marriage, which she favors, and social reforms such as compulsory school desegregation, which she opposes. The force of this distinction is demonstrated by Andrew Sullivan's application of it in defense of the legal recognition of same-sex marriage (Sullivan 1995, 1997).

his wealth to a public accounting to avoid a liturgy.[12] No one who stepped forward as a public speaker could hope to keep his private life or character beyond the reach of public debate, because each speaker's true convictions as a friend or enemy of the democratic regime were always in question. Speakers had to simultaneously distinguish themselves from the many in political knowledge and experience, and identify themselves with the many as loyal democrats who aimed only at what would benefit the citizens of Athens. To show that his rare knowledge was combined with a "common touch," a politically active Athenian man would have to prove repeatedly that he acquired and disposed of his wealth, and that he loved and hated in a manner becoming of a friend of the Athenian people.[13]

In Athens, the citizens' knowledge of their political leaders came principally from Rumour, deified as the goddess Phēmē.[14] Character was thus always an issue, and those now infamous categories, the "personal" and the "political," were not be demarcated in Athens in a fashion beyond the reach of rhetoric to transform. As the orator Aeschines states the Athenian view:

> To the lawgiver it did not seem possible that the same man could be worthless in private and worthy in public; nor did he think that the orator ought to ascend the platform having prepared his words beforehand, but not his life.[15]

All are agreed that some boundary divides public from private, city from household, but the boundary is marked out by the orator in order to demand that on both sides of the boundary one ought to maintain a consistent character, thus making private conduct into public reputation.

If we are to look to rhetoric to ease the strains of joining men and women together as equal citizens, we can hardly ignore the bad name that rhetoric has acquired. Rhetoric, as an art, is concerned not with what ought to persuade but with what does, in fact, persuade. Our suspicions of rhetoric, like those of the Greeks, have much to do with rhetoric's claim to "make the weaker speech the stronger," to discredit the traditional commonplaces and invent new arguments that overturn received moral understandings. The city fathers of Athens charged the teachers of rhetoric accordingly when they accused them of corrupting their youth. Yet this very charge ought to remind us that Socrates, who

---

[12] On the role of the Athenian courts as sites for elite conflict see Ober 1989; 1996, chap. 7; Cohen 1995.

[13] See, e.g., Thucydides 6.12; Yunis 1996, 11, 104; Ober 1989, 126–7; Kochin n.d.

[14] Aeschines 1.127–31, cited by Moore 1984, 157n. On the role of gossip in disciplining the Athenian elite see Ober 1989, 148–51; 1996, 182.

[15] *Prosecution of Timarchus* 30; Moore 1984, 154.

was not a professional teacher of rhetoric, suffered execution for the same crimes generally ascribed to the rhetorical masters.

It is a matter of historical fact that political philosophy, the attempt to know the truth about the human things, emerges in the writings of Plato and Aristotle out of the rhetorical situation. In Aristotle's ethical writings, to start with the easier case, the phenomena that are to be explained by philosophical inquiry are the judgments that mature citizens express and act upon. The general knowledge that political science can achieve is thus a purified version of the probabilities on which the orator relies in fashioning a rhetorical proof in an individual case.

With regard to Aristotle, the philosophical encomiast or praiser of practical reason and of human beings as "political animals," the rhetorical origin of political philosophy is not so surprising, perhaps. But Plato, the scourge of the orators, mocker of Protagoras, Gorgias, Thrasymachus, Lysias, and Isocrates?

In the *Symposium* the idea of the beautiful appears at the crowning moment in an encomium of Eros delivered in obedience to a decree offered by Phaedrus and passed by an assembly of fellow drinkers. The contest over the claims to power and artfulness of rhetoric in the first half of the *Gorgias* paves the way for the encomium of the just life that Socrates blends from arguments ad hominem, insults, and myths of the afterlife in his struggle against Callicles.

In the *Republic*, Socrates is once again compelled to praise justice, speaking for himself against Glaucon's "unjust speech" offered on the grounds of natural right and against Adeimantus's "just speech" that appeals to the opinions of fathers, priests, and poets. Glaucon's celebrated challenge, the challenge in the second book of the *Republic* that invites Socrates' prolonged and complex response, is not only to show that the just is worthy of choice in itself but that it is so worthy because "justice itself is more choiceworthy in terms of happiness than injustice itself."[16] The philosophical concern with the meaning of justice becomes an example of the general deliberative, and thus rhetorical, effort to distinguish between apparent and real goods.[17] In legislating for the second-best city of the *Laws*, the Athenian Stranger makes the laws "come close to philosophizing" by adding persuasive preludes to the laws' commands

[16] Reeve 1988, 33. Neither in Plato nor in Aristotle is there any notion of moral goodness apart from happiness, even if the happiness that justice brings is strictly psychic or even present only in a future life, whether that future life is here on earth or in "another place." As John Rist writes, "The notion that a defence of morality must be conducted without any reference to what is expedient is unknown in Greece or in Greek philosophy" (1982, 117).

[17] Cf. *Republic* 357b–358a with 505.

and prohibitions, and in doing so persuades his interlocutors, the
Cretan Kleinias and the Spartan Megillus, "to endorse the language of
persuasion."[18]

Plato not only criticizes rhetorical forms, he also "adapts and
transforms" them, so that "the entire corpus of dialogues contains the
full articulation of an alternative view of what is truly praiseworthy."[19]
As Harvey Yunis writes: "Plato was – explicitly so – a rhetorical theo-
rist of the first order; and he deserves our attention for his engagement
with political communication no less than the sophists who preceded
him" (1996, 17).[20] Plato's use of examples and images, in particular,
reflects the rhetorical necessity of grounding all claims, no matter how

[18] The last words are quoted from Nightingale 1993, 294. As Cicero says: "But I think
that I should follow the same course as Plato, who was at the same time a very learned
man and the greatest of all philosophers, who wrote a book on the regime (*de re publica*)
first, and then in a separate treatise described its laws. Therefore, before I recite the law
itself, I will speak in praise of that law" (*De Legibus* II.vi, cited by Rutherford 1995,
303 n. 93; slightly modified from Keyes' Loeb translation). Cicero's claim that the *Laws*
describes the laws of the regime of the *Republic* appears, however, more problematic
(see Section 5.1).

[19] Rutherford 1995, 244; Monoson 2000, 204. Thomas Cole's even more radical claim
that the word "rhetoric" and the concept of an art of persuasion are themselves
Platonic inventions has not found favor with the critics (cf. Cole 1991 with O'Donnell
1991; Wardy 1996).

[20] In two important respects, my arguments for Plato as rhetorical master depart from that
of Yunis. Relying on a radical distinction between the rhetoric addressed to the masses
and the speech of private persuasion, Yunis sees a conscious effort to redesign rhetoric
beginning only with the *Phaedrus*. As he puts it, "In both the *Gorgias* and the *Republic* the decisive political fact is the utter recalcitrance of the multitude which incapaci-
tates communication between political expert and masses" (1996, 202). Yet although
Plato's new art of rhetoric in the *Phaedrus* is an art of turning around individual souls
(*psychagogē*), it is in virtue of his practice of private advising, which would seem to be
the veritable true rhetoric of the *Phaedrus*, that Socrates claims in the *Apology* to be a
public benefactor and in the *Gorgias* to be the only political man in Athens. His
attempted *psychagogē* of Polemarchus, Thrasymachus, Glaucon, and Adeimantus is likewise a political and rhetorical effort.

   Having asserted a radical dichotomy between public and private speech, Yunis then
claims that Plato can revalue public speaking in the *Phaedrus* because the masses act as
if they had one soul (1996, 204), thus bridging the gap between the need to address
many at once and the claim that the true art of rhetoric addresses itself to the type of
each soul. It is more reasonable to say that if rhetoric must be able to grasp the type
of soul of the addressee, speaking to many at once is only partially artful, just as in
the *Statesman* the doctor, trainer, or lawgiver who prescribes for many and varied
individuals cannot fully apply his skill in judging particulars (see Section 5.4 and
Kochin 1999a). Rhetoric becomes philosophic in Plato's dialogues when it consciously
confronts the variation in types of souls and thus its own real but limited capacity to
persuade all, given that diversity. Yunis's radical separation of public speaking and
private counseling obscures this confrontation by dichotomizing where Plato sees a
matter of degree.

abstract or universal, in the things that illustrate them (Allen 2000, 271–2).

Yet for all the rhetorical talents that Plato's Socrates displays, he remains the Socrates who refused to stand up in the assembly and chastise the Athenians all at once. Socrates presents this, however, as merely a judgment of his rhetorical situation. In the assembly, Socrates says, at best he would fail to persuade and at worst would be condemned for his advice (*Apology* 31c–32a). Instead, Socrates converses about political subjects in private conversations. He claims in the *Gorgias* that this made him more a public man than Themistocles or Pericles.

For Plato the central exemplification of the rhetorical situation occurs when a speaker with knowledge faces an audience that does not readily recognize the justice of the speaker's claim to know. This is an account less foreign to us than the Athenian democratic understanding wherein the rhetorical situation allows a pooling of the knowledge of the many and the few. Plato's account is less foreign because it was readily adapted to the politics of the Enlightenment by its advocates, from Francis Bacon to John Stuart Mill and beyond. Indeed, the contemporary notion of a political community as made up of individuals with fixed preferences about social outcomes is simply an egalitarian version of Plato's understanding of the rhetorical situation, in which each citizen is granted what can be described interchangeably as perfect knowledge or invincible ignorance, since under either description he or she has nothing to learn about common concerns and possibilities. Plato's partial alienation from the rhetorical situation, as understood by ancient citizens of classical polities, anticipates our own estrangement from the rhetorical and hence from the political (see Latour 1999, 216–65). For that reason, the study of Plato's rhetoric is a vital propaedeutic for the revival of the rhetorical that we must undertake if we are to grapple politically – as citizens and not just as objects of state administration – with gender questions.

1.2 GENDERED COMMONPLACES AND THE UNITY OF THE VIRTUES

In Plato's dialogues, philosophy and its politics and rhetoric contest with the manly life of public speaking, political activity, and success.[21] Plato's

---

[21] Here is an important point of comparison between Platonic political philosophy and feminism: Both are theories that "emerge from those whose interest they affirm," to use Catherine MacKinnon's phrase (1989, 83), insofar as political philosophy speaks in the first place in and for the interest of philosophy and philosophers. Perhaps, however, the distinction is more important: Political philosophy emerges from the perspective of the few on themselves, whereas feminism emerges from the perspective of the many, or claims to so emerge. The philosophic few do have a view as to the true interest of the unphilosophic many, but that view is secondary to the philosopher's

apologies for or defenses of philosophy must operate against a field of rhetorical commonplaces in which every aspect of political life was colored with gendered language. In Athens only men were citizens in the fullest sense, sharing in ruling and being ruled as members of the autonomous political community of the city. The men of Athens, the *andres athēnaioi*, did not conceal this from themselves with a false universality. They saw themselves as men, not in the generic sense of standard English usage before the age of inclusive language,[22] but as real men and not mere human beings (see Xenophon, *Hiero* 7.3). They entered into politics and war to prove their manly valor and steadfastness before womanly passions, and put at risk their lives and reputations to win the fame of men who proved noble and good (*andres kaloi k'agathoi*). In continually competing to prove their manhood, the *andres athēnaioi* were repeatedly purging themselves of what they saw as effeminate. Plato, for his part, saw this purgation as in important respects a corruption of men's souls.

Plato describes this corruption by developing an account of the soul as a hierarchy of desires.[23] The soul or psyche is healthy, Plato says, when its desires are in proper alignment. The individual then governs his or her life by the rational desire for knowledge of how to live (Reeve 1988, 256), and the other desires pursue only their peculiar objects, in obedience to reason's plan for the whole self. Such a rational hierarchy of the desires is possible only if there is in truth, and not only in speeches, a single hierarchy of the human goods, whose capstone is the final human good. The single human good would provide a single standard for human excellence.

The possibility of a single standard of human excellence valid for all human beings is called into question by the division of gender roles in actual Greek cities (see, e.g., *Meno* 71e ff.). In Homer and in tragedy, women are frequently condemned for performing acts that are respectable or even praiseworthy when performed by their husbands (Adkins 1960, 37). The Greeks assigned gender to the virtues because they separated gender roles radically. The radical separation of Greek gender roles is often described spatially: Men work and act outside;

---

view of their own interest (see Kochin 2002). MacKinnon intends the claim that feminism is the first theory to emerge from those whose interest it would affirm to contrast it with Marxism, which emerged from bourgeois reflection on the condition of the working class.

[22] Defoe (1971, 215–19) is an amusing exploration of the ambiguity of supposedly inclusive language.

[23] As James Peters (1989, 174) writes: "Each part of the psyche, including the rational element, seeks its own distinctive kind of pleasure and is fueled by its own particular kind of desire."

women, inside.[24] The entire sphere of political life belongs to the outside: Merely to be mentioned in public is compromising of women's honor.[25]

The Greeks had thought of *aretē*, excellence or virtue, as in some way composed of other virtues. Although *aretē* itself somehow belonged especially to men,[26] two of its component excellences are frequently assigned separately to both genders: courage or manliness (*andreia*) to men (*andres*) and moderation (*sōphrosunē*) to women. In Xenophon's *Oeconomicus* the young bride says to her husband:

What would I be able to do together with you? What is my ability? Rather, everything is up to you. My work, my mother said, is to be moderate. (*Oeconomicus* VII.14)

The excellences of women that Aristotle declares are relevant for the orator are "excellences of body, beauty and stature; of soul, moderation and a love of activity that is not illiberal."[27] For both married and unmarried women of the fifth and fourth centuries B.C.E., moderation "is the most common of all tributes inscribed on memorial reliefs and tombstones."[28] Men gain honor when other men recognize their manliness in public speeches uttered or preserved in monuments, while women retain honor only as long as their chastity, the core of women's moderation,[29] is publicly or rhetorically unquestioned.

While manliness or courage is simply male, ordinary Greek opinion assigned gender to moderation in a more complex manner.[30] Two different and contesting Greek conceptions of the good man, which I will call the "civic" and the "heroic" conceptions of masculinity, are distinguished by their views of the status of moderation. The

[24] Xenophon *Oeconomicus* VII.22ff.; Salkever 1986, 234; Cohen 1991, 72.
[25] Thucydides 2.45; Cohen 1991, 64; Gould 1980, 45; Schaps 1977.
[26] The word *aretē* when not qualified means male virtue simply (Loraux 1987, 27; cf. Brown 1988a, 60; Jaeger 1945, 1.6–7). For example, Laches claims to have seen the *aretē* of Socrates during the retreat from Potidaea: This would imply that Socrates' *aretē* is reducible to the martial and manly virtue he manifested through the rigors of that march (*Laches* 189b4–5; Schmid 1992, 89).
[27] *Rhetoric* 1361a6. These references to Aristotle and Xenophon are from Cornford 1912, 252. See also *Poetics* 1454a20–4, where Aristotle advises the poet crafting characters for the stage that "to be manly or clever is not suitable for a female."
[28] On moderation as the womanly virtue see also North 1966, 41; Loraux 1986, 386 n. 31.
[29] See Aeschylus *Suppliant Maidens* 1012–13; North 1966, 37; Cohen 1991, 160–1.
[30] We can get a good sense of the complications from Sophocles' *Ajax*. Ajax moves from understanding moderation as his wife's silence to understanding that he, too, ought to be moderate (586, 677–8). As the Greek proverb had it, "Suffering is learning," but the suffering that enables Ajax to learn the value of moderation destroys him.

true man, the civic conception of masculinity proclaims, masters his desires; his desires never overpower him and compel him to do anything unlawful or shameful. For a grown man to submit to his desires for food, sex, or drink is not merely immature but actually effeminate. In *Against Timarchus*, Aeschines describes the dissipated Timarchus as "a male and masculine in body, who has committed feminine transgressions."[31]

The second Greek ideal of masculinity, the heroic ideal of the warrior, explicitly excludes self-control – Homer's Achaeans hardly exemplify moderation. The civic ideal of masculinity must therefore contend with the heroic tradition, inherited in part through the reception of Homer, and with the constant war that beset Greek cities. Both epic idealization and military necessity appeared to the ordinary Greek citizen to validate the notion of manliness as assertive valor, and to proclaim the good warrior as the best or the only type of man.[32] As Kurt Raaflaub writes, for the aristocrats within the *polis* "there was a constant tension between personal and communal obligations – a tension that was frequently resolved in favor of the former and cause the community much harm. Such attitudes were as much alive in the fifth century as they had been in the archaic age" (1994, 129).

---

[31] Aeschines 1.185; see also Aeschines 1.42; Demosthenes 60.3; *Laws* 633d–e; Aristotle *Rhetoric* 1361a3–4; Dover 1974, 208; Loraux 1986, 45; Just 1989, 158, 166. Pace Alford, the aim "to persuade the sons of Athenian aristocrats that *sōphrosunē* is the mark of a real man" (1991, 67) is not Plato's "solution," but a crucial element of the ideology of all settled Greek regimes and in particular of the Athenian democracy.

[32] *Laws* 626b7–c2; for a general discussion see Adkins 1960, 1970; Gutzwiller and Michelini 1991, 69–71. Admittedly, the hoplite standing shoulder to shoulder with his fellow citizens in a phalanx was not the Homeric hero who rides to the battlefield in a chariot to engage another hero in single combat, though the *Iliad* itself describes the clashes of massed troops in a fashion consistent with hoplite combat (Pritchett 1971–91, IV, 11–15, 42–4; Bowden 1993). This contrast did not, however, become a conflict between heroic courage and civic discipline. The soldiers massed together in the phalanx saw themselves both collectively and individually as seeking to prove their heroic *aretē* on the battlefield (Wheeler 1991, 123). In Tyrtaeus 10 the poet commands the soldier: "let each man close the foe, and with his own long spear, or else with his sword, wound and take an enemy, and setting foot beside foot, resting shield against shield, crest beside crest, helm beside helm, fight his man breast to breast with sword or long spear in hand" (29–34, tr. Edmonds 1931). In Tyrtaeus's image, the clash of disciplined lines is itself a clash of fighters striving manfully in single combat. Victor Davis Hanson, the leading contemporary authority on hoplite warfare, puts the issue thus: "Hoplite battle, like other aspects of Greek culture, must have required a unique duality of spirit in the warrior: at once a reckless barroom fighter who would brawl his own way through the flesh and bronze of the enemy in his face, and yet, mindful all the while to do so in orchestrated effort with those at his side" (1989, 169).

The political life of free Greek men remained viable because the warrior ideal was balanced by the civic conception of masculinity that included self-control. The warrior ideal required internalized control of fears: The ideal of the citizen requires internal control even of desires.[33]

A twofold account of Greek femininity emerges as the negation of the civic and heroic ideals of Greek masculinity, wherein women are seen as lacking both heroic courage and civic moderation. Women are weak, prone to excessive lamentation, incapable of resisting their fears; they are also rapacious in their appetites, abiding no limitation of their desire for food, drink, and intercourse. The common opinions that structure the ideals of Greek manhood thus endow women with the traits that male citizens must control if civilization is to survive. Women must be ruled by manly citizens who are themselves courageous before fears and self-controlled before pleasures.[34] Women represent the forces that the city exiled beyond its bounds, mythically with the Greek defeat of the Amazons,[35] actually with the exclusion of women from the public spaces of the city when in political use. Any action by a woman that has a publicly visible impact is transgressive and therefore tragic. Even women's role as mourners of the honored dead, slain in battle with the city's enemies, must be carefully restricted if the passions the women represent are not to overwhelm the civic order.[36]

Plato sought to redefine male excellence because he saw the actual Greek conceptions of masculinity as diseases of the soul, as misalignments of the hierarchy of desires. He describes the civic and heroic conceptions of masculinity as two sets of symptoms, the first less virulent but prone to be transformed into the second. The first set of symptoms, the mild form, is that exhibited in the manly ideal of the citizen, who in Athens, at least, was always male. The citizen's manly illness remains mild because he is self-controlled. Yet, as Plato points out, the city commands its citizens to control their desire to enlarge themselves in the long run. The citizen is taught to aim at self-expansion as an individual by achieving glory in the competitive political culture of the city.[37] He is also taught to aim at the joint aggrandizement of all of

---

[33] Though Adkins' account of the development of Greek moral ideas is widely criticized (Long 1970; Lloyd-Jones 1983; Williams 1993), these criticisms focus on Adkins' account of the role of justice in Homer and not on the role of *sōphrosunē*, which is uncontroversially exceedingly minimal (see Long 1970, 123). Justice is the virtue of "mine and thine," while the paradigmatic instances of *sōphrosunē* involve what is one's own.

[34] Aeschines 1.183–5; Just 1989, 192–3, 216.   [35] duBois 1982; Just 1989, 243.

[36] Allen 2000, 112–21; Loraux 1998, 26 and *passim*.

[37] See, e.g., *Alcibiades I* 105, *Theages* 124a, *Gorgias* 485d.

the citizens by conquering other cities and enslaving their inhabitants.[38] The citizen's self-control is for the sake of unlimited self-aggrandizement in the long run, whether as an individual who achieves glory in the agonistic politics of the city or as a member of a city that dominates other cities as a master does slaves (*Laws* 625e–626c). The citizen is commanded by his city to control his desires only when these desires threaten their eventual maximal satisfaction. The city teaches the citizen to be moderate so that he can realize the city's immoderate ends.[39] Civic mores are thus but an instrument for the pursuit of heroic values.[40]

The citizen's individual self-control depends on repression and a high degree of control by others: Plato will argue in the *Laws* that the Dorians, who were most successful at internalizing in their citizens the control of fears, depended not on self-control to moderate the desires but on control of the self by the city and its laws. Such enforced control is generally resented rather than welcomed, at least at an intellectual level.[41]

The heroic ideal of masculinity, for its part, discards moderation even as a contingent good. When reapplied from the battlefield to the city within the walls, the heroic ideal sees politics as a ceaseless struggle of all against all (*Laws* 626c–628): Classes, families, and individuals contend for the prize of unlimited tyranny over the lives and possessions of all the inhabitants. The heroic ideal in its most pristine form undermines any notion of obedience to law, for what free and spirited man wishes to be a slave, even a slave to the laws?[42] Plato shows that the heroic ideal threatens to destroy political life and subverts the civic ideal of masculinity that actual Greek cities sought to foster. It idealizes not citizens but mercenaries, men who will fight anywhere as long as the

---

[38] *Laws* 625e–626c. Compare Leo Strauss's distinction between the version of the natural right of the stronger as proclaimed by the Athenians in the Melian dialogue, which uses "the stronger" only of cities, and the version of Thrasymachus and Callicles, which uses "the stronger" to refer to individuals within a city (Strauss 1978, 193–4, 195–6).

[39] As Arthur Adkins points out, while a citizen might admit his inferiority before other citizens, it would be far more painful for him to admit the categorical inferiority of his city, even as the Melians cannot resign themselves to civic slavery at Athenian hands (1976, 312–13).

[40] It is thus only a partial, if still fundamental, truth that "the 'warrior ideal' in democratic Athens was subsumed under [the] overarching democratic morality" (Ober 1999, 158). The city demands such a subsumption from her citizens, but the city itself relies upon this subsumption in her own unrestrained pursuit of the heroic or warrior ideal.

[41] See the discussion of Glaucon's account of the origin of the city in a contract not to do injustice and to punish any man who does in Section 3.1.

[42] Adkins 1960, 263; compare *Laws* 922a. For a harsh condemnation of such slavery to the laws (by Plato!) see *Theaetetus* 172c8–173b4, cited by Vickers 1988, 129.

material reward is sufficient, with no concern for the justness of their cause or for moderation in its pursuit (*Laws* 630b).

Plato claims that by inculcating both the civic and the heroic ideals of masculinity, actual Greek regimes taught that self-controlled male citizens ought to seek to rule over uncontrolled female citizens, and simultaneously taught that self-control or moderation is unmanly and thus itself suitable only for women. Plato's Callicles, for example, attacks moderation as unworthy of a real man:

> This is the noble and just according to nature – which I will explain to you now because I speak freely – namely, it is necessary for the man who would live rightly to allow his own desires to be as great as possible, and not to check them, and to be competent to attend to these desires when they are as great as possible, out of manliness and intelligence,[43] and to fill himself up of whatever his desire comes to be at any time. But I think this is not possible for the many, so they, out of weakness, blame the men of this sort, and thereby conceal their own impotence. And the many say that want of check is shameful, as I said before, so that they can enslave the human beings best in their natures. And the many themselves, because they are unable to provide fulfillment for their pleasures, praise moderation and justice due to their own unmanliness. (*Gorgias* 491e6–492b1)

Callicles says frankly what the city promulgates covertly: The city itself praises the aggrandizement of the city even as it condemns immoderation in the citizens (517b–519b). Callicles' frankness is all the more remarkable because it leads him to express openly and subversively his resentment of the pretensions of the many to rule the man who is stronger by nature (483e–484a, 489b–492c). Many among Athens' aristocratic elite, including some of Plato's relatives, had learned from the Sophists who educated them to see the unity of the city as a myth, and to discredit it along with the other myths whose charms were dissolved by the philosophic inquiry into nature. Philosophy had dispelled the civic understanding of manly excellence for this elite, while the heroic understanding stood firm and thus became the most available alternative.[44]

---

[43] *Phronēsis* is usually translated as "practical wisdom," but Plato does not distinguish between practical and theoretical wisdom or (outside of the *Sophist* and the *Statesman*; see Kochin 1999a) between philosophy and political science. Reason has only one function: to rule the whole in the light of the good. Accordingly, it is difficult to know how to distinguish *phronēsis* from *sophia* in Plato, although to translate *phronēsis* as "practical wisdom" in accordance with Aristotle's division of practical and theoretical reason gives an untenable interpretation of Plato.

[44] On the relation between the Sophists and the heroic conception of masculinity see Scolnicov 1988, 4–5. In the *Protagoras* (315cd), Socrates compares the Sophists assembled in the house of Callias to the mindless ghosts of the heroes that Odysseus encountered in Hades.

The resulting tension between manliness and moderation emerges not only in the subversive grumblings of the resentful aristocrat Callicles but even in the city's characteristic practice, making war. To be successful in war, these men must practice some form of moderation or self-control: Citizens must endure the privations of campaign and must not always be turned toward the fruits of peace.[45] Yet the purpose of this constant self-denial is civic self-aggrandizement, success in aggressive war – the rape and enslavement of enemy cities. Through their laws and public speeches, cities inculcate the civic ideal of masculinity among their own citizens in order that these citizens may practice the heroic ideal of masculinity toward other cities.[46] As long as citizens do not question the unity of their city, they see the city as the place of concord among citizens and the area beyond the walls as the place of strife with the city's foreign enemies. Through this bifurcation of space, citizens can simultaneously but separately practice the two ideals of masculinity, as the city demands. Yet every failure of civic unity threatens to bring the heroic, manly strivings of aggressive war into the political spaces that ought to be governed by the civic conception of masculinity, the civic conception that includes moderation or self-control.

Plato aims to establish the superiority of the just life to the unjust life – of the life of the philosopher to the life of the tyrant – but to do so, he must replace the Greek ideal of masculinity with a *human* excellence (*anthrōpinē aretē*) of individuals distinct from and superseding the excellences that the actual city assigned separately to men and women.[47] An individual can achieve the single human excellence only by transcending what Greek men understood and spoke about as the masculine excellence of manliness or courage (*andreia*) and the feminine excellence of moderation (*sōphrosunē*). The gendering of the virtues in actual Greek regimes occurred through opinions instilled by laws and unwritten conventions. It is by legislating for his cities-in-speech that Plato challenges the customary division of the excellences of human beings.

---

[45] This contrast between the rigors of war and the pleasures of peace forms the theme of Aristophanes' *Acharnians*.

[46] Loraux (1986) shows how the officially mandated funeral oration describes Athens as a unity, without classes or factions. Greek democracy did not so much replace aristocratic values as enable the demos to act on them: "Democracy stood, in antiquity, for a limited extension of the circle of loyalty, not for a principled abandonment of the circle of inborn superiority" (Rahe 1992, 193; see also Meier 1990, 50, 145).

[47] See, e.g., *Republic* 332d, *Meno* 71e–73b.

2

Plato's Psychopolitical Justifications

A man's maleness is certainly partly conditioned by his upbringing, to an extent that it does not seem sensible to think of his body as so conditioned. Thus his maleness must in part be a consequence of some portion of his character, not just of his anatomy. Plato finds the origin of maleness in a set of passions, and he aims to rationalize political life by understanding these "male" passions and subjugating them to reason.[1]

All human needs and aspirations, Plato claims, must be brought under the control of reason, because reason alone is competent to evaluate their relationship to the good of the whole individual. Such a rational self-justification requires one to discover the reasons behind one's desires, to justify one's motives to oneself, and to refuse to act on those desires whose reasons do not turn out to be adequate. Such a justification is for Plato the only way that one can come to own the motives one already has, both those that grow up spontaneously and those that are inculcated by the existing civic education. The great hope of this Platonic project of self-inquiry is that the desires can be brought into order – that a human being will not be left with desires the reasons for which he or

---

[1] Feminists critics of moral rationalism such as Luce Irigaray have erred in seeing Plato's drive for a rational understanding of ourselves and our world as essentially male (see, e.g., Irigaray 1985 or Elshtain 1981). According to Plato's Callicles, the philosopher is not masculine but effeminate (*Gorgias* 485b–d). The dubious masculinity of the philosopher in the *Republic* is noted by Arlene Saxonhouse (1976, 1985) and by Wendy Brown (1988b). As Michèle Le Dœuff argues, the trope of reason as male was first deployed by philosophers following Rousseau to justify the exclusion of women from philosophic circles. In Descartes, reason has no sex (1989, 102–3; 1991). Or to put it in another way, "The feminist critique of the particularizing, implicitly gendered, character of all attempts within modern philosophy to construct a timeless metaphysical image of human subjectivity" (Johnson 1994) has a target only in a certain strand of modern philosophy, the line that runs from Rousseau to Sartre through Kant and Hegel.

she cannot impugn, when all other reasons for action are weighed, but whose demands conflict.[2] Plato's argument for the life of self-inquiry aims to overcome the obstacles that stand in the way of the realization of this hope.

In Plato's texts the two greatest obstacles to the rational unification of the human goods are, first, the authority of law that commands and dissuades without apparent regard for the good at all, and, second, the plurality of apparently incompatible goods recognized by the laws and mores of actual cities. The plurality of goods, in turn, implies a plurality of individual virtues required to attain those goods. To understand this plurality of virtues we must understand its connection to the plurality of roles and, in particular, the assignment of radically different roles to men and to women.

The actual Greek city's understanding of the virtues presents us with an irreconcilable multiplicity of good lives, so that it is impossible for its law to be articulated and defended in the way that Plato demands. In the *Meno*, Meno initially asserts that virtue is not a difficult concept to explain, since it has no common structure: There is the virtue of a man, the virtue of a woman, the virtue of a child, an elder, and a slave. Every sphere of action and every age group has its own peculiar virtue (71e–72a). Meno finds it easy to say what virtue is in each case precisely because referring to the capacity for action in each case as a virtue is to say very little. It is always possible to speak of someone's virtue as his or her capacity for realizing his or her role in the *polis*, but this kind of talk fails completely to get at any of the issues regarding the goodness and the compatibility of the virtues. Socrates forces Meno to admit that the functions of men and women can be redescribed so as to make clear their need for some common capacities. Both men and women, he gets Meno to concede, must show moderation and justice in governing, women when governing the house and men when governing the city (*Meno* 73ab; Osborne 1979, 71).

Without a new understanding of the political, however, this analogy is of unclear force. An actual Greek city is governed so as to force the households within it to show moderation and justice to other households, but so as itself to show injustice and immoderation toward other cities. Manliness is needed to be successful in such exertions of *pleonexia*, the rapacious and insatiable desire to have more than one's rivals. This manliness is seemingly radically incompatible with any form of moder-

---

[2] Plato's grappling with the problem of the plurality of goods is one of the major themes of Nussbaum 1986 (see esp. chaps. 4 and 5). On the theme of the *Republic* as the overcoming of variety by unity see the very beautiful essay by Charles Segal (1978) and Saxonhouse 1992.

ation that is not subordinated to pleonectic ends. Justice thus seems to conflict with manliness, as we will see when we examine the critiques of justice offered in *Republic* II by Glaucon and Adeimantus. Glaucon states in his attack on justice, it is the unjust man who is manly and strong and most truly a man.[3] Adeimantus shows, moreover, that this attack on justice as proclaimed by the city ought in fact to be ascribed to the official or lawful teaching of the city and to the poets it licenses![4]

Courage clearly conflicts with moderation in the contrast of the behaviors and the statements of those whom the city regards as the moderate and the courageous. Even wisdom may conflict with any putative affective virtues: Unless all human goods, and thus all the virtues, both cognitive and affective, are reconcilable, wisdom may be merely a conditional good, because rationality may not always be in one's own best interests. If the recognition of the irreducible plurality of goods reduces my individual commitment to pursuing the good of my own way of life, knowledge of the good, or rather of the goods, will prove rather a bane than a boon to my ability to choose and succeed in any particular good life.

An explanation of the unity of all of the virtues thus requires an understanding of the purpose of the city that departs from actual Greek norms. Plato's new understanding of the city is rooted in an account of human nature, which in turn is founded in a new account of the human soul.

2.1 THE LAW IN THE SOUL

For Plato's Socrates and Athenian Stranger there is no promise that an adequate justification of political life is available, or if it is available, that such a recasting can be put into practice or legislated. Every city claims that the just is the lawful, but every city's young men, like Glaucon and Adeimantus in the *Republic*, demand that the just be shown to be the good. Law, Plato argues, cannot be fully justified as good, yet Socrates and the Athenian Stranger demand an (albeit qualified) adherence to the law of one's own city in spite of its defects.

Worse, even our opinions about the good, when we come to inquire into it, are learned in the first place from our laws. The cave, Socrates says, is "the first home" (*Republic* 516c4); all of us are initially, and some of us are always, bound in our judgments to the common opinions of those around us. Among the most important of these judgments is our judgment of ourselves. Like the prisoners in the cave, bound in our perceptions and judgments to the common opinions of those around us, we

---

[3] *Republic* 361b, 359b; Nichols 1987, 61.   [4] See Section 3.1.

are only shadows of ourselves (515a). We understand ourselves as having the desires and interests that the law understands us to have, and thus we understand the good for ourselves as the law proclaims it. We have other desires and other judgments of what is good, but if we adhere to the image of the human being presented by the law, we cannot own these desires or judgments.

The regime, Plato claims, changes the desires of its citizens and subjects. The law presents an image of the desirable to those who are governed by it, and citizens internalize this image as a particular hierarchy of desires within themselves.[5] Yet the law also generates desires opposed to it: By defining compliance, the law creates the desires to comply but also the desire to deviate, what Plato calls "law-abiding" and "lawless" desires (*Republic* 571b–572b). The structure of these compliant and deviant desires in an individual reflects the particulars of his or her law, and also his or her place within the city governed by that law.[6] To quote Andrea Dworkin (1987, 167): "There is a false appearance of freedom from law when one is simply following the sexual topography the law itself has created. The law says what is lawless with precision, in detail, drawing lines the lawless adhere to."

Most citizens do not, however, distinguish between what the law judges to be good and what they judge for themselves; to use the language of the image of the cave, most depend on the images of the good that the legislator has embodied in his written statutes and unwritten customs. The good as the legislator sees it can only be available to a few, because most have no other standard than the law itself by which to judge the good. Plato concedes that any law, even the best, necessarily embodies an inadequate judgment of the good, and so the law ought to be changeable. Yet though the law can and at times must be changed, this ought to be concealed by a public proclamation that the law is absolutely unchangeable. It must be concealed most of all from those who obey the law's judgments rather than deliberate for themselves.[7]

Plato's political science teaches that the laws have intentions, just as a human agent has intentions: The laws contain a judgment of what is good, and ordain actions and create institutions as means to the realization of the good as the law judges it. The laws' intentions and judgments may not be consistent with each other, for the laws may exhibit a con-

---

[5] Among the most important images that the law uses to shape the souls of its citizens are the myths of civic heroes that law enacts as models for emulation (Hobbs 2000, 59–68).

[6] The desire to have sexual intercourse with gods, whose only existence is in the myths told by the law, is such a lawless or illegal desire (*Republic* 571c; Benardete 1989, 205–6).

[7] See Section 6.5.

flict of desires just as human beings exhibit conflicts of desires. Plato's single science of the analysis and dissolution of such conflicts, which one could call his "political science" or "psychology," but which I will call his "political psychology," brings out such a conflicted intention.[8]

To speak of the law as having an intention is already to challenge the authority of prescription. The law is no longer authoritative simply because it is *our* law or even because it is divine. We can judge the law on the correctness of its end and on its success in achieving that end. Our judgment of divinity turns out to depend on our judgment of the ends possible for a law: A divine law ought to have the best end.[9] The Dorian laws posit success in war as their sole aim, Kleinias claims (*Laws* 625c–626b). In response the Athenian Stranger asserts that any law ought to have its end in virtue (*Laws* 631b–d; Rogers 1991, 92). The Dorian laws err in their exclusive focus on success in external war, and they fail to achieve this success because they fail to inculcate the virtue of manliness needed for success in external war in their men and women to the extent necessary (814b, 838e–839b).

Not only ought the law to aim everything at one end, but it ought to look to all of virtue (688b1, 705e). This requirement assumes that the virtues and the ends with which they are correlated can be brought into harmony. If our ends are not really capable of being brought into coherence with one another, then consistency is no virtue in laws or in human beings. Only if a citizen who lives within the law is able to inquire into the goodness of the law can there be a true unity of the goods, because only then can the life of inquiry or the philosophic life and the life under the law or the political life be in harmony with one another.

The intentions, judgments, and desires of the city as expressed in its written and unwritten laws become the intentions, judgments, and desires of its citizens. Implanted in the citizens when they are young, these abide. The Athenian Stranger expresses this with his extraordinary myth of man as puppet:

These passions, present within us like sinews or cords, pull us and, being opposed to one another, pull in opposite directions toward opposite actions,

---

[8] The notion of the science of city and soul as a single science is due to Jonathan Lear (1992). The language of the analogy of polis and psyche is present not only in the *Republic*, where it is thematic, but also in the *Laws*. The parts of the soul that feel pleasure and pain, the Athenian Stranger says, are the *dēmos* of the soul (*Laws* 689b1–2).

[9] *Laws* 630e; Blitz 1991, 188. Piety, the virtue of reverence toward the authority of the gods as such, is thus, at best, a secondary or subordinate virtue. This is, of course, a consequence of the problem posed explicitly in the *Euthyphro*: To know that the gods are good, we must know what goodness is independent of our knowledge of the gods and their actions.

wherein excellence and baseness are distinguished. The account says that it is necessary to follow one of the pulls and never to let go of that one, and for each to pull against the other sinews. And this pull is the sacred and golden pull of calculation, called a common law of the city; but the others are hard and iron, while this one, because it is golden, is soft, and the others are similar to all sorts of forms. It is necessary to assist the noblest pull of the law always. For because calculation is noble, but gentle and not forceful, its pull requires assistants, in order that the golden kind may win out for us over the other kinds. (644e–645a).

The golden cord is the pull of the calculation that is called the law.[10] The law is in essence a calculation regarding pleasures and pains, a moral calculus of which pains ought to be endured and which pleasures ought to be refused in achieving the good as the law judges it (*Laws* 644cd; see Cohen 1993, 305). This calculation is "present within us," just as our other passions are: It stirs us to action, though it is not our strongest drive.[11]

Our law's calculation may be perverse (cf. *Protagoras* 345e–346b), it may conflict with the true account of human justice and the human good, but, says Plato, it is nonetheless psychologically effective within us no matter how firmly we reject it rationally. The rightly educated man will love what the law loves and hate what it hates (*Laws* 653a–c, 659d; Morrow 1993, 301). He loves and hates as the law does because the intention of the law is itself operating within his psyche, and some of his other desires recognize this intention and respond to it. Education is the drawing and pulling of the children toward the argument said to be correct by the law, to the point where this argument, the "calculation called a common law of the city," is operative within them (*Laws* 659d, 645a1–2).

Insofar as we can choose our own way of life, it is up to us to decide how far we should assist the golden cord of law's calculation by training our other passions to pull together with it. We cannot, however, simply ignore the standard set by the law, for since we have already inter-

---

[10] Christopher Bobonich (1994) stresses the importance of this passage for understanding Plato's psychology, but he compromises his interpretation by ignoring the crucial mention of law here.

[11] Since the intention of the law is a part of our psyche, both the corruption that an imperfect law begets in the soul and the corruption from resistance to the pull of the golden cord cannot be said to come from without. To use the terminology of Nightingale (1995, chapter 4), the law is an alien speech that is already implanted in the soul when each person attempts to make his or her own speeches. Disease and vice, then, cannot be said to originate simply from outside the soul (contra Derrida 1981, 101–2; Nussbaum 1986), for we cannot strip away that golden cord within us that internalizes the judgments and intentions of the city.

nalized this standard, to ignore it is to remain ignorant of our moral selves.[12]

2.2 JUSTIFYING JUSTICE

For Plato the quest for self-understanding is a quest for the understanding of our desires. In the *Republic*, Glaucon and Adeimantus have a problem with justice because they are and want to be just but are unsure whether they should want to be (347e, 368ab; cf. Bruell 1994, 265). Their quest for happiness is largely a quest to determine what sorts of desires they ought to have in order for them to be happy. In the city of sows in *Republic* II, the only desires portrayed are the desires for food, drink, sex, and the other purely bodily satisfactions. While this kind of regime may be satisfactory for whatever kinds of creatures could possibly live in it, human beings could not be those creatures. We humans have desires that transcend the search for filling up and emptying of the appropriate bodily vessels. To acknowledge these desires is to acknowledge in ourselves our need for connection with others, for honor, friendship, respect, and love.

The love of my self, as I currently understand my self, generally stands in the way of desiring the good for myself as it is in truth.[13] To take only the most extreme formulation, according to the Athenian Stranger my self-interest may dictate deference to one who is better than I am if he or she has superior knowledge of what is good for me (*Laws* 731d–732a).

Plato argues that we are bundles of desires, where these are particularized as desires for specific things by our positions relative to other such bundles. In some cases these bundles to which we relate are other people; in some cases these bundles are political regimes. I do not desire honor in the abstract, but honor given willingly from some particular person or group. I do not desire to be loved, but to be loved by someone whom I can love in return. The human soul for Plato is a mixture of conflicting desires, of desires that do not simply pull us in opposed directions but, as in the example of the deviant desires produced by the law, actually represent and contradict other desires. Whereas Socratic

---

[12] Compare Richard Crossman, who claims, as he sees it, against Plato that "I am not free to renounce the morality of my home and country and civilization; I cannot do it because it is part of my personality and a mainspring of my will" (1959, 126–7). Substitute spring for "mainspring" (and, as I have been arguing, soul for "will") and Crossman's attack on Plato becomes the view expressed by Plato's myth of the human being as puppet.

[13] In that sense one might merely seem to be a friend to oneself, but in fact, because one is ignorant of one's own good, one might be one's own worst enemy (cf. Craig 1994, 16).

intellectualism, as expressed in the paradoxical assertion that knowledge is virtue, transforms vice into ignorance, the partitive psychology of the *Republic* transforms vice into mental illness (Kenny 1969).

Plato's parts of the soul have often been understood as different faculties having different functions within the person.[14] On this understanding the calculating part (*to logistikon*) exclusively calculates, taking into account how the desires can best be satisfied. The appetitive part alone has desires, and the *thumos* or spirited part is the origin of those impulses directed against desires that do not seem to reflect any kind of ratiocination.[15]

This facultative interpretation fails, however, to explain conflict within the soul, for parts radically differentiated in function in this way could not come into conflict (Moline 1981, 57–9). Functional parts could not plot a coup within the soul because such parts simply do not have what it would take to try to run the show, any more than a word processor could attempt to chair an editorial staff meeting. Nor can a facultative partition explain how psychic unity could be restored once conflict had erupted, since, if functional parts somehow came into conflict, this conflict could not be mitigated. If desires are blind and inherently insatiable, they cannot be persuaded by reason, as Socrates says they are in the *Republic*, but could only be held down by psychic force (cf. Williams 1973). Yet such a psychic force cannot find a place within a functional account of reason as exclusively calculative.

Since Socrates divides the soul in order to explain conflict within it (*Republic* 437bff.), the facultative interpretation renders his psychology useless for its intended purpose. Socrates in fact distinguishes the parts of the soul not by the presence of desires, since each part desires, but by the objects each desires and the structure of the desires themselves.[16]

The appetitive desires are numerous, perhaps even innumerable. We are frequently beset by desires that we cannot simultaneously satisfy, as when I lie in bed too hungry to sleep and too tired to get up and eat. This is not, however, the sort of conflict that Socrates uses to found par-

[14] Jon Moline gives a list of scholars who have understood Plato's psychic parts as faculties (1978, 1–2 n. 2), but he wrongly includes Cornford and Robinson (see Cornford 1929–30, 213–15; Robinson 1970, 43 n. 23).

[15] For passages in the *Republic* that seem to support the interpretation of the parts of the souls as different faculties, see *Republic* 439d–440b, 441c–e.

[16] See also Cornford 1929–30, 215; Robinson 1970, 43 n. 23. Moline 1978; Kelly 1989, 196. Aristotle notes that division of the desires is required by Plato's (or perhaps he means any) tripartite psychology: "if soul is three parts, in each part there will be desire (*orexis*)" (*De Anima* 432b7–8). Ferrari correctly rejects the facultative interpretation of partition, yet he fails to grant the proper significance to the structural distinction between spirited and appetitive desires (1987, 200–1).

tition. Each appetitive desire longs independently for the stirrings of other appetitive desires and has no cognizance of them.[17] My desire to stay in bed is not a desire not to eat or a desire not to satisfy my desire to eat. Because appetitive desires have no reference to other desires, there is no problem of *akrasia* or self-contradiction within the appetitive part.[18] *Akrasia* requires that some desire overpower a decision made on behalf of the whole person, but conflict of appetitive desires is a simple conflict of forces (Reeve 1988), and there is no overall judgment of what is best within the appetitive part for the winning desire to counteract.

Both in the *Laws* and in the *Republic*, spirited desires, unlike appetitive desires, refer to other desires. Leontius shows his spirit by getting angry *at his desire* to see the corpses (*Republic* 439e). The partly spirited desire to eat meat includes a desire not to live on a vegetarian diet suitable, the soul thinks, only for pigs.[19] Desires that can have reference to other desires have in that sense a picture of the self to which they belong: Thus spirited desires, unlike appetitive desires, contain within themselves a self-image and also a self-ideal at which the spirited desire aims.[20]

---

[17] Irwin 1995, 206ff.; cf. Aristotle *Nicomachean Ethics* 1111b15–16.
[18] Pace Bobonich 1994, 10–14. [19] V. *Republic* 372d, and see Section 3.2.
[20] Joseph 1935, 67; Annas 1981, 125–6; Cooper 1984, 16. Because the two kinds of desire are structurally different, a partition between spirit and appetite exists of a different kind than the distinction between different appetitive desires. Appetitive desires do not interact so as to *contradict* one another. Any appetitive desire lacks an image of other desires (whether appetitive, spirited, or rational); thus it cannot contradict a claim of which it is unaware (Plato's appetitive desires are analogous to Freud's unconscious wishes in that neither are contradictory assertions; see Freud 1963, 134). A spirited desire, on the other hand, is well aware of the appetitive desire that it contradicts or supports, because it has an image of the appetitive desire. For this reason, Plato locates the spirited desire in a part different from that of the appetitive desire that it represents to itself. The conflict between spirited and appetitive desires appears in the *Laws* as the conflict between spirit and pleasure, for "pleasures" (*hēdonai*) in the *Laws* frequently means the pleasures of appetite exclusively (*Laws* 631e, 633de, 634a–c, 635b–d, 636b–e, 637a, 645d, 647a–d, 649d–650a, 673e, 710a, 714a, 782e, 783a, 836d, 838b, 840c, 841a, 863, 864b, 886a, 888a, 934a). The Athenian Stranger mentions but does not answer the question of whether the opposition between spirited and appetitive desires is of such significance as to regard spirit as a separate part or as a mere passion, presumably of the whole soul (863b). He says repeatedly, however, that there are numerous pleasures that are opposed to thumos: "We do not call pleasure the same thing as thumos, but we say that it holds sway from a force opposed to thumos – by persuasion with deception, not by force, [we say] that pleasure does any thing just as the intention of it wishes" (863b6–9; cf. 636d). A pleasure has an intention (*boulēsis*): In that sense it is analogous to what Bobonich (1994) calls an agent-like, opinion-connected, desire of the appetitive part as described in the *Republic*.
  Socrates posits psychic parts to explain why some human beings desire money, others desire learning, while still others are spirited and desire honor (*Republic* 435d–436a, 581b). The parts of the soul are *genē* or *eidē*, kinds of desires; each contains numerous

Plato can present us with a single science of *polis* and psyche because he regards both as complexes of desires. The *polis* has within it the intention of the law, as well as the intentions of the various classes of citizens, slaves, foreigners, and criminals. We too have a variety of not-always-compatible desires – desires for food, desires to be loved and honored, desires to understand our desires. Neither in actual cities nor in most actual individuals do these desires come together in a unified persona. Thus both cities and individuals need to own their desires by bringing them into unified and coherent structures; a regime, whether in the soul or in the city, is such a hierarchy.[21]

The life of injustice is judged, in Plato's writings, by appeal to the good. This is not a superordinate, impersonal good that hangs over us or that constitutes the good of an organic state of which we are dependent appendages. In giving a self-interested justification for justice, Plato needs to show how justice in our interaction with others can be for the good of each. Platonic justice demands not that we rise above our self-concern, but that we understand what is good for ourselves as fully as possible and follow it wherever it leads. Both the self and its interest must be redefined from the conceptions we have inherited from our education and our laws. Because we already see ourselves as citizens, as participants in a political order, our understanding of our own good as

particular desires. This is clearest in the case of the appetitive part, which contains the desires for food, drink, sex, warmth, and so on. Indeed, Plato frequently speaks of this part as *to epithumētikon*, the desiring part simply (see, e.g., 580e2). The spirited part too is in this sense complex: Through it a person desires reputation, honor, distinction, and victory (*Republic* 581ab; Schmid 1992 and Craig 1994 have suggested that the distinction between *philotimia* and *philonikia* in this passage bears substantial psychological significance). It is the spirited part of the soul that expresses itself in the "masculine" virtues and affects. Finally, the object of the rational part is knowledge – most important, knowledge of what is good for the individual as a whole (*Republic* 441e, 580b, 582de; Murphy 1967, 91; Guthrie 1975, 475–6). The desire for knowledge of how to live would seem to be what Nietzsche called the "will to truth": Nietzsche's anti-Platonic wrath would seem to be directed at the right target.

Logistic reason takes the desires as given and has no desires of its own; this logistic reason is virtually indistinguishable from the Humean reason, which is "the slave of the passions." Plato's desiderative or erotic conception of reason is superior to the logistic or facultative in that his desiderative conception can account for the malleability of our desires and the fact that we have preferences concerning them.

We can form second-order desires, desires to have desires, and we have views of what our desires ought to be (Frankfurt 1971). One of these views comes from the views of our friends, family, and fellow citizens on the credibility of various desires, and from the intention of the law regarding which desires are to be praised and which blamed. If we are to articulate the structure of our desires for ourselves as individuals, we must come to terms with the articulation that the law has already put inside us, as a golden cord pulling the desires that we have.

[21] *Republic* 590e, 591e; Lear 1994, 142.

cultivated by our laws may indeed be contrary to our true self-interest. Indeed, since on Socrates' account in the *Republic* most citizens and subjects of any regime will remain forever chained to the wall of the cave, unable to glimpse themselves directly and thus utterly dependent on their inferior regime and its laws for their self-images and their understanding of the good, most will perpetually find their inclinations at odds with their true good.[22]

Formidable obstacles stand in the way of a justification of justice in terms of one's own good. Justice in its ordinary conception has to do with doing right by others and abstaining from wrong toward them, while bracketing, or at least tempering, one's concern for one's own good. Both in the speeches of Thrasymachus in *Republic* I and in Socrates' own reply, justice is most emphatically viewed as the good of others (*Republic* 338–339a, 341c–344c, 345b–347d). In Glaucon's attack on justice the charge is more sophisticated: Justice is the good of the naturally inferior, but it comes at the expense of the natural superior, the "true man" (*hōs alēthōs anēr*).[23]

Indeed, the link between Socrates' conception of justice – which as psychic health is almost self-evidently in one's own best interest[24] – and the conception of justice implied in the laws and mores of actual Greek cities is far from clear. Socrates asserts that the just man will abstain from such vulgar injustices as embezzling deposits, theft, temple robbery, adultery, neglect of parents, or failure to care for the gods, but he presents no real argument at the level of the individual.[25] Nor does the *Laws* offer

---

[22] *Republic* 514a, 515a; cf. 516a; Annas 1981, 112–13; Craig 1994, 141; Murphy 1967, 191.

[23] *Republic* 359b. It is a scholarly commonplace to compare Glaucon's contractarianism with that of Hobbes (see, e.g., Allen 1987b). Hobbes, however, uses the notion of contract to argue *for* submission to the state on the assumption of *equality* of the parties in their powers. Hobbes appeals, at bottom, to the ability of any human being to kill any other human being in the state of nature. Plato's Glaucon uses the notion of a contract as the origin of the city and its justice to argue *against* submission, on the assumption of *inequality* in the capacity for injustice between "true men," and, to use Xenophon's phrase, the "mere human beings" who are the contracting parties. As Michel Despland writes of the Sophists' account of the origin of the city that Glaucon echoes, "Their very account of the origin of cities, born of weak helpless men protecting self-interest, opened the door to those who professed to be stronger than the rest and saw in morality the reflexes of sheep" (1985, 110).

[24] *Republic* 445ab; cf. 579d–580c.

[25] See *Republic* 442e–443b. The lack of any argument to connect Platonic justice and justice as prephilosophically understood is the "fallacy" of the title of Sachs 1963 (for a survey of this literature see Jang 1996). This lacuna occurs only at the level of the individual in the analogy of city and soul. Socrates argues that the city will refrain from the civic counterpart of vulgar injustice, aggressive war against other (Greek) cities (see Section 4.3).

a thicker account of the connection between justice as the psychic health of the individual and justice as abstaining from wrongdoing toward others. The Athenian Stranger calls upon legislators to uphold the goodness and pleasurability of justice, but adds that it would be expedient to proclaim the pleasantness of the just life even if that life were not, in fact, most pleasant (663). This combination draws our attention to the absence of an argument for the goodness of justice as abstaining from crimes, adulteries, and the breaking of oaths and contracts.

Plato's apologies for justice are best understood by focusing on their target. These apologies are, explicitly, defenses against the *manly* life of injustice, which reaches its individual extreme in tyranny and its political extreme in the tyranny of one city over others.[26] Plato's account of the human soul thus cannot be separated from his views on gender and politics. He argues for justice by claiming that injustice is bad for the soul of the unjust man. In particular, he argues that the fathers of Athens and other Greek cities make their sons into adult citizens with manly desires too great to be reliably satisfied. By understanding the life of injustice as referring specifically to the life of *manly* injustice, we will see why Platonic justice entails abstention from injustice.

---

[26] Plato's principal interlocutors mention the unjust aspirations of women in actual cities only briefly, generally to illustrate or support their critiques of male injustice (as at *Republic* 549c–550b; see also Section 4.5).

3

Manliness and Tyranny

The *Republic*'s radical proposals for communism of property, the abolition of the family, and the egalitarian assignment of men and women to occupations based solely on considerations of individual merit have been the subject of concentrated attention in the secondary literature for more than thirty years.[1] This literature, however, apart from the Straussian contribution, has dealt with these proposals by isolating them from the theme and structure of the *Republic* as a whole.[2]

The true power of Plato's teaching on gender and politics appears only when the three waves are situated as part of an extensive drama designed

---

[1] The modern controversy about women in Plato has two very different proximate sources: the "Second Wave" of Western feminism, and the "Interpretive Essay" of Allan Bloom (1968). For a survey of the literature through the mid-1980s see Bluestone 1987 and, more recently, Tuana 1994. The question is too often discussed as if it could be answered by assessing Plato's "feminism." Feminists seek to expand women's possibilities in civil society and secure rights from the modern state. Yet since Plato and his fellow Greeks experienced neither civil society nor the state (see Holmes 1979; Berent 1998, 2000), the question of Plato's feminism gives us very limited insight into his project, as well as that project's relation to Plato's understanding of human nature and to actual Greek *poleis* and their mores.

[2] Wendy Brown (1988b) discusses the role of gender in Plato's philosophic politics and defense of philosophy against sophistry and eristic, but she refrains explicitly from coming to terms with the arguments of the first two waves. Angela Hobbs (2000) has now provided us with an extensive treatment of Plato's view of Greek manliness and its limitations, but she does not follow through to the consequences Plato draws from this view for the reform or reconstruction of laws and institutions. Both Jaeger and Friedländer see the discussion of the first two waves as designed to distract the reader so as to heighten the tension before the high note of the work, the introduction of the philosopher-king (Friedländer 1969, 3:103; Jaeger 1944, 2:242–6). Murphy (1967, 76) claims that Plato shows us that the investigation of marriage and the education of women are irrelevant to the main issue by raising it via an interruption from Polemarchus and Adeimantus.

to turn the reader around from admiring the political life inspired by the Greek ideals of masculinity to admiring the political life inspired by the true human ideal of the philosopher. The shocking and striking arguments of *Republic* V are in fact well integrated into the general argument of the *Republic*. Expounding Plato's prescriptions for the equality of women and for the communism of the family as his complete view of women, or as his entire teaching on gender and politics, obscures the true importance of gender in every book of the *Republic*. Yet even sympathetic interpreters of the arguments for equality of women and the abolition of separate families in *Republic* V have generally failed to appreciate the relation between Plato's defense of sexually egalitarian communism and his general political/educational project, founded in the political psychology laid out in Chapter 2. This connection between Plato's views on gender and the family and his views on the true human ideal is crucial to his political teaching.

Straussian writers have attempted to place the arguments of the first two waves in relation to the remainder of the *Republic*. These writers claim that Socrates argues for equality and communism solely in order to point to the eventual unmanning of the tyrant, and to exalt the life of the philosopher over the life of "manly" political action.[3] In moving so quickly to the discussion of philosophy, these writers obscure the political character of Socrates' arguments in defense of philosophy, arguments that have much to say on the education of individual males and females, on the constitution of the family, and on the place of war in political life. These writers also obscure the role of philosophy in human life, which for Socrates and Plato is not the mere contemplation of universal moral truths but constant and rigorous investigation of the choices that confront actual individuals in actual regimes.[4]

In the structure of the *Republic* as a whole, the arguments of the celebrated "three waves" of the fifth book (equality of men and women, communism of children and property, philosopher-rulers) have a crucial place, for it is the three waves that bring us from the city of the guardian-

[3] See, e.g., Strauss 1978; Bloom 1968, 1977; Nichols 1983; Saxonhouse 1976, 1985. On the problem of irony these writers raise, see Section 4.7.
[4] Arlene Saxonhouse's analogical interpretation of the *Republic*'s statements on the female (1976, 1985), for example, is highly suspect because of the account it implicitly gives of philosophy. As Martha Lee Osborne points out (1979), if Plato does not really endorse the claims about women, as Saxonhouse states, then he cannot really endorse the claims about the philosopher whom the female supposedly represents. Unlike Saxonhouse, Nichols, Benardete, and Planinc are at least consistent, if implausibly so, when they claim that Plato neither endorses the sexual egalitarianism of the *Republic* nor approves of the account of the way of life of the philosopher as described by Socrates (Nichols 1987, 72–3, 100–1, 118–23; Benardete 1989, 139–40, 145–6; Planinc 1991, 127 and passim).

warriors of *Republic* II–IV to the city-in-speech ruled by philosophers of *Republic* V–VII. Socrates insists on an extensive discussion of women and the feminine to solve the problems that male sexual desire and masculine pride pose for justice. One important clue to the place of the three waves in Socrates' complete argument can be found in his own description of the connection, right before he launches into the argument for sexual equality: "Perhaps thus it would be right, after the male drama has been brought to a conclusion, to complete, in turn, the female drama" (451c). Socrates' argument in books II–IV is in a very simple sense the male drama: He has described the education of *males* as guardians, in part by contrast with the Greek ideal of masculinity proclaimed as manly excellence (*andros aretē*) by the poets.[5]

In the *Republic* Socrates prescribes directly for the symptoms caused by the disease of Greek masculinity in its far more severe heroic form. Achilles, whose desires and passions, as Plato describes them, are completely uncontrolled, stands behind the valorization of the tyrant as seen in the views of Thrasymachus and Glaucon.[6] Whereas the citizen, in his illness, seeks a private realm of self in the private appropriation of material possessions and a private family, the tyrant aims at the unlimited extension of himself: All the citizens' property, all their women, every nook of their household is his to take and ravish as he will.[7] To control oneself is unmanly, the apologists for tyrants claim; the most manly life, the only truly manly life, is the life of the tyrant who never hears the word "no," whether from his parents, from his fellow men, or even from the gods (*Republic* 359ab).

Socrates responds by deploying the civic ideal of masculinity against the ideal of the tyrant, and thus implicitly against the heroic conception of masculinity that validates tyranny. Socrates makes the tyrant's lack of self-control appear to the manly citizen as characteristic of the woman whose mind and spirit are too weak to resist temptation or to hold fast against passion and grief.[8]

To make use of the rhetorical force of the Greek ideals of masculinity, Socrates justifies his new ideal of the warrior as truly manly, whereas he describes the ideal he aims to replace, the heroic ideal of the warrior exemplified by Achilles, as "womanish" (*Republic* 469d). Many writers have claimed that Socrates' appeal to misogyny shows that Plato's

---

[5] See Halliwell 1993 ad loc. 451c2.
[6] *Republic* 388a, 390d–391c. Socrates' critique of Achilles is expounded usefully in Hobbs 2000, 199–219.
[7] *Republic* 568d, 574a; Ophir 1991, chap. 1.
[8] *Republic* 578a, 579b–e; cf. 395de. For an account of Socrates' complex condemnation of grief as effeminate see Spelman 1997.

ambition in the *Republic* is to use political and educational reform "to efface female difference from his ideal city."[9] Yet Socrates' use of manliness in the *Republic* can only be rhetorical, because he has evacuated manliness as conventionally understood of its essential component, aggressive war. The city-in-speech of the *Republic* refrains from the wars of civic aggrandizement that are fundamental to both the heroic and the civic ideals of masculinity.[10] Socrates' new ideal of human excellence leads to a new account of war, the paradigmatic manly activity, as educational and concerned with the soul. Socratic war is thus no longer the arena for spirited contests of bodily faculties, so excellence in war requires more than manliness as usually understood (*Republic* 469de, 471a). If female gender difference disappears, Plato's critiques of Greek manliness make male gender difference, *as his audience would have understood it*, vanish as well. Socrates indeed contends that no art or practice is distinctively female (454d–456a), but he does so not in order to rid his city-in-speech of all feminine qualities, but in order to argue that virtue is not distinctively male.

The general method of Plato's critique of the Greek ideal of masculinity in the *Republic* is to turn male prejudice against itself.[11] Greek custom, religion, and law identify the more highly valued practices with the male role. Indeed, Greek men understood their political life in part as a defense against women and the forces they represent.[12] Yet Greek men also valued those practices that were male simply because they were male. Thus, in order to revalue such seemingly masculine practices as courage, competitive aggression, training for war, and agonistic political participation, Socrates will argue that these practices are essentially no more male than female. To revalue the virtue of moderation, by contrast, Socrates must argue that it is no more female than male. Socrates claims that moderation is truly manly, while immoderation is effeminate, allying

---

[9] The quotation is from Rosenstock 1994, 373, but this claim has been maintained by scholars from widely separated portions of the philosophic universe. For Straussians see, e.g., Bloom 1968, 382; Nichols 1987, 105; Saxonhouse 1992, 153. For a communitarian and "maternal thinker," see Elshtain 1981, 22–4; from a liberal feminist, Annas 1976, 329; from a Lacanian poststructuralist, Irigaray 1985, 156–7. Vlastos would agree, while stressing that the female difference to be eradicated is merely the accretion of conventional traits caused by the Athenian corruption of women's nature (1989, 276).

[10] Although according to *Republic* II the origin of war lies in the conflict over resources (373de), in Socrates' account in book V the city-in-speech makes war not to aggrandize itself but to educate. Through war the best city teaches her children and educates fellow Greek cities in moderation toward other Greeks (466e–467e, 469b–471c).

[11] For some helpful general comments on Plato's critique of manliness see Salkever 1990, 174–8.

[12] See Elshtain 1981, 142–3; Gould 1980, 56; Saxonhouse 1992, chap. 3.

himself, for rhetorical purposes, with the civic conception of masculinity against the heroic conception.

We must continually recall that Socrates attacks the pretensions of masculinity before an all-male audience. His occasional use of sexist language is a concession to the limitations of his audience before his speeches have done their work. Greek men understand what is good as what is manly; whatever Socrates can portray as *womanish*, whether it be Achilles' excessive lamentation or his defiling Hector's corpse, his male listeners will henceforth see as bad if his regendering of these practices is successful.[13] As Elizabeth Spelman puts it, "Although the description of behavior as 'womanly' never seems to have a positive valence, this does not mean that the behavior itself can't come to be seen as acceptable, or even desirable – it only means that, should this happen, the behavior will no longer be describable as womanly" (1997, 174). The force and totalizing range of the Greek ideal of masculinity empower Socrates' reappropriation of what we would call patriarchal sentiments in an antipatriarchal cause.

3.1 TYRANNICAL SOULS

In *Republic* I–IV, Plato transforms the question of justice from a problem of relations between persons into a problem of healthy relations between parts of the soul. By examining the psychological roots of moral behavior, he seeks to show us that the question of how we ought to live cannot be separated from the question of who we are, which is to say, what we want. Socrates' interlocutors, who are men of various psychic types,[14] reveal their most profound conflicts, conflicts both between their desires, and between their understandings of their desires and the desires they actually have. In the statements of Cephalus, Polemarchus, Thrasymachus, Glaucon, and Adeimantus, the Greek male comes on stage as riven by conflicts between male sexual desires, inherited norms, love of one's peers, and the desires for self-aggrandizement, wealth, and reputation. Most important, the Greek male is torn between his immediate wants and his desire to follow his opinion of what is best for himself. Each interlocutor presents a different side of the conflict

---

[13] *Republic* 387eff, 391b, 469d. Many have cited these sexist statements to characterize Plato as a misogynist; see, e.g., Wender 1973, Pomeroy 1974, Elshtain 1981, Irigaray 1985. Pomeroy's argument is refuted in Fortenbaugh 1975a and more fully in Osborne 1979. Susan Levin (1996) rightly points out, following Gregory Vlastos (1989), that Socrates' charges apply only to women in actual, flawed, cities. She does not explain why he makes these charges in such a misogynist form.

[14] As H. D. Rankin puts it, "In the presentation of the characters in a dialogue, there is something of the novelist's or dramatist's appreciation of individual human types" (1964, 14).

between the Greek ideal of masculinity and the ideal of a single human excellence.

Socrates' ideal of the philosopher is intended to quiet these raging intrapsychic storms and make it possible for a human being to live a complete, coherent, and decent life. Socrates argues for the life of the philosopher by claiming that this life alone, not the manly life of political action – or its extreme form, the tyrannical life – can provide us with what is good for us as whole individuals (*Republic* 586d–587a, 591a–592b).

Each of Socrates' interlocutors presents a different but still incomplete anthropology in his account of justice and injustice. Plato allows Socrates' own account of the whole human being to emerge through the contrast with the views and characters of his partners in conversation. Socrates' account of the political good for us must somehow reconcile all the traits that his interlocutors both describe and illustrate. The threads of the Socratic description of the human condition are thus spun from the speeches and actions of his interlocutors; only once they are spun will Socrates weave them into his political psychology. Tracing the threads will reveal Plato's account of our desires in their structured multiplicity. This account grounds Socrates' new science of politics, the political science that demonstrates that the regime of communism, equality, and philosopher-rulers is best.

The reader does not get very far into the *Republic* before he or she is thrown into the problem that the desires pose for virtue, before he or she sees the storms in the soul brought on by the mighty and terrible male sexual passion. Socrates asks Cephalus, his elderly host, to describe the experience of old age. Cephalus, in turn, relates that while many of his age-mates bewail their fate, he himself, and others he has met, do not suffer so:

And indeed once I was present when the poet Sophocles was asked by someone "Sophocles, how are you regarding sex? Can you still have intercourse with a woman?" And he said "Do not blaspheme, person; I escaped it most pleasingly, even as one escaped from a mad and savage master." Even then [Sophocles] seemed to me to speak well and now no less, for in old age great peace and freedom from these things come in every way. When the desires cease straining and relax, in every way Sophocles' thing comes about: it is to be freed from very many raving masters. (329b7–d1)

To live well, Cephalus implies, is not to subjugate one's desires, for that is impossible. They, not we, are the masters (Benardete 1989, 13). We can thus live well only insofar as the desires no longer pull us,[15] and only

---

[15] Nussbaum 1980, 405; 1986, 137.

divine intervention (which we entreat through pious acts) can save us from the consequences of our service to these mad masters. The desires, especially the sexual desires, are simply alien and disruptive to the business of living.[16] If, however, to live in the fullest sense includes having sexual desires, then the task of living well includes controlling them properly while they are still active.

The way of Cephalus is the way of death more thoroughly than the way of the philosopher even in its most body-hating extreme in the *Phaedo*: The philosopher aims to live *with his desires* as far as possible as though he had no desires (*Phaedo* 81–3), while Cephalus wants (and wanted even as a young man) to have no desires simply. "Even then, Sophocles seemed to me to speak well, and now no less," Cephalus admits.[17] The way of Cephalus thus denies the possibility of a good life and holds out nothing but the consolation of a good death – if we do not cease appeasing the gods and thus win sufficient favor to avoid suffering in some future existence.[18] There is no harbor from the storms of our passions, Cephalus claims, and especially from the tempest of male sexual desire, except in the shadow of the grave. Then, at last, passion dies, fears triumph.

Polemarchus, the heir to his father Cephalus's argument, defends justice as aiding friends and harming enemies (332ab). Polemarchus expresses the typical Greek view of the *agathos kai dikaios anēr*, the good and just man.[19] As Socrates jests, Polemarchus could easily have learned his account of justice from Homer (334ab).[20] If our friends are those who are useful (*chrēstoi*) to us, Socrates points out, each individual would be his own best friend (334c). With the help of this Socratic, utilitarian emendation of "Homeric" justice, Socrates characterizes Polemarchus's definition of justice as suitable for a tyrant, the only man whose self-interest appears unbounded by any ties of affection to others.[21]

---

[16] Strauss 1978, 66; and compare the account of oligarchic man at *Republic* 554.

[17] In his impressive analysis of Cephalus's character and opinions, Peter Steinberger sees him as exemplifying democratic man, whose desires are governed by a kind of chance equality (1996, 185–9). Yet the anxiety that Cephalus expresses and – more importantly – claims always to have felt about his desires does not fit with Socrates' subsequent image of democratic man allowing himself to be governed equitably by his desires in regular rotation (561a–562a).

[18] Cf. Nichols 1987, 54.

[19] Adkins 1960, 269. Friedländer incorrectly labels Polemarchus's view as characteristic of the money-loving spirit of a successful merchant (1964–9, 2:53, 57). Polemarchus's view is rather that of every Greek hero and warrior; see, e.g., Sophocles, *Ajax* 95–117.

[20] On the sources of Polemarchus's views see Rahe 1992, 848 n. 37.

[21] *Republic* 336a. Note that since the tyrant's soul is ruled by the lawless desire to sleep with parents and gods, he is not independent but radically dependent on others (571cd, 574a–c; Benardete 1989, 207).

Good-natured (*euēthēs*) as he is, Polemarchus fails to follow this "Homeric" view to its logical conclusion. Gentlemanly Polemarchus readily admits that tyranny is necessarily evil, so Socrates' critique forces him to vacate his proposed definition of justice.

Yet although Polemarchus yields, his definition of justice poses an abiding problem. We do, in fact, have friends and enemies, kinsmen and strangers, whom we have somehow managed to acquire without much regard for their usefulness to us.[22] Socrates simply assumes here that we can and ought to reconstruct these ties based on our judgment of how we will benefit from them.[23] In the *Protagoras*, Socrates interprets another poem of Simonides as claiming that we ought to credit our actual ties even when they bind us to perverse relations (345e–346e). The Socrates of the *Euthyphro* is not so ready to concede that a man's obligations to his father are so easily overridden by claims about justice and the general good. The best regime of the *Republic* requires the abolition of our actual family ties in favor of a new political superfamily; we must wonder whether the goodness, naturalness, and justice of the regime should persuade us to concur in this abolition.

Whereas for Polemarchus the just man is truly manly, for Thrasymachus the life of injustice is the manly, grown-up life because it promises the greatest material abundance (343a–344c). Thrasymachus agrees with Socrates that all human relationships are founded on the expectation of some good, but unlike Socrates he restricts the goods to the tangible (343e). According to Thrasymachus, the tyrant lives best because he plunders most from every quarter (344a). Thrasymachus describes man as desiring only the grossest material possessions; his man has no use for honor or any of the goods that come from reputation. For Cephalus the sexual desires make psychic reconciliation impossible, but Thrasymachus leaves out these desires in his description of man: He does not think to mention that all the women of the city are the tyrant's for the taking (see *Republic* 344a–c). His speech or theory takes no account of motives or desires arising from human interaction and no account of the desires that Socrates will later describe as spirited.

Yet by his own behavior, Thrasymachus refutes his simplistic picture of man as seeking only material rewards. He claims to want to speak for the sake of the promised wage, but he clearly wants to speak for the applause and approval he believes will come to him for his superior

---

[22] See Cross and Woozley 1966, 19.

[23] Mary Nichols writes that "Polemarchus seems to have given up his friends for the sake of justice" (1987, 46–7). I would say rather that Polemarchus qualifies friendship to the point of abandoning it for the sake of the good.

definition of justice (338a). Nor does Thrasymachus hesitate to impute the desire for honor (*philotimia*) to Socrates (336c). By portraying this inconsistency between expressed judgment and sophisticated explanation, Plato shows Thrasymachus as failing to reflect even on his most recent judgments. Thrasymachus's answer to the question of justice fails because he fails to put himself into the scope of the question; his life manifests desires for respect and reputation that his account of the human good omits.[24] In terms of the psychological theory Socrates will develop in book IV, man as described by Thrasymachus lacks spirited desires and, perhaps more strikingly, even sexual appetites.

Glaucon's apology for injustice at the beginning of *Republic* II is based on a depiction of human desires more comprehensive than that of Cephalus or Thrasymachus. Glaucon shows us the desires of Everyman, under conditions of utter license, through the tale of "the ancestor of Gyges the Lydian," who found a ring that could make the wearer invisible at will (359). When this ancestor of Gyges realized the power of the ring, his first move was not to rob, as a Thrasymachean tyrant would, but to seduce. After he had perceived the power of his ring, he arranged to be sent to the king of Lydia. "After he arrived, he seduced the king's wife; then plotting with her, he killed the king and took over his position" (360ab).

The protagonist's motives in Glaucon's myth seem oddly mixed. His first desire is to sleep with the queen, and only after he has plotted with her does he seek to usurp the king's power in addition to his wife. Yet why would someone who in virtue of his invisibility was "equal to a god" (360c) seek to rule among men? For the man possessing the ring of Gyges, it is possible "to take what he wishes from the market without fear, and going into others' houses to have intercourse with whomever he wishes, and to kill and free from bonds whomever he wishes" (360bc). An invisible man can take whatever he pleases without putting on the yoke of office. If the hero of Glaucon's tale wanted to be king, ruling itself must satisfy some desire of his that simple taking could not.[25] Glaucon's anthropology thus includes some sort of desire for recognition, for being *visibly* honored, that is different from the merely material lusts Thrasymachus has described. Socrates will ground this lust for domination in the soul by adding a spirited part to the desiring part that

---

[24] C. D. C. Reeve and Angela Hobbs both correctly describe Thrasymachus as a lover of honor (Reeve 1988, 41; Hobbs 2000, 170), but it is equally important to note that Thrasymachus's own character is richer than his account of our desires.

[25] Gyges does not wish to remain invisible but rather takes off his ring in order to rule and to be seen ruling. This saves the view of happiness he instantiates from the adolescence charged by Despland (1985, 365–6 n. 213).

is the only irrational part implied by the speeches (not the character!) of Thrasymachus.

It is no accident that Glaucon speaks of men rather than human beings, for his case against justice, like that of Thrasymachus, relies in part on the proclaimed manliness of the life of injustice. He who is "truly a man" would never agree to abstain from injustice, and anyone who would refrain from injustice when he could get away with it would appear "most weak" and "senseless" (359b, 360d). The perfectly unjust man who appears just lives the active life of a citizen, while the just man who appears unjust ends his life as a base victim of civic injustice (361e–362c).

Glaucon agrees with Cephalus that we are at bottom slaves of our desires, that no power within us can save us from the temptation of the unjust life. If anyone could acquire a ring of Gyges, "no one could be, as it would appear, so adamantine as to abide in his justice and to dare to withhold himself from what belongs to others and not to touch it" (360b). No opinion or knowledge could save us from our desires, apart from the fear of punishment from our fellow citizens. Our life together must therefore always frustrate our deepest, best, and most natural urges, the urges that the most manly among men satisfies best.

Glaucon appeals to nature to argue that political life must always repress our manly desires unnaturally (358e). From that point of view, a defense of justice would be a defense of the city against the pretensions of masculinity. Yet Socrates' apology for justice must also respond to the politically more dangerous claims of Adeimantus, Glaucon's more moderate brother. Adeimantus shows that the fathers, the city they constitute, and the poets these laws license preach the superiority of the manly life of injustice, as long as that life conforms to the duties toward one's family and fellow citizens and the pieties toward the city's gods that the laws impose. Any defense of justice as good must therefore include a revision of civic dogma.

Fathers and poets, Adeimantus claims, praise not being but seeming just (363). The poets and priests teach us that to practice justice is more difficult and less profitable than to practice injustice. Nor can the just man expect any special reward from the gods: These same poets and priests quote Homer to prove that those who have committed injustices can earn pardon from the gods through prayer and sacrifices (363e–365a). We men are all persuaded by our fathers, our poets, our paternal laws that injustice is better and manlier than justice, says Adeimantus. Because of the actual force of this persuasion, even a man who knows that justice is superior to injustice knows that "apart from someone who by a divine nature is ill-disposed to doing injustice or who abstains from it because he acquired knowledge, no one else is willingly just, but only on account of want of manliness or old age or some other weakness condemns doing injustice, because he is unable to do it" (366cd). The just man recognizes that all pursue injustice not least because the city's case for injustice stands unrefuted.

Adeimantus presents a more critical account of actual political life than Glaucon, for he sees the city itself as an ally of manly injustice, not as an institution for the repression of manly drives. Yet even as Adeimantus condemns political life as corrupting, he implies a view of the individual that is much more harmonious. In contrast to Glaucon and Cephalus, Adeimantus portrays us as persuaded always by our *opinion* of what is best for us. We practice injustice because the city teaches us that to do injustice is the greatest good. If the city and her poets taught us that to do injustice is the greatest evil, that opinion alone would compel us to act accordingly. "Each man himself would be his own best guard, fearing lest doing injustice he would dwell with the greatest evil," Adeimantus claims (367a). Our actions follow our opinions – there are no mad desires to overmaster them, as Cephalus claimed – but our opinions are formed by our inherited traditions without regard for the truth. Glaucon claimed that no man was so adamantine as to resist the temptation of injustice without fear of punishment. Adeimantus claims that every man is adamant (the pun can be no accident) in pursuit of what he believes to be best.

According to Adeimantus, those who would educate the young men to always act justly can succeed if they but replace the city's praises of injustice with praises of justice. To accomplish this replacement, Socrates indeed carries out his theological and moral purge of Homer in *Republic* II and III with Adeimantus as his interlocutor. We might wonder, however, how the fathers, priests, and poets would respond to such praises and to those who offer them, since they would challenge the core of the city's conception of masculinity.

In making opinion sovereign in the self, Adeimantus has broadened the account of man yet again, for in his anthropology a man is governed always by his belief about what is best for the whole self. Socrates must provide an account of justice that upholds the goodness of the just life for an individual who combines the despotic desires of Cephalus and Glaucon with the sovereign opinion of Adeimantus. He must defend justice against both the seemingly philosophic claims of natural right, put forward by Thrasymachus and Glaucon, and the opinions of the city embodied in law, ritual, and poetry, appealed to by Adeimantus. Socrates cannot do all this and simultaneously retain as good our conventional relations, our actual divisions between friends and enemies, kin and stranger, to which Polemarchus, the heir to Cephalus's argument, had alluded. It is these ties, we shall see, not some lacuna in Socrates' concept of human nature, that make the fullest realization of his political project unlikely.

3.2 GENTLING THE DRIVE FOR DISTINCTION: MAKING MEN IN TWO PREPHILOSOPHIC CITIES

Glaucon and Adeimantus have described the individual as a locus not of simple unity, but of constant conflict. To defend justice as the good for human beings against the arguments of Glaucon and Adeimantus, Socrates makes his famous analogy between soul and city (*Republic* 368c–369a). The attacks on justice have shown that both the city and the soul have within them varying and seemingly contradictory intentions or desires. The soul has within it appetites for food and for sex, desires to rule and dominate, and an acquired opinion of what is best for the individual. The city is made up of rulers and of ruled, and of the naturally strong and the naturally weak. Yet difference need not mean disharmony. We are each different in nature and suited for different jobs, so to fulfill our natural wants we must come together, Socrates claims, in a city that is simply a collection of artisans (369–71).

Initially it appears that Socrates' first city is a city only of men. "The most necessary city," Socrates says, "is made from four or five *men* (*andrōn*)" (369d11). Yet when the necessary city is fully populated, Socrates portrays the citizens of this first city as "having sweet intercourse with each other, not making children beyond their estate, bewaring poverty and war" (372bc). Already Socrates has presupposed that childbearing itself does not preclude participation in an art, since the artisans *themselves* are described as "having sweet intercourse with each other."[26] Socrates in the end includes women among the citizens of the city of artisans, so that in the first city women and men are each engaged in the art that suits their individual natures.

The men and women who make up the first city come together solely in order to satisfy the needs of the body. The needs of the body, the desires that Socrates will eventually describe as appetitive, can in principle be completely satisfied, and are satisfied in the first city. In the city that exists only for the sake of satisfying these bodily needs, men and women are equal.

---

[26] Bruce Rosenstock claims that we have here a myth of fraternal reproduction, just as he rightly sees in the "noble lie" of *Republic* III (1994, 369–70). Despite the use of *andres* at *Republic* 369e1, the reference at 372bc to intercourse "with each other" shows that both men and women are included among the artisans of the first city. Socrates is merely smuggling in an assumption that will become explicit in *Republic* V, that childbearing, and thus female sexuality, do not preclude participation in an art. Women are included among the craftsmen, since the craftsmen produce offspring by having intercourse with one another.

If the account of our desires to be found in the first city were complete, we could find in its citizens' moderation and health the single human excellence available to both men and women. Yet the citizens of the first city possess only parts of the full human complex of desires, and cannot therefore help to solve the problem of human justice. Despite Socrates' apparent claim (369a), then, justice cannot be found in the first city. The citizens will live, as long as they control their population, under circumstances of abundance relative to their wants. Since everyone has enough, no one will want more; thus, no one will commit any unjust act for the sake of gain.[27] The citizens of the first city have comforts without honor, since honor can be won only in political competition within the city and in military action beyond its boundaries. Without justice the first city has no internal politics, and living in perpetual peace with its neighbors, it has no external affairs either. The first city is attractive to Adeimantus, whose implicit account of the individual portrayed us as simple slaves of our opinion of what is best for us. Adeimantus had mentioned nothing of any illimitable desire, nor in particular the unquenchable thirst for rule and reputation. Malcom Schofield writes that the first city Socrates describes, although a "highly abstract and artificial model of one dimension of human social activity," is nonetheless "an excellent paradigm to think with" (2000, 213). The first city is useful as a paradigm not because of what it tells us about the human condition, but because of what it illustrates as the manifest limitations of a certain way of thinking about the human condition. This way of thinking Plato shows to be a systematic error natural to certain human types, such as the type that Adeimantus exemplifies in the *Republic*.[28]

The first city fails to be the good city for us, because we have the spirited desires that Adeimantus's understanding of human nature neglects (cf. Dobbs 1994, 266). We will fail to find the true justice that is *human* excellence in the first city, because its inhabitants, in lacking spiritedness, fail to be human.[29]

Adeimantus's brother Glaucon, whose implicit description of man included the illimitable lust for rule, is unsatisfied with the first city, and

---

[27] Pace Vlastos (1978, 175–7), it is the absence of the unhealthy desires that cause injustice that prevent the appearances of unjust inequalities in the city of sows. Justice as it appears in the cities that Socrates subsequently describes is absent in this first city.

[28] To see the "spiritlessness" of Adeimantus's psychology, note that his later description of the happiness the guardians forgo includes no political goods (*Republic* 419a; Ophir 1991, 65).

[29] The inhabitants of this first city "sing to the gods" (372b), but the spirited, fully human response to the gods is not to praise them but to question them (see Section 6.3). Birds and beasts too praise the Lord, but even the most devout and grateful man is wont to ask, "O Lord, who is like you?" (cf. Psalm 148 with 35:10).

rightly. He interrupts Socrates' description of the city, complaining, "Without treats (*aneu opsou*), as it appears, you make these men feast" (372c). After Socrates has praised the simple pleasures of the diet in the first city, Glaucon bursts in again:

If you were furnishing a city of sows, Socrates, with what other food than these would fatten them?

But how, Glaucon, is it necessary [to feed them]?, I said.

[Feed them] the customary things, he said. I suppose that those who are not to suffer hardship are to recline on couches, and to dine from tables, and [to eat] dishes (*opsa*), the ones they have now, and also desserts. (372de)

The Athenians denoted by *opsa* the variety of foods one could eat with bread, including the whole range of seafoods from the sprats eaten by the poor to the choice eels and grayfish consumed by the sybaritic rich.[30] Glaucon's desires for luxuries turn out not to be appetitive desires simply, but also desires for the distinction involved in being a consumer of luxuries, which by definition only some can have. Whereas Adeimantus is satisfied with a life of bodily comforts without honor, Glaucon will be satisfied with a life of honor that lacks bodily comforts (Nichols 1987, 81).[31]

Glaucon's honor-bearing luxuries bring on honorable war. The necessary goods, those that satisfy the healthy, and consequently strictly appetitive, desires, are available in abundance, but the desire for luxuries creates scarcity and scarcity leads to war (373e).

Since war presumes warriors who will be guardians of the city, suddenly the nature of the citizens of our city has altered radically. No longer can we imagine that our city is made up of men and women participating according to their natures in the necessary arts. Instead, Socrates has introduced a class of artisans whose excellence appears exclusively male. Skill in soldiering seems most closely tied to physical strength, and the moral qualities of the good soldier are those that actual Greek cities put at the core of their ideal of the masculine.[32] Human excellence has no place in the city at war, it would seem; instead, there is the manly excellence of citizen-soldiers and the excellence of women, about which the city, as in the funeral oration of Pericles, prefers to say nothing.[33]

---

[30] See the masterful discussion of this passage in its material context in Davidson 1998, 3–35.

[31] It is Adeimantus, not Glaucon, who later will question the happiness of the auxiliaries because they live an existence purged of every luxury (*Republic* 419). Unlike his brother Glaucon, "most manly in everything" (357a), Adeimantus – or at least man as described by Adeimantus – wants the material goods in themselves. Adeimantus seeks the honor-bearing pleasures because they are pleasant, not because they are honored.

[32] Adkins 1960, 208; 1970, 78; Loraux 1986, 73–4.

[33] Thucydides 2.45; cf. Lysias 2.4–6.

Manly anger is not the sole attribute that the warriors of the just city are to manifest. These warrior-guardians must somehow simultaneously combine in a single soul gentleness toward their fellow citizens and great-spirit (*megalothumos*) toward the city's enemies (375c). To inculcate both spiritedness and gentleness the guardians must be educated in both gymnastics and music, but they will begin first with music, which conduces to gentleness (377a).

This first music consists of the false speeches and tales of gods and heroes, but, as Adeimantus claimed, the existing myths that form the education of all actual cities, the tales told by Hesiod and Homer, are unsuitable. That is to say, a crucial part of the city's understanding of itself and its past must be banished for the sake of the city's proper ends (see Adams 1988, 64). The inherited poetry must be purged before it can be incorporated into the education of (so far male) warrior-guardians, because it encourages its listeners to become excessively spirited, that is, to become excessively manly in defending themselves from injustices done by city or kin (377e–378d).

First to be purged are tales of immoderate anger. Cronus punishing his father, Uranus, Cronus eating his own children and his son Zeus revenging himself upon him. All these (false) stories told by Hesiod must be excised lest some young man think it just to do to his father what the greatest of the gods did to his (377e–378b). Indeed, any verse in which the gods get angry and make war on each other must be eliminated so that each citizen will think it most shameful and unholy to get angry and lash out in anger at his fellow (378cd).[34] The warrior-guardians are to be taught to abstain from just requital of injuries suffered if their relationship with the injurer is too close. The guardians will learn from a poetic curriculum suitably mutilated by the excision of tales of mutilation that the bond between father and son or that between fellow citizens sometimes ought to trump considerations of justice that pay no respect to the particular persons involved.[35]

Instead of displaying deeds of manly vengeance against enemies and kin, the poetry of the warrior's city will teach self-control. Our guardians, says Socrates, will avoid excessive lamentation, for they do not fear death as an evil (387d). Accordingly, he states, we will censor the lamentation of supposedly virtuous and manly men, such as Priam

---

[34] The poetry of actual cities is, on Socrates' view, further from the truth about the gods than the reformed poetry would be (pace Steinberger 1989, 1217). The noble lie is to be told not about the gods, but about the origin and upbringing of the citizens.

[35] On this point, too, one ought to compare the *Euthyphro*, as well as Socrates' interpretation of Simonides in the *Protagoras*. The subordination of religion to political necessities that struck contemporary readers as blasphemous in Machiavelli is thus an element of his teaching that he could have learned from Plato and Aristotle.

and Achilles (387e; see Rankin 1964, 16). Nor will Socrates and Glaucon allow their guardians to hear of excessive laughter among the gods, and the guardians will be taught, through poetic speeches, never to lie to their rulers (388e–389d). Socrates' reformed poetic education will teach the guardians moderation (*sōphrosunē*), that is, "to be obedient to rulers, and themselves to be rulers over the pleasures concerned with drinks, and sex, and concerning feasting" (389d9–e1). The poetry of actual cities teaches immoderate indulgence: Even the reward of virtue is said by the traditionally esteemed poets to be an eternal drunk.[36] The reformed poetry of the just city will teach moderation instead, though moderation conflicts with the heroic conception of masculinity as promulgated in the myths told by actual cities. There will be no terrible rapes of Perithous or Theseus to warm the loins of *our* guardians, Socrates says.[37]

Achilles, the very embodiment of the heroic ideal of masculinity, bears the brunt of the purge of poetry. He is an immoderate money grubber (390de), impious and hubristic toward gods and men (391a–c). Odysseus, by contrast, comes off better, earning mention in the reformed poetry for his self-control.[38]

Although Socrates intends his poetry to teach manliness (*andreia*) in the face of death, it is a very different kind of manliness from that of the Homeric heroes who are the exemplars for the young men of actual cities (see Salkever 1990, 187). The Homeric hero is courageous in the face of fearful death. The Socratic guardian is confident, by contrast, that death is no evil for him, because he maintains his belief in the city's teaching concerning the afterlife through all pleasures and pains.[39] These two affective states have in truth nothing in common, and Socrates' so-called manliness seems to be some sort of faith but no passion.[40]

What Socrates describes as the goal and crown of the musical or poetic education is radically opposed to the ideal of masculinity in actual Greek cities. The music education is to inculcate moderation in pleasures, and especially in sex, the keenest pleasure of all (402e–403a). Socrates leads Glaucon, an erotic man (474d), to assent to a prohibition on the consummation of pederastic affairs:

---

[36] Republic 363cd; Howland 1993, 85. See also *Republic* 390ab.

[37] *Republic* 391c; Elshtain 1987, 53.

[38] *Republic* 390d; On Socrates' elevation of Odysseus at the expense of Achilles see Hobbs 2000, 239–40.

[39] *Republic* 386–7, 429c–430c; cf. *Apology* 37b, 40b–42a.

[40] See Aristotle's contrast between the manly man and the man who is of good hope because of his experience (*Nicomachean Ethics* 1115b1–4).

You will legislate in the city that is being settled that a lover be with and touch his beloved as a son, for the sake of his beauties, if he persuades him; but [it is necessary for any lover] to relate in other respects toward whom he is serious such that he will never appear to go farther in intercourse than this. But if [the lover] does not [so relate] he will suffer the reproach of unmusicality and inexperience in the beautiful. (403bc)

It is true that this law relates only to appearances, but it is the appearances that determine what and who are honored in the city.[41] In Athens, and even more in Sparta, for a man to engage in active intercourse with a boy or youth was honored as a sign of manhood, but Glaucon's warrior-guardians will express their moderation through repression rather than their manly virtue through consummation.[42]

When the purgation of diet and poetry is completed, Socrates proceeds to describe, in partnership with Glaucon, the task of the now-educated guardians in the city. Having been taught to care for themselves, they must now be taught to care for the city.[43] Yet the conviction that they must care for the city as their own cannot be reliably implanted by an education that relies solely upon the truth. Perhaps it goes too far to say that the city is not in truth one's own, but we can say that the process by which it comes to be one's own is not a purely rational one. Accordingly, the prospective guardians must be tested, and those who fail to retain the conviction that "it is necessary to do whatever they judge to be best for the city for them to do" must be purged from the regiment (413c–414b).

The conviction will be sealed in the minds of those who survive this final purge by the application of a lie, "some noble thing to persuade and thereby deceive the rulers themselves most of all, but if not them, then the rest of the city" (414bc).[44] What provokes our incredulity about

---

[41] Cf. Howland 1993, 103 with Arendt 1958, 199.

[42] On pederasty as a sign of manliness see Dover 1989, 81ff.; Foucault 1985, 47; Halperin 1989; Rahe 1992, 128–33. Since the love of boys is connected to the condemnation of women and the female fostered by the Greek ideal of masculinity, Socrates' stern limitation on the consummation of pederasty may serve to turn the affections of a guardian to a suitably beautiful woman. The possibility of a new heterosexual erotics appears to stand behind Plato's critique of conventional pederasty in the *Republic*. On this point compare *Laws* 838eff., where the Athenian Stranger's first proposed sexual law, which prohibits males from having intercourse with males, will make men "loving relations to their own wives (*gunaixi te autōn oikeious einai philous*)" (*Laws* 839b1). G. M. A. Grube calls this "a tantalizing hint, left unexplored" (1935, 118–19), but Plato leaves it unexplored because his interest in the regulation of sexuality is determined by the ethical consequences of pederasty and not by a ranking of forms of sexuality as in medieval and modern natural lawyers.

[43] 412b–e; cf. 403e–405a.

[44] My translation follows Dobbs 1994, 276–7 n. 11.

Socrates' Phoenician tale is the provision about the different metals in the different souls.[45] But Glaucon, the Athenian aristocrat, is more perturbed by the claim, the quintessential claim of the Athenian democracy, that since all are literally sons of their earth and motherland, they ought to defend it as sons defend a mother and ought to regard the other citizens, regardless of class, as "earth-born brothers."[46] Even the supposedly aristocratic myth of metals is used first in the city to justify a most unaristocratic institution, the preferment of the young on the grounds of merit alone (415cd). The guardians must harden their hearts against considerations of family preferment, the essence of a hereditary aristocracy, in service to the good of the city.

The second use of the myth of the metals is to justify communism. The guardians will in no way "capitalize" on their position; instead, they will live on a wage that the city provides without any surplus or deficiency (416e–417a). Unlike the ruling class of "Equals" (*homoioi*) of Sparta, our guardians, Socrates says, will have no private houses in which to store up private wealth. Their entire life is publicly disclosed, open for continual inspection by all.[47]

The *all*, the public here, is not merely the collectivity of the guardians but the entire city. The Spartan "Equals", or, as Vidal-Naquet would translate it, "Peers", were equal only to each other, and their entire way of life taught them contempt for their unequals, the semislave helot farmers who gave their exclusively military life its economic foundation (Vidal-Naquet 1986, 100 n. 2). Through their gentling education, through the myth of civic brotherhood, through the purge of all those who do not care for the city as a whole from the guardian and auxiliary classes, through communism, a perpetual audit of their entire lives, the warriors of the city of the *Republic* are to be made and kept brothers and protectors, not masters and exploiters, of the economic classes (416ac). These guardians are what the Athenian dead are claimed to be in the democratic funeral oration: heroes made the city's exclusively and forever.[48]

---

[45] See, e.g., Karl Popper's diatribe against Plato's "racism," or Edward Andrew's statement that the essential falsity of the noble lie, for Plato, is the claim that there are significant natural differences between human beings that the rulers can discern before educating them (Popper 1963, 1:46–56; Andrew 1989).

[46] Cf. *Republic* 414e with *Menexenus* 237bc; Loraux 1993, 7–8. One author who does note this antiaristocratic and thus democratic side to the noble lie is Strauss 1994, 262. The myth also teaches the citizens to defend the city's land as their own even if some of it was seized in aggressive wars of conquest (*Republic* 373e; Pangle 1998, 383–5).

[47] Cf. *Republic* 548a; Strauss 1978, 103.

[48] See Loraux 1986, 24–5, 278, and passim. On the Athenian myth of democratic unity see also Saxonhouse 1992, 50–89; Saxonhouse 1996; Ober 1999, 39–40, 67–9; Monoson 2000, 14–15, 21–50; on Plato's relation to it see Nichols 1987, 59, 78; Saxonhouse 1992, chap. 5, 111–31.

3.3 SOCRATIC *REALPOLITIK*

To this military idyll, Adeimantus has a "realistic" objection. The warriors could have everything in the city, since they are its only armed
element, but in fact they profit from it not at all (419a). They live like
soldiers on perpetual campaign, and so never are promised and never
will receive the fruits of victory, the things of the vanquished that ought
to belong to the victors.[49] As Socrates adds, raising the stakes, as it were,
in response to the challenge of Adeimantus, these warriors are left with
nothing more than a subsistence wage. They live *for* the city as a whole
and *for* the economic classes, when they could live *from* the city,
the farmers, and the craftsman. Adeimantus wants to know what the
warriors of the best city could possibly gain from such an arrangement. Adeimantus thus denies, at first, that the city is a natural whole
united in pursuit of a common good.

Socrates does not answer so much as evade the question. Adeimantus
wants to know whether these men would be happy, but Socrates answers
that their existence is not for the sake of their own happiness, but for
the city as a whole (420b). These warriors are parts of a whole that is
greater – they are not wholes and so cannot be happy. On the city side
of the analogy between city and soul, happiness belongs only to the
whole of the city. We might wonder, however, whether the city can really
be happy if none of the citizens who make it up are happy, any more
than it can be spirited without spirited citizens or best without the best
citizens (435d–436a, 456e, 544de). Despite his earlier caveat about the
supposed harmony between the guardians and the economic classes,
Adeimantus now accepts a vision of the city as a natural whole made up
of "polispart" citizens who have no right to happiness.[50] Adeimantus's
"realism" – his denial of the ideal unity of the city in favor of the natural
unity of the individual – is easily dispelled. He would, in that sense, make
a good ruler or auxiliary of the city under discussion, for he would easily
sacrifice his personal happiness out of concern for the city.

When Socrates banishes wealth not only from the guardian class but
from the city as a whole, Adeimantus makes another "realistic" objection: If the city will fight as a whole for a single aim, how can Socrates
deprive it of the money it needs to finance its wars (422a)? Socrates first
gives an answer in line with the vision of the city as a whole that

[49] Adeimantus states this objection as if it were being made by an external observer
(419a2). Since, as we have seen, Adeimantus believes that opinion in fact rules unquestioned over the soul (see Section 3.1), he does not object that the warriors who have
been cheated of their proper share of material comforts will overthrow the repressive
yoke that the city and its laws have educated them to bear.

[50] *Republic* 419a; the term "polispart" comes from Lear 1992.

Adeimantus was quickly brought to share. As long as the enemy cities are many, the guardians of the best city can contrive to fight them one at a time, either by applying their military skill to strike quickly and decisively at each in turn or by offering to ally with any particular aggressor against another city that, unlike the best city, has gold and other luxuries to steal. In the latter case they can offer exceptionally favorable terms of alliance, since they will not demand any share in the proceeds of such aggression.

But what if the cities do not remain many? Adeimantus asks. What if one city unites all the wealth, and thus all the power, of the many cities (422de)? Now Socrates himself returns to the denial of the unity of the city that Adeimantus initially expressed. One city cannot unite the wealth of many cities, Socrates claims, because no actual city is truly one. Each city is in fact divided into many, or into at least two, rich and poor (422e–423b). By approaching one of these internal many within another so-called single city and offering it the favorable terms already discussed, Socrates claims that the city that is truly one will always maintain its independence.

The policy that Socrates has laid out is thus realistic in two senses: First, it treats every other city as it really is, many cities that only appear as one. Second, this policy appears to sacrifice all considerations to those of security. It is as though the Athenians, attacked unjustly by the Thebans, buy off the Thebans with an alliance against the Corinthians, who, let us say, had wronged neither. It may not be *unjust* to deprive an unjust city of the wealth or freedom it possesses, since an unjust city has no better claim to its own possessions than the madman of Socrates' dialogue with Cephalus in book I has to his own spear.[51] Yet it is at best not just, neither just nor unjust, to yield up to the aggressing unjust city or class the spoils of the victim. Even if being looted does not wrong the Corinthians, receiving the booty does not benefit and may harm the Thebans, on a Socratic account of justice. The best city's wars of preemptive joint aggression thus appear not just, but not unjust either. Nonetheless, it would seem unlikely that a city's warriors could constantly act as accomplices in robbing other cities without themselves being corrupted by lust for a share of the booty.[52]

---

[51] *Republic* 331cd. On the distance between justice as described by Plato's Socrates and the ordinary justice of "mine and thine" see Shklar 1990, 21–5.

[52] Though Gregory Vlastos denies it in regard to slaves, it would seem that in regard to gold and silver at least, Socrates does indeed "cast the utopians in the sordid role of procuring for others merchandise whose use by themselves they would consider immoral" (Vlastos 1981, 143). The role is indeed sordid and, as argued in the text, corrupting.

If the perpetual insecurity of the international or interpolitical environment is so unfriendly to justice at home, how can Socrates vindicate justice for a city as a whole? And if, as Socrates maintains against Adeimantus, it is the city as a whole in their argument that is supposed to stand for the real, whole individual, justice as conventionally understood would require that we constantly be ready to wrong innocent parties in maneuvering to defend ourselves. Socrates' account of war to Adeimantus at the level of the city, when brought back to the level of the individual, leaves us each as individuals in perpetual war with each other, and in a kind of war where a realistic concern for one's own survival, much less happiness, frequently trumps any considerations of mere justice. War as understood by the city at this point in the *Republic*, at the end of book IV, seems to demand radical unconcern for justice. War originates in a desire for luxuries that justice cannot credit or in an unceasing pursuit of security in which justice has no place. If war is the fundamental activity of a city and her citizens, courage must be the paramount civic virtue, where courage means the virtue needed for success in aggressive external war.

3.4 THE MALE DRAMA CONCLUDED

Socrates' male or manly drama through the end of *Republic* IV is devoted to a critique of the Greek ideal of masculinity. He revalues the most important aspects of a Greek man's identity, from his courage in battle to his sexual desires and activity. Yet Socrates' critique of manliness is not yet complete. The guardians, until the end of book IV, live in a kind of purified Sparta. They are moderate in the face of pleasures and courageous in the face of fears, but they are devoted solely to military pursuits.

In making self-control a vital component of his guardians' character, Socrates is indeed challenging the heroic version of the Greek ideal of manliness, as exemplified in the actions of Achilles and the view of Callicles, that he who is most truly a man is most excessive in both his desires and his emotions. Yet Socrates seems to accept another version of the ideal of manliness wholeheartedly: the citizen's ideal that sees conquering the passions as manly and submitting to them as effeminate.

Socrates' attack on the poets in *Republic* III, for example, frequently appears to identify the womanly and the immoderate. The lamentations unfit for men are to be given to women – "and not to those women who are serious" (387e). Nor will we allow our guardians ever to imitate a woman, Socrates says, "whether young or old, or abusing her husband or quarreling and talking big with the gods, thinking that she is happy, or being among disasters and miseries and wailings; and we are far [from allowing our guardians to imitate a woman] who is sick, whether in love or in labor." The guardians must not imitate a woman undergoing suffering or giving vent to her emotions, lest they learn the womanish habit of slavery to the passions (395de).

From the civic ideal of masculinity, Socrates can recover a praise of psychic health through self-control to oppose to the heroic tradition's praise of manly excess in both desires and passions. Self-control as Socrates has lauded it so far, however, appears to be but an instrumental good. Self-controlled, we can carry out our plans sensibly and coherently; lacking self-control, we are driven before the mighty gusts of the emotions. Self-control thus described would serve any plan, even the plans of real, hard-headed tyrants, who cannot afford the fantastic emotional excess of the dream-tyrants of Callicles, Thrasymachus, and Glaucon.[53] Socrates has yet to demonstrate that the purposive and even seemingly single-minded pursuit of excessive ends must undermine the order among the desires needed for any continued purposive action.

The wisdom, the manliness, and the moderation of the city of the warrior-guardians can be instrumental virtues even as the moderation of the citizen-warrior is but an instrument in the unceasingly quest for civic aggrandizement, or even civic security, through aggressive war. Wisdom could mean mere calculation (*logismos*); manliness, simple and unceasing fidelity to the rulers' commands; or moderation, control of passions that threaten to interrupt any purposive action.

The education of the guardians described through *Republic* IV has failed to meet the challenges of Glaucon and Adeimantus on two counts. First, the internal psychic harmony of the guardians and the harmony of their city could be in the service of unjust, even tyrannical, domination over others.[54] Second, the guardians themselves are just, they abstain from the activities and properties of the other classes, not because they know justice to be good for themselves, but because they are deceived and constrained. They are deceived by the noble lie into believing that they have a common interest in the welfare of the city, and they are constrained by their absolutely visible and entirely public life, which makes it impossible for them to transgress any of the city's boundaries and retain the gains of their transgression.[55] Their psychic health supports a plan that is not their own and that is not necessarily aimed at their own good.

---

[53] On Glaucon's ideal of tyranny as more dreamlike than real see Voegelin 1957, 77.

[54] This is the civic version of the alleged "fallacy in Plato's *Republic*," as formulated by Sachs 1963 and discussed in the large literature that followed him.

[55] 412de, 414e, 416d–417b; Ophir 1991, 81.

The guardians' life thus cannot illustrate the superiority of justice chosen without regard for its consequences, since they choose justice because they are threatened and deceived by their rulers. Nor does Socrates intend it to: The guardian class, as presented so far, is only a part of a city, which *as a whole* is analogous to the individual (420bff). It is the good city as a whole that is supposed to be exemplary, and thus the whole that provides the analogue of the just and good individual.

Yet Glaucon has no doubt that the guardians whose education has been described in *Republic* II–IV are in fact the best of the citizens (456de). Glaucon seems to see their (admittedly revised) manliness, and especially their psychic health, as overwhelmingly attractive, because he himself is torn by the desires pictured in his description of the human condition. He is satisfied with the life of the guardians as so far described because, by licensing their spirited desire for honor, the city trains the guardians to use their spiritedness to suppress their material desires. Glaucon wants the objects of sensual desire not in themselves, but for the honor they bring. He, as he is by the end of book IV, would choose a life that offered none of those objects but all of the honor associated with their possession in actual cities, because this life promises him psychic harmony through the complete subjugation of the appetitive desires.[56]

The life of a guardian-warrior can serve as an example only for those whose need for relief from their despotic desires outweighs their attachment to truth and their faith in the goodness of truth for life. Glaucon may have been seduced by the moral heteronomy of the guardian-warriors' life, but the life of the guardians in Glaucon's city[57] fails to provide a model that can answer our (or even Glaucon's) questions about justice. We therefore require a fuller account of the human good that somehow transcends the partiality of Glaucon and also the partiality of the guardians of the city as so far described.[58] Only by radicalizing even further the critique of manliness can Socrates show the ideal human type in the philosopher-ruler, who may be either male or female.

---

[56] *Republic* 440–1; 445ab. As Christopher Bruell writes: "Only after the discussion of the education has had on Glaucon an effect akin to that which the education itself is intended to have on the soldiers, can Socrates reveal to him that it has rather, 'without their noticing this,' purged the city of those very desires which had made expansion appear to be necessary" (1994, 269).

[57] *Republic* 427c6; and see Friedländer 1964–9, 3:93.

[58] It is difficult to see how the education in opinion that the guardians receive could be a preparation for the education in the love of knowledge and truth of the future philosopher-rulers, as Peter Steinberger points out (1989, 1219–20); for a starker formulation of this objection see Benardete 2000, 114n16, 248–9.

4

Justice and the Ungendered Self

4.1 THE FEMALE DRAMA: EQUALITY

The argument for the equality of men and women and the community of marriage, like the argument concerning justice within which it is contained, is given only after Socrates has once again apparently been compelled.[1] Socrates is about to go on to describe the unjust regimes when Polemarchus and Adeimantus demand an argument for *how* the common possession of women and children will be arranged. While his interlocutors desire merely to hear a description of these novel institutions, it is Socrates himself who raises the question of sexual equality (452d). It is Socrates, who too, demands an explanation of the possibility and superiority of the communism of women and children (450c). Socrates insists on arguing for the goodness and possibility of communism and equality because these arguments about the political place of gender serve to distinguish the ideal of the philosopher from the civic ideal of masculinity inculcated in the warrior-guardians of *Republic* II–IV.

In arguing for the equality of female human nature, the fundamental bodily difference between the sexes, "that the woman bears and the man mounts" (454de), must be made as insignificant for human excellence as possible, as insignificant as the difference between the bald and the hairy (454c).[2] The burden of child rearing must therefore be borne by the whole community, not by women alone. "You assert a great ease for their childbearing of the women among the guardians," Glaucon says to Socrates (460d).[3]

---

[1] *Republic* 449–50; Murphy 1967, 76; Bloom 1968, 379; Okin 1982, 40.
[2] For a helpful examination of the conflicts within human nature that are revealed in *Republic* V see Forde 1997. My primary concern is, however, with the work that Plato's Socrates does on the Greek *conventions* of masculinity.
[3] Nancy Tuana has charged that the duty of childbearing itself will impede the education of women, especially since the best women will bear more frequently (*Republic* 458e),

Until *Republic* 455, Socrates has not yet argued for the equality of the natures of men and women in respect of the arts. Socrates uses the analogy to dogs merely to show that if men and women are to be used for the same things, they must be taught the same things (451d), but that does not show that women and men *can* be used for the same things. The celebrated carpenter–doctor argument just begs the question: Socrates says "We were saying that a man doctor and a woman doctor have the same nature in respect to soul; or do you not think so?" "I do indeed," Glaucon replies (454d). Socrates has not yet given us any argument that women doctors exist, let alone women guardians.[4]

Socrates finally *argues* for the equality of natures by asserting that men as a class are superior to women as a class in everything (455bc). Julia Annas comments, "It is hardly a feminist argument to claim that women do not have a special sphere because men can outdo them at everything" (1976, 309). Yet unless Socrates is simply to beg the question by asserting full female equality, this sort of argument is needed to show that sex ought to be irrelevant for politics as Socrates understands it. If women by nature excelled at any of the arts,[5] the rulers might have to restrict them in occupation to ensure that their peculiar functions are carried out by those who are naturally suited for them. Only if there is no task for which all women are better than all men can women be assigned to tasks solely according to their individual capacities, without regard for their sex.[6] Competent women might have to be restricted from entering some occupations in order to force them to pursue those for which they were uniquely suited as women. Only if women are superior to men in nothing can their excellence be the same as the excellence of men.

---

and the years of bearing from twenty to forty overlap greatly with the years of philosophic education from twenty to thirty-five (1992, 20). Yet unless the city acts to minimize the consequences of bodily inequalities by lifting the burdens of childbearing from women, as 460d demands, women's putative equality of natures will never be expressed.

[4] Sarah Pomeroy asserts that Plato is here arguing from the existence of women physicians in fourth-century Athens (1978). Pomeroy believes that Plato is making an argument from analogy in his appeal to the female physician: "Just as men and women may be suited by the quality of their souls to be educated for the practice of medicine. so both men and women may be suited to be educated for the administration" (1978, 498). Yet Plato's main point, which he proves by the *example* of the physician, is that to be suited for an art is fundamentally a quality of soul, not of body.

[5] Recall that in the city of sows the rearing of children is not among the arts but is apparently an activity of another sort (see Sections 3.2).

[6] Christine Pierce writes (1973, 3): "If anything, the argument from female inferiority shows that women have no place." See also Benardete 1989, 116, who makes a similar point. Averroes oddly contradicts this in his commentary on the *Republic* when he says that women might be more diligent at some activities than men (53.10ff).

The argument from inferiority is a class, not an individual, argument. Socrates claims merely that women *on average* are inferior at every task. As Glaucon says "many women, however, are better than many men in many things." Socrates then asserts that women are varied in nature, so that some are fit for guarding.[7]

Equality of occupation is *possible* because there exist women with the appropriate nature. It is *just* according to Socrates' definition of justice in the city as each doing the occupation for which he (and now she) is suited by nature (Vlastos 1978, 185). Strangely, Socrates argues for the superiority of equality of opportunity in occupation without appealing explicitly either to its naturalness or to its justice. Instead, Socrates claims that women must be admitted to the guardian class because there is nothing better for a city than that its "men and women come to be as excellent as possible" (456e6–7). Since the guardian men are the best possible men, the guardian women must be the best possible women.[8] Yet what Socrates means by the best possible man or woman, we, the readers of the *Republic*, do not yet know. If we are not seduced (as Glaucon was) by the Spartan charms of the guardian lifestyle as it has been explained thus far, we cannot yet recognize ourselves in the guardians of the just city.

4.2 EQUALITY AND COMMUNISM

Having escaped the first of the three waves (*Republic* 457bc), Socrates then points out the second wave: the possibility and desirability of the community of women and children (457cd). The relation between the first and second waves has, however, long been disputed among readers of the *Republic*. I will argue that the collectivization of the family is a necessary condition for the equality of men and women in occupational assignment.

Jean-Jacques Rousseau is perhaps the most famous authority for the opposite claim, that the communism of the family requires the equal occupational treatment of men and women: "Having removed private

---

[7] 455d–456a. That the argument from inferiority is a class argument is noted in Pierce 1973; Calvert 1975; Jacobs 1978; Lesser 1979; Smith 1983; Thornton 1986; and Halliwell 1993, 147, although the best work on this question is that of Osborne (see Osborne 1975, 1979). Joyce Trebilcot (1975) provides a useful account of how little is implied merely by the claim that one sex is on average inferior to another at some task. A strikingly similar argument appears in Mill's *Subjection of Women* (Mill 1988, 19). Those who see sexual inequality as founded on natural differences in physical stature are reminded that "if physique were legislated as the sole criterion of gender, the border between masculine and feminine would be laid in a new and iconoclastic place" (Cocks 1989, 169). Note, however, that because of their physical weakness, women will generally receive lighter tasks (*Republic* 457a).

[8] Literally, Socrates asks whether the guardian men "are not the best of the other citizens (*polites*)" and "won't these women be the best of the women?" (456e). Socrates is using *polites* in the usual Athenian sense in which citizens are all male (see the Introduction).

families from his regime and no longer knowing what to do with women, he found himself forced to make them men" (1979, 362). Yet even if women are unsuited for the job of guardian, the best women could bear male children for the guardians' pen without taking up the work and training of the guardians.[9] Equality of occupation is therefore not a necessary consequence of Socrates' abolition of the family.

The proposals for communism and female equality are nonetheless not strictly logically independent, although Socrates must argue for their superiority on independent grounds.[10] Some sort of communal child care, if not communism of women and children, is necessary to support the "working mothers" in the guardian class and allow them to do their own work (see Burns 1984, 139). Yet if the problem were simply that the city cannot afford to waste the talents of its best women on child rearing, the children could simply be raised in public crèches by members of the economic class and still be acknowledged by both parents. Insofar as the burden of child rearing is made public, children are made children of the city, as opposed to children of their parents. To that extent, at least, the equality of women requires the communism of children, if not of women (cf. *Laws* 804d).

Communal child care, in some fashion, is thus necessary to allow men and women to work together as equals. Yet, according to Socrates, such occupational integration, together with public acknowledgment of paternity, violates what Glaucon calls "erotic necessities" (*Republic* 458d). Socrates tells Glaucon that we cannot expect that men and women will live their entire working lives together, especially if they jointly engage in (always nude) gymnastics, without coming to desire one another and acting on that desire (457ab). The mixing of men and women in tasks, required by their equal training and occupation, will lead perforce to sexual mixing, Socrates says (458cd).[11] If no measures are taken, this

---

[9] Allan Bloom's view that the women are admitted to the guardian class to ensure the reproduction of future (male) guardians falls prey to the same objection (cf. Bloom 1968, 383 with Pierce 1973, 10; Tovey and Tovey 1974, 598 n. 35; Osborne 1978, 71; Vlastos 1989, 288; Buchan 1999, 6, 79). Seth Benardete claims that women are given to the guardians in violation of strict justice, which would require that women, who are inferior, be relegated to other tasks (1989, 113). Yet Benardete too seems to neglect the alternative that the guardians could have a collective harem of nonguardian women.

[10] Pace Annas 1976, 308 n. 5; Tarcov 1985 and Hyland 1990 point out that Socrates argues for communism of the family and for the equality of women on two different grounds. Equality is necessary in order that the men and women of the city come to be the best possible men and women, and communism is necessary for the sake of the unity of the city (456e, 462ab).

[11] Socrates does not wish to desexualize relationships between male and female guardians, as some have argued (Bloom 1968, 382; Tovey and Tovey 1974, 593–4). Rather, he acknowledges and seeks to appropriate for the city the force of these erotic necessities (see, e.g., 468c).

sexual mixing in the workplace will produce offspring of unknown pater-nity.[12] Socrates appeals to the great fear that was institutionalized in Athenian law and custom: Unless women are repressed and restricted to life indoors, sexual mixing between women and men in places of occu-pation cannot be prevented, and the father's ability to know his own off-spring cannot be assured. Paternity thus requires the support of law or convention in a way that maternity does not.

Equality thus requires at least partial communism of the family. The abolition of separate paternity is a necessary consequence of freeing women from the unequal regulation of their sexuality (though Socrates substitutes a strict but equal eugenics) so that they will have equal oppor-tunity to participate in all public and private occupations.

Yet surely the most striking consequence of Socrates' abolition of the family is that apparently natural mother-right goes the way of appar-ently conventional father-right: For example, those who supervise the nursing must "devise every device so that no mother will perceive her own offspring."[13] The abolition of particular paternity is justified on the grounds that it is necessary to free women from patriarchal restraint to allow the best possible men and women to develop in the city (cf. 457ab, 460cd); the abolition of particular maternity requires some other ground to prove its goodness. The communism of maternity is thus logically independent of the equality of women, unlike the communism of paternity.

Socrates provides such a new ground when he commences to argue directly for the superiority of the community of women and children:

Do we have any greater evil for a city than that which scatters it and makes it many instead of one? Or any greater good than that which binds it together and makes it one?

We do not.

Doesn't the community of pleasure and pain bind together, when all the cit-izens to the highest degree delight and are pained when the same people are born and die?

Yes, in every way.

---

[12] In Xenophon's *Constitution of the Lacedaemonians* (1.7–8) and in Plutarch's *Life of Lycurgus* (15), the Spartan legislator is said to have limited men's sexual monopoly over their wives in order that the best children would be produced regardless of marriage ties. Socrates, however, does not use eugenic considerations to justify the abolition of separate families. The eugenic scheme is part of the manner, and not the justification, for the communism of the family (see 457e–458b, 461e). Having argued for equality of the sexes in education and occupation, which he claims will bring about sexual mixing of men and women without patriarchal restraints, he imposes a system of eugenic restraints on their "erotic necessities" (458c–e).

[13] *Republic* 460c9–d1. See O'Brien 1981, 121; Saxonhouse 1985, 45.

Doesn't the private possession of these sorts dissolve [a city], when some become exceedingly pained, and others exceedingly pleased at the same experiences of the city and of those in the city?

How not?

Doesn't that come about from the following cause, when they in the city do not utter simultaneously this phrase, "mine" and "not mine," and concerning what belongs to another likewise?

Entirely so.

Then in whichever city the most at the same time in respect to the same things say this, "mine" and "not mine," this city is best settled?

Very much so (462ab).

Separate rejoicing at births and deaths will undermine the unity of the city, so the regime dissolves every individual's tie to any particular birth and death by rendering paternity and maternity unclear beyond hope of resolution.[14] Private paternity will be abolished through the community of women and children, while private maternity will be abolished through the arrangements for communal wet nursing (460cd, 464a8–9). Instead of respecting particular family relationships, the whole guardian class will treat one another as relatives.[15]

Socrates does not propose to abolish the family but to enlarge it. The guardians will have parents and children, and corresponding obligations

[14] On the role of common feelings of pleasure and pain in binding the city together see Spelman 1997.

[15] *Republic* 463cd. Aristotle already raises the question at whether communism will be instituted for the guardians alone or will extend to the farming, artisan, and laboring classes (*Politics* 1264a37–1264b3), but he claims that the *Republic* leaves this question open. Contemporary interpreters of the *Republic* have generally assumed that the lower classes will retain private families and property (see, e.g., Barker 1947, 211; Rankin 1964, 72; Klosko 1986, 141–4). Halliwell writes (1993, ad loc. 450c1) that "Book 5 clearly limits the idea [of communism] to the Guardian class" – something of an overstatement; more correctly, book V discusses the communism of the guardian class alone. The best evidence for the view that communism is for the guardians alone is perhaps *Republic* 417a6–7: "when these [guardians] will acquire private land and houses and moneys, they will become householders and farmers instead of guardians." Yet this passage is more ambiguous than some modern readers have realized: It is unclear whether a guardian who acquires property is being compared to a farmer or householder in the best city, or to such as exist in actual cities. Note on the other side that the system for promoting and demoting children (*Republic* 415b) would conflict sharply with the putative family life of the lower classes, and that Socrates' argument for communism as good is explicitly about "all the citizens" (462b5; Halliwell 1993 ad loc.). Averroes alone among postclassical commentators states simply that communism will extend to all classes (43.1–13), relying upon Socrates' argument at 420–1 that the acquisition of wealth corrupts the practitioners of any art, pottery, carpentry, and farming as much as fighting, judging, and ruling. The question remains unresolved on the authority of Aristotle, though Averroes' argument appears strong. For views similar to my own see Dobbs 1985, 29–30 n. 2; Mayhew 1996, 233 n. 9; 1997, 129–37.

of filial reverence and paternalistic concern, but they will be tied by such bonds to every member of the guardian class (463c–e). "But fathers and daughters, which you were mentioning just now, how will they distinguish one another?" Glaucon asks. They won't, Socrates answers, but one will call all children born in the tenth month and the seventh month after his wedding sons and daughters, and they will call him father (461d).[16] These bonds are to have not merely the name of kinship ties, but some of the real affections as well (463e, and contrast 425b). No young man will dare hit an older one, Socrates says, because he will be ashamed to lay a hand on his father, and he will fear lest the other guardians come to the older man's aid as sons, brothers, and fathers (465ab).[17]

Socrates professes a great faith in the power of these bonds if he feels that they can retain this measure of strength when the class of relatives has been so greatly enlarged.[18] Yet given the power and moral importance that Socrates imputes to these kinship ties under communism, it is safe to assume that the kinship ties in actual cities are no less powerful and have at least equal moral significance. In this light, the superiority of communism to a regime of private families and private property appears insufficient to excuse the citizens of an actual city in breaking their existing familial obligations to found the just city, as Socrates implies will be necessary if the just city is to come about in the way that is quickest and easiest (541ab).

4.3 PLATO'S COEDUCATIONAL ARMY

The city described in the *Republic* is the best city in part because it contains the best men and women, and the guardian women, Socrates says, are the best of women because they share in the education of their male fellows (456de). Yet Socrates initially described this education as the edu-

---

[16] For a persuasive attempt to sort out the difficulties of this institution see Grube 1927.

[17] As James Adam says on 461d (Adam 1963 ad loc.), "the Aristophanic parallel here [*Ecclesiazusae* 635–42] is very close." Yet such a parallel (present also at 461d) does not appear sufficient to prove Plato's comic or ironic intent, as Allan Bloom has claimed (Bloom 1968, 380–6; 1977). The same passage from the *Ecclesiazusae* is paralleled at *Laws* 879b–881e, where the Athenian Stranger legislates that whoever is twenty years or more of age should be considered as a father or mother, and never beaten, and that anyone who sees a younger man beating an elder must defend the attacked as he would a relative. Those who argue from Aristophanes to demonstrate the irony of the first two waves of the *Republic* are bound to provide an ironic interpretation of the *Laws* as well (or at least of *Laws* 879bff).

[18] Aristotle's strongest criticism of the community of women and children in the *Republic* is precisely the claim that familial ties will not survive this enlargement (*Politics* 1261b16–1262a14).

cation of a warrior, albeit a warrior who is supposed to be fierce to strangers and gentle to his (and now her) fellow citizens, and who understands self-control as an essential aspect of his (or her) manliness. When Socrates describes the work of the women guardians at the end of the first wave, he says that "it is necessary for the women among the guardians . . . to share in war and in the rest of the guarding concerning the city, and it is necessary for them to do nothing else" (457a6–8). War is the principal task of the guardian class. Their other tasks, "the rest of the guarding concerning the city," Socrates leaves unspecified (425).

In the Western world before the reception of revealed scripture, the notion of perpetual peace in a world of distinct human communities was unimaginable: "War was a part of the fabric of society, on a par with earthquakes, droughts, destructive storms and slavery."[19] In his writings Plato portrays a condition without war, but he limits that condition in the *Republic* to a city of sows, as we have seen, or, in the *Laws*, to the survivors of some devastating worldwide catastrophe that disrupted a prior world of cities and their wars (*Laws* 678e–679e). That condition of peace is thus either illusory for human beings or a transient moment in the cycle of civilization.[20] It is not merely, as Adi Ophir has written, that the just city will engage in war shows that the *Republic* is a "political act within an existing political order," not a utopia located nowhere with respect to the current political situation (1991, 83). The very possibility of a perpetually peaceable utopia did not exist for Plato. The city of the *Republic* exists in time, it was legislated, it will decay (546a–547a). To be in time is to be in motion, and the best city in motion, as Socrates says in a different context, goes to war (*Timaeus* 19c).

If the condition of war, as understood by actual Greek cities, is the fundamental human condition, the city's best warriors (whether male or female) are the city's best human beings. Socrates' attempt to prove the goodness of justice for an individual seems to have miscarried, for if the good city is to be a model for the good man, it provides a model not only of internal harmony but also of external savagery. Indeed, the good city appears to provide a model of internal harmony *for the sake of* external savagery. If the city-in-speech makes war in the normal manner of

---

[19] Pritchett 1971–91 pt. V, 312; cf. pt. I, 82.

[20] In an image used both in the *Laws* and in the *Statesman*, Plato describes the peaceful age of Cronus, when human beings were ruled by superhuman daimons under the supervision of the god (*Laws* 713a–714b, *Statesman* 268d–274e). Yet although the age of Cronus is supposed to describe *human* life, it is a life in which speech and thus human reason have no place (see Kochin 1999a). As the Eleatic Stranger states gently and euphemistically, we cannot tell if the human beings of that age engaged in philosophy (*Statesman* 272b–d). The age of Cronus is a condition of peace, but like the city of sows in *Republic* II, it fails to be a *human* condition.

Greek cities, then the individual who takes his or her moral guidance from its example would value justice toward others merely for its external consequences, even as free cities are, and apparently ought to be, just only from policy (Bloom 1968, 378). The effect of Socrates' first two waves would then be to make the Greek ideal of manliness (in the civic version that includes self-control) the ideal for both men and woman. The manly tyrant who stably pursues his own satisfaction, undistracted from long-term gain by short-term pleasures, would stand vindicated and the just human being condemned.

Furthermore, if the role of the warrior in the just city is much the same as it is in actual cities, few women will in fact be fit for guarding. If war is understood primarily as a method of external coercion for the aggrandizement of the city, then natural competence in that kind of war requires great physical strength, in which respect women are naturally inferior to men (456a, 457a). In aggressive war, women, no matter how well trained, must always play a secondary role (cf. 471d). If aggressive war is the defining purpose of the city's rulers, women would never be equal participants within the guardian class.

In order to show that the just city is to provide a paradigm of justice as the single human excellence, relevant both for men and for women, Socrates interrupts his discussion of an equal and united city to present us with a new account of war (466de). According to *Republic* II the origin of war lies in the conflict over resources (373de), while according to book IV it lies in the desire of each city to preserve itself by preserving its own unity, in part by uniting its factions against other cities (422e–423c, Section 3.3). But in Socrates' account in book V, the city-in-speech makes war not to aggrandize itself or simply to preserve itself but to educate.

The first part of the guardians' art of war that Socrates mentions in book V is their use of actual battles to provide their children with on-the-job training (466e–467e). The aged and experienced soldiers will serve as leaders and tutors of these child-apprentice soldiers (467d). War thus appears in the first instance as a necessity for breeding good guardians, and the first use of war for the city-in-speech is as a practical part of the city's system of guardian education. The rewards of the valiant warrior, next to be mentioned, are intended to improve the guardian stock and play a crucial role in its cultivation. At first Socrates leads Glaucon (and us) to believe that the prize of valor will be sexual satisfaction.[21] Socrates points out, however, that the reward system for

---

[21] Or at least the partial satisfaction implied by the use of *philein* (468c2) rather than some word that more usually denotes sexual consummation (LSJ s.v. *phileō*; cf. 402e–403c). On Ares and Aphrodite in modern total war, see Gray 1967, 59–79.

valor in war is not intended to provide an erotic stimulus to virtue so much as to ensure more frequent wins in the city's eugenic marriage lottery to the meritorious warrior "in order that as many offspring as possible be produced from a person of this sort" (468c7–8).

Glaucon saw these sexual rewards from the point of view of the young male warrior-pederast, but Socrates redescribed them as part of the city's role as an institution of reproduction. As an institution of reproduction the city's sexual laws must transcend the male outlook, and all the more so the outlook of the pederast. As an institution of reproduction, the best city must govern not only its men but its women as well (cf. Canto 1986).

The good warriors will also be honored with hymns, presumably so that by singing these hymns other guardians will be inspired to imitate their deeds (see *Republic* 607a). The city will set banquets with meat and wine for good warriors. Yet these warriors will eat meat not just as a mark of their elevation but because this seeming luxury contributes to their military prowess, and thus to their performance as warriors in the service of the whole city (468de).[22] Those who die in battle will be honored by the burial rites and grave cult of the "divine and daimonic" – yet here we the readers get our first notion of the limits of the warrior ideal, for these rites will also be bestowed on "anyone who dies of old age or in some other manner of that number who are judged good (*agathoi*) in their lives" (469b2–3). In actual cities, military valor was the fundamental component of manly excellence. In the just city there is another, presumably peaceful, kind of goodness, which will also receive the highest and most sovereign honors in the city.[23]

Up to this point, we readers have seen the city-in-speech engaging in war either to educate future warriors, or to run a kind of contest of virtue among the soldiers to provide models for its education. Not only, however, does the just city make war an educational practice, but its external motives for making war are themselves educational, brought on by a desire to teach rather than to despoil its opponents:

First of all, concerning slave-taking, does it appear just for Greeks to enslave Greek cities, or not even to permit another [Greek city to enslave Greeks] as far as possible and to accustom them in this, to spare the Greek race, while taking care against enslavement to barbarians? (469bc)

---

[22] Cf. *Iliad* 12.310–21, where Sarpedon encourages Glaucon (!) to fight by reminding him that both of them receive the places of honor and the hero's portions at the feasts of the Lykians.

[23] Josiah Ober's claim that the fallen of the best city will be the subject of individual veneration does not seem to me to have a basis in the text he cites, since the honored dead are repeatedly spoke of in the plural, without any mention of rituals that would separate or individuate them (see Ober 1999, 230 and n. 134; *Republic* 468e–469b).

Not only will our city refrain from enslaving other Greeks because it is unjust, but it will aim, through its foreign policy, to habituate other Greek cities to refrain likewise. In the "realistic" war policy of book IV, the city stirred up civil war in cities that threatened it by offering to some "the money and the powers of the others, and even the others themselves" (*ē kai autous*; 423a3–4). In the new educative policy, lives are not booty: Enslavement of the citizens of other Greek cities is neither to be practiced nor condoned. The mere practice of war is mute, but the common language of the Greeks allows the city-in-speech to use war to train its neighbors out of their savage and unfamilial habits.[24]

When they go out to war, our guardians will refrain from excessive contempt of their enemies, whether Greek or barbarian. They will neither strip the dead nor mutilate their corpses, because by doing so they would strengthen vicious habits of thought and deed:

Does it not seem illiberal and covetous of wealth to strip a corpse, and characteristic of a small, womanish mind to believe the body of the dead your enemy after the enemy has flown away, leaving behind that by means of which he fought? Or does it seem that the one who does this acts any differently from bitches, who vex the stones that have been thrown, but do not touch the one who was throwing them? (469d6–e2)

The very behavior of Achilles with the body of Hector (*Iliad* 22.337–405) is here said to be characteristic of a small, womanish mind and no different from the baying of bitches! Our warriors will go out to war intending to practice moderation and restraint, rather than the excess – no longer the manly excess – of Achilles.

From their practice of war, too, the soldiers of the city-in-speech will learn to look upon the soul of a human being as his or her identity and essence. The soul that has departed *is* the enemy, Socrates says, not the soul's material tools (Robinson 1970, 46). By thinking of the person of

---

[24] For more on war as a mode of education see Averroes 26–7. As Horst Hutter pointed out to me, Socrates does not say that the city will initiate war in order to teach Greek cities not to enslave Greeks, but that it will engage in such wars as arise in a manner (*tropos*) that will educate both its own citizens and other Greeks (see *Republic* 466e2). Yet one wonders whether the city can be so moderate as never to seize an opportunity to moderate another city.

    Leon Craig contends that "beneath [this] discussion lies a natural, and not merely conventional, distinction between Greek and barbarian" (1994, 13). Yet Socrates gives us no sign that the best city, if Greek, is to use any distinction between Greek and barbarian other than the conventional one. The distinction as it exists is conventional, but it serves the natural end of marking out a group of regimes with which a more moderate warfare may be possible. In the language of contemporary rational choice theory, the Greek cities are a small group of potential cooperators in an unorganized and therefore hostile world of Greek and non-Greek regimes.

the enemy as identical to his soul, the warrior will come to think of his or her own body as a contingent part of the self, and will come to understand the apparently most bodily of human activities, the use of force in war, as primarily educational and therefore directed toward the soul (compare 410a).

With regard to other Greeks, the warriors of the city-in-speech will conduct themselves not as punishers but as "moderators" (*sōphronistai*).[25] At Athens the *sōphronistai* were indeed educational officials: namely, the officers appointed by the city to oversee the training of the ephebes, youths between the ages of eighteen and twenty.[26] So too, the guardians are to see themselves as the (self-appointed) moderators of all Greece. Having joined moderation to manliness, the guardians will teach other Greeks to do likewise, albeit through war. Such wars are not so much honorable as necessary, so they will not be commemorated by dedications of spoils to the gods.[27]

Even if the city does have ineducable enemies who cannot be moderated, these are always the few. Thus, by judicious raiding, the warriors of the city-in-speech can teach their many nonenemies to compel these few enemies to stop the war (471ab). Even the harshest aspects of the city's military policy, the suffering of those innocent of aggression that leads the innocent to overthrow the guilty, are described as educational.

Women are fit to be warriors because war itself ought to be human rather than manly, more concerned with the activities of nurture, rearing, and reproduction. The just city conceives of war as part of rearing and protecting the young (467ab), and of reproducing the traits of the best through the system of sexual rewards. Socrates thus deprives the practice of war itself of its manly character. By bringing women into the city's army, Socrates breaks the connection between the manly activity of war and actual men: The warrior's life will no longer seem overwhelmingly appealing because it is no longer the exclusive sphere of the valorized gender. Socrates aims to persuade his interlocutors, especially Glaucon, that war is less noble since women can do it too.

The transformation of manly military practice into human educational practice makes war compatible with justice, the *Republic*'s candidate for the single human excellence. Justice in war turns out to be not Polemarchus's manly "helping friends and harming enemies" (*Republic*

---

[25] *Republic* 471a7. This is paralleled almost exactly by Agesilaus in Xenophon's encomium, who says, refusing to storm the walls of Corinth, "it is not necessary to enslave Greek cities, but to moderate them" (*Agesilaus* 7.6; also see Pritchett 1971–91 pt. V, 299).

[26] Aristotle, *Constitution of the Athenians* 42.2; Cornford 1912, 257.

[27] *Republic* 469e–470a; Pritchett pt. V., 132 n. 157.

332a), but the cultivation of human goodness – even in the city's enemies. The individual who models himself or herself after the just city will give rein to anger and aggression only in order to transform enemies into friends, even as the just city seeks to tame and moderate its fiercest opponents.

4.4 OF COMMUNISM, SOULS, AND PHILOSOPHER-RULERS

Socrates' account of war has given us a much clearer notion of the human beings of the just city. Now we see that the guardians are not to be mere dogs of war but veritable Socratics of the battlefield, who teach using a militant elenchus or refutation when the peaceful elenchus through speech fails. In that sense, the guardians are more complete human beings than we might at first have feared when Socrates introduced the analogy between city and soul, for the guardians as described in *Republic* V must carry out their military duties with regard for the city's politics of reproduction and its educational regime.

Yet the wholeness of the guardians appears threatened by Socrates' defense of communism, which, as it appears, requires each citizen to regard himself or herself as one part of the single civic body (462cd). If, as some writers have claimed, the ultimate purpose of Socrates' proposals is nothing less than the destruction or dissolution of the self into parts, in order that the parts be merged into the city as an organic whole,[28] the city of the *Republic* would be without significance as a model for a city of whole human beings such as we. Socrates' argument for the superiority of communism would then be of the form "you all would be better off if you were not individuals, as you are now." This argument is, one might say, modally incoherent, for we can identify no listener to whom this argument could be addressed across the gap between the actual situation of private families and property and the proposed communist alternative. There would be no person for whom we could say that he or she would be better off under communism, for there would be no person who could be said to exist both under the current condition of persons as selves and in the future condition where no selves, as we understand them, can be identified.[29]

The guardians of Plato's city do in fact have firm conceptions of themselves, even if each has nothing of his or her own except his or her body. Once we have saved the self in Plato's account of communism, we can use that account to provide a political critique of private property and

---

[28] See, e.g., Nussbaum 1980, 410–15; Benardete 1989, 126; Lucas 1990, 225.
[29] For a discussion of a similar problem in the comparison of planned and market economies see Przeworski 1990.

private families meaningful to us "householders" – who certainly cannot see ourselves as possessing anything less than full selfhood.

Back in his conversation with Cephalus in *Republic* I, Socrates drew an important distinction between oneself and what belongs to one:

Just as the poets love their own poems and the fathers love their own children, thus the money-makers too are serious about their money because it is their own work, and also for its use, as others are. Thus they are hard to be with, for they wish to praise nothing other than their wealth. (330c)

It is quite possible, then, for one's concern for one's own to become excessive, and this is especially likely regarding something of one's own that one has made oneself. We have not answered the question of what is good for an individual when we have discovered what is good for something that belongs to that individual.

As an individual, a man is already related to others under a variety of descriptions: he is a lover, a father, a son, a husband, a brother – and a citizen. On occasion, he is willing to subordinate some of his desires to the desires that he possesses because of these relations, but he does not regard such a sacrifice as altruistic, for it is, after all, his interests and desires as father, lover, or citizen that are coming to the fore: I am not selfish enough if I think that my interests stop at the edge of my skin (Allen 1987a, 11). A man makes such a sacrifice in the service of his "extended interest," to use the term coined by Richard Kraut (1973), in the service of the good of whatever belongs to him through some affective tie.[30] Kraut distinguishes extended interest from "proper interest," the individual's interest in what is good for himself or herself, in contrast to what is good for someone or something that belongs to him or

---

[30] In Homer, for example, the family seems to be a moral unit, and the lives of the children are seen as morally bound up with the lives of the parents, so that punishment of children for the offenses of their parents is unproblematic (Dodds 1951, 34; Adkins 1960, 64, 68). Note also that one very important modern attempt at the justification of political life also relies upon the family as a moral unit. John Rawls asks us to think of the parties to the social contract as "heads of families" or "representatives of families" in order to justify their sense of obligation to future generations (Rawls 1971, 128). As Susan Moller Okin points out, this means that Rawls's account assumes that questions of justice do not arise between family members and that the family itself is not an institution in need of justification (1989, chap. 5). Okin, however, overstates her case when she puts a great deal of weight on the phrase "heads of households" and claims that Rawls's account is thereby prejudiced in favor of the interests of male heads of households as against other household members (1989, 94). Rawls's heads of households are representatives of families in their relation to other families, and rather than take the side of fathers he seems to abstract from any conflict between fathers, mothers, and children (see Rawls 1993, xxix).

her. A complete account of the soul must make reference to the relational desires that make us members of families and citizens, and thus to our extended self-interest, if it is to include the desires that we, even as individuals, actually express. Plato argues for the goodness of justice on the basis of extended self-interest rightly understood.

Now the extended interest of the guardians, their individual interest in things and people they call their own, is to be thoroughly collectivized (Kraut 1973, 334). The guardians are not to know their own children, much less have any material possessions of their own, and they are to look upon themselves as members of a single great household. They are to view their fellow guardians as relatives and their subjects, the farmers, artisans, and laborers, as "wage-givers and nurturers" (463b–c).

Note well that the guardians do not confuse their own persons and bodies (their proper interests) with those of their fellows. A man who has pain in a finger says both that he is hurt and that his finger is hurt (462cd). So too the guardians, when a citizen is hurt, will say both "that person there is hurt," speaking in terms of their own proper interest, which distinguishes them from the victim, and "I am hurt," speaking in terms of their extended interest, as when we say that a mother is pained at the death of her child.[31] The guardians are, therefore, to retain a separate but narrowed proper interest. Each individual is to have exclusive guardianship over his or her own body, and the public bodies of the city will in no way intervene in a case of outrage or assault (464e–465a). Each will, of course, have his or her own sexual pleasures (458d, 468cd). Even in the best city where positions, spouses, and children are all held communistically and maintained by the regime, each guardian is responsible for the care and defense of his or her own body.

The guardians, and a fortiori the other citizens of the city-in-speech, do have selves, for they recognize their bodies, and presumably their souls, as their own. We can thus find in the unrealized alternative of the city-in-speech a counterpart to our own selves, and once we have found this counterpart, we can render coherent and evaluate Socrates' argument that communism is a superior regime for *us*.

Socrates' argument for communism provides us with an important insight into the psychological roots of private property and families. By collectivizing the extended interest in property and offspring and simultaneously retaining the guardians' particular interest in their bodies as private, Socrates implies that the desire to have things of one's own is

---

[31] One could restate Aristotle's strongest objection to communism (Section 4.2, n. 18) as asserting that one's extended interest can hardly be broadened to encompass an entire class or city, as Socrates demands, and still have any peculiar or particularizing force (*Politics* 1262b).

not simply a need of the body, nor is private property per se required to satisfy any healthy appetitive desire.[32] In the city of sows of *Republic* II, where merely bodily needs are amply fulfilled, the whole question of "mine" and "not mine" will never arise as a political question. Only when the spirited desire for distinction is commingled with the appetitive needs of the body will material needs be met through privatization of material possessions.

The guardians are psychically healthy in part because they do not displace the spirited desire for honor onto what are properly the objects of the appetitive desires. They do not acquire private property to supply their physical wants or take private wives or private husbands to fulfill their sexual needs. Their paternal or maternal longings will be fulfilled by the collective parenthood of the city, which provides them with children through its conventions regarding the marriage lottery (461de), even as actual cities provide men with children of their own by sanctioning and enforcing patriarchal boundaries (see *Crito* 50d).

Communism itself thus seems to imply that at least some of the citizens of the city-in-speech are just in their souls. These just citizens must desire the satisfactions of the body only for their own sake. They must seek honor and distinction in the deeds of war and public life, which are the proper objects of the spirited desires, and not through the private appropriation of corporeal goods (581ab; Ophir 1991, 84).

If the guardians of the city, who are supposed to be mere parts of the city-in-speech, are to be psychically healthy, then in the end they are to resemble the city-in-speech as a whole. Just as in Socrates' final image of the human soul as part lion, part chimaera, and part human being (588–9), the city-in-speech turns out to have as a part that which is said to be analogous to the whole: the just, virtuous, psychically healthy guardian.[33]

Now it is clear why Socrates expanded the demands of his interlocutors at the beginning of book V, to discuss not only the manner of the community of women and children in the best city, but also its justification. When the city is conceived strictly in terms of the city/soul analogy, as a collection of parts that as a whole is analogous to the human soul,

---

[32] Aristotle would seem to agree with Plato that the origin of private property is not to be found in a mere appetite or bodily need. In arguing against the *Republic*'s communism, Aristotle points to a virtue, a necessary component of the good life, that depends on the privateness of private property – that is, the virtue of liberality (*Politics* 1263b11–14).

[33] Perhaps this complication explains why Socrates omits any mention of the analogy of city and soul in his discussion of the three waves and the education of the philosopher-rulers from the beginning of book V through the end of book VII, as Andersson notes (1971, 15). Every city has a part analogous to the whole, since every city has laws, which constitute an opinion about everything in the city (see Section 2.1).

the goodness of communism does not pose a problem. If we accept the unity of the person, we want our souls to be united by a common concern for the welfare of the whole soul, and we would abhor any attempt by a part of the soul to impose its object of desire as the object for the other parts. We thus will grant easily that nonrational parts, whether of the city or of the soul, will have to be persuaded by nonrational means. When we are forced to recall that the city of the city/soul analogy is to be truly a city, made up of individuals each of whom has a claim to be regarded as a whole and not a mere part, as the parts of the soul are mere parts, then the goodness of communism appears doubtful. In order to show that communism is the best regime for *us*, Socrates must justify it for the city of individuals made whole by their separable particular interests.

Through his defense of communism, Socrates shows us that existing cities, through their laws and customs, foster an unhealthy attachment to private acquisition and private families. Socrates attempts to produce healthy individuals in this unwholesome environment by showing them that their happiness depends on recognizing what is good and useful in the objects of appetitive desires. Thus they will abandon unnecessary pleasures and seek the necessary appetitive goods alone. These individuals, if they are to be healthy in their souls, must come to see as vain any attempt to acquire honor and distinction, much less happiness, through the private appropriation of material possessions, women, and offspring.

4.5 CITIES MANLY AND UNJUST

After completing the description of the just city and the just individual, Socrates moves at the beginning of *Republic* VIII to the account of their degeneration, and to the typology of unjust cities and individuals. Socrates has thoroughly reconstructed the ideal of Greek masculinity. Now the new ideal, that of the philosopher-ruler, will be contrasted with the professed ideal citizens of actual cities and with the true or hidden ideal man according to the two Greek conceptions of masculinity, the tyrant. Socrates' tale of decline itself contributes to his critique of manliness, for in it he describes actual patriarchies as doubly flawed. We see the manly political life of actual cities degenerate into tyranny, and we see actual patriarchal households destroy themselves in the conflict between father and son.

The best regime, which Socrates calls aristocracy, degenerates first into the regime ruled by the lovers of honor, the timocratic city. The timocratic regime is inferior to the aristocratic regime because it is excessively spirited, and the timocratic man is inferior to the just man for the same reason (*Republic* 548c, 548e–549a). In the timocratic man, spirit rules in the soul over reason and appetite, so that he transforms the desires of each part by commingling with them the peculiar desire of spirit for honor and distinction. He thus seeks to acquire honor by acquiring the objects of the desires of the appetitive part of his soul.

The timocratic man becomes excessively manly in reaction to his mother's constant harping on his father's apparent unmanliness (549d–e). Instead of pursuing truth and knowledge of how to live, the timocratic man uses his reason to pursue honor and victory, the goods of spirit, through the life of conquest and rule. Yet the human good is not to be found in this life of domination, and so the timocratic man's quest for the good is inherently unsatisfiable. Incapable of satisfaction, the timocratic man thus comes to possess an unlimited desire for domination. He thus studies and practices nothing but war and acts harshly to his slaves beyond necessity (547e–548a, 549a). The rule of spirit transforms the timocratic man's quest for satisfaction of his physical desires into an urge to appropriate. This excessively spirited man wants all other men to recognize what he uses as his *own* because he seeks honor and distinction from his pursuit of wealth and offspring. To be capable of honor (and thus of rule), he thinks, is to have women whom one can protect.[34] He demands sons of his own instead of the communal sons and daughters of the city, so he needs a wife of his own whom he must keep locked up within walls (547c, 548a). The timocratic man creates the private in order to preserve the identity of his progeny, and thus to ensure that he receives the respect due to a father.[35]

In secret, the timocratic man does not merely *desire* gold and silver – he *honors* gold and silver (548a5–6). The timocrat's appetitive desires are no longer the healthy desires of the just man, but are rendered excessive or feverish by the rule of spirit. The appetitive desires now become unlimited, since under the rule of spirit, the soul seeks to gain honor by acquiring the objects of appetite, an honor that material possessions cannot satisfactorily supply. In public, the appetitive desires of the timocratic man are restrained by his ruling desire for honor and domination, so that outside his household he seeks to appear an incorruptible and high-minded Cato. In private, however, where the timocrat is concealed from the glare of public life and denied the reputational goods that public life contains, his spirited desires do not find their appropriate object and so are drawn to the objects of the appetitive desires.

[34] In Livy's history of Rome, the patricians claim the right to rule from the king in avenging the violation of Lucretia, while the plebs claim a share in avenging the death of Verginia (Livy 1.49, 3.44–5, 3.49); and see Kochin 1999c.
[35] Compare Aristophanes, *Ecclesiazusae* 635–42.

Accordingly, timocracy conceals within it the psychic germ of oligarchy: The timocratic man is a timocrat in the public sphere of contest and an oligarch in the private household of material production.[36]

Timocracy is transformed into oligarchy when the regime's rulers cease to love honor and victory at all, and instead act both politically and privately only for the sake of wealth (*Republic* 550d–551a). The oligarchic *man* is ruled continually by his desiring part, more precisely, by the "necessary" desire for wealth (*Republic* 559b–d). The distinction between oligarchic and timocratic man is thus not in the desires they manifest so much as in the organization of those desires into a particular psychic regime of rule and subordination. Like the timocratic man, in honoring wealth the oligarchic man displaces the spirited desire for honor onto the pursuit of wealth. Unlike the timocrat, however, the oligarch does not restrain himself in public, but honors wealth even in the open, when the reputational goods that are the objects of spirited desires are available. Because oligarchic man is ruled by an appetitive desire, he manifests no independent desire for the goods peculiar to public life.

In the democratic city, by contrast, no one claim to the good is ennobled above all others, and in democratic man, no set of desires rules the whole soul in the name of their peculiar good alone. All claims about what is good for us are available in the democratic city, and the pursuit of any of these visions is licensed by the regime (*Republic* 557b–d). Democratic man takes his desires as they are and attempts to satisfy all of them without ranking them or purifying them (561a–d). His desires include the commingled and the feverish, not just the healthy desires of one part of the soul alone, and he regards the shameless pursuit of all of his desires as manliness and their moderation as unmanliness (560d; Benardete 1989, 201).

In the democratic city, all human types claim equal dignity and respect, whether male or female, slavish or free (563b). Women's claim to equality in the democratic city is unjustified even as the slave's claim is unjustified, because for all its rhetoric of fraternal equality the democratic city remains patriarchal. In (Athenian) democracy, women are confined in private households and are denied public opportunities (cf. *Republic* 549c–e; Rosenstock 1994). Actual women are oppressed in actual democracies; in consequence of this oppression, they are not truly the equals of democratic men (see Vlastos 1989; Schreiber 1996).

Last to appear in the parade of regimes is tyranny, the darkest slavery arising, in Plato's tale, from the utmost license (563d–564a). The demo-

---

[36] For a discussion of the resulting compound or disunited structure of timocracy, and indeed, of all the unjust cities, see Ferrari 1987, 101–2; Lear 1992, 1994.

cratic regime fostered a manly freedom among its citizens, but this manly freedom leads in the end to a valorization of the insatiable and indomitable tyrant. Publicly each citizen fears the potential tyrant in his fellow, but privately he strives to be that tyrant, or, at best, to join with fellow citizens in order to rule tyrannically over the rest of the city and over all other cities.[37] In fear of the harsh rule of the rich, the citizens of a democracy come to erect over themselves the very tyrant they most fear and most admire (564–6).

The tyrant strives to live in reality as did the hero of Glaucon's myth. The tyrant, like a man who wears the ring of Gyges, is reputed in poetry to be equal to a god (*isotheos*).[38] Just as one who wears the ring of Gyges could enter any private space as long as he was invisible, so too the tyrant can trespass any boundary, whether sacred or profane.[39] Whereas the just city is transformed into a single household for the sake of fostering a feeling of kinship among its citizens, tyranny transforms a city into a single household in order to reduce all citizens to the status of slaves within it (Averroes 85.18ff). Democratic man has no single ruling principle in his soul, but the tyrant's soul is ruled by sexual desire (*Republic* 572e–573e). Unlike Gyges, who sought to rule when complete and perpetual satisfaction of his material desires was possible without ruling, the tyrant seeks to satisfy all of his desires through physical objects alone. In seeking power in order to satisfy sexual longings, the tyrant confuses sex and power; he demands the sexual possession of his own mother in order to seize paternal power for himself (571cd, 574bc).

The tyrant, like a woman, cannot participate in the manly public sphere. No one honors him except flatterers, and in fear he must do away with the most manly and virtuous among his subjects until he has neither friend nor enemy of any worth (567bc, 575e, 576a). The tyrant, ironically, fails to achieve political success, since honors from decent men and contest with worthy enemies form the drama of *polis* life. The tyrant wishes to have Gyges' ring of invisibility in order to perfect his tyranny, but the life of the male citizen is available only to one who wishes to be visible among men (cf. Arendt 1958, 199). Plato's critique of the Greek ideal of masculinity culminates in a depiction of the allegedly most manly life of the tyrant as in fact the most womanly. The tyrant, for fear of his life, is shut up in his palace like a woman in her house (579b). The life that common opinion thinks is the most unbounded turns out to be in fact the most physically constrained.

---

[37] On Plato's criticism of democracy as a regime of many (potential) tyrants, see McGlew 1993, 33–4, 184.

[38] Compare *Republic* 568b with 360c.

[39] *Republic* 568de, 573c, 574a. On this point see Nichols 1987, 62; Ophir 1991, chap. 1.

4.6 THE MYTH OF ER AND THE STRUCTURE OF CHOICE

The goal of the *Republic* is to vindicate the human ideal of the just life against the manly life of citizens and would-be tyrants. Socrates aims to show that only the human life lived in accordance with justice, the life of the philosopher, can promise psychic health and true individuality. The Greek ideals of masculinity, even the self-controlled civic form, are unstable, Socrates argues. Both the civic and heroic ideals point ultimately to the life of the tyrant as the most manly life. In order to call these ideals into question, however, Socrates has to call into question the gender identities that shore it up, as we have seen. Socrates can revalue the love of honor, the love of knowledge, and the love of physical pleasure only after he has broken apart the connection between these inner drives and the physiological facts of sex.

The good life, Socrates shows us, is the life ruled by reason, the life of examining and choosing how best to live (cf. 344de). Socrates has taught Glaucon, through the critique of manliness and the three waves, that if he makes all the aspects of the Greek ideal of masculinity necessary components of his life as an individual Greek man, he closes his mind to the true breadth of the choices available to him. To live the just life, the philosophic life, Glaucon must remove the bonds by which law and myth tie him to their own conceptions of the good man, or at least remove these bonds in thought.

Yet despite his long attempt to vindicate the just life as the philosophic life, Socrates finally acknowledges that the human situation is not fully meaningful in this life alone, because our choices are restricted by our circumstances in a way that cannot be humanly justified (see Morgan 1990, 153; Sartre 1956, 83). It makes sense to speak of a choice of lives, as Socrates portrays in the myth of Er (617d–620d), precisely because our lives are in fact constrained by our congenital character, our paternal and maternal upbringing, and the regime that rules over us. "For Plato," as Ferrari writes "our moral lives are not led *in spite of contingency* ... but become complete through proper dealing with contingency" (1987, 137). It is this lesson that the myth of Er delivers, abstracted from the element that our choices in life are not made once and for all but lived through and continuously renewed. Not all are born with philosophic natures, Socrates admits, and of those natures, many are corrupted by their environment (490eff). Only the prospect of reincarnation, Socrates hints, can save our condition from this tragic incoherence, since our ability to live well in this life, to live according to philosophic examination, is partly dependent on arbitrarily distributed external circumstances.

Yet the myth of Er still teaches us that the proper way of life for all is the life of choosing how to live (618b–619a).[40] Most men and women do not choose how to live: The justice of ordinary men depends on their accepting the laws, and thus the lies, of their respective cities.[41] The most serious of these lies are the city's lies about human desire, for the laws of actual cities inculcate a false account of the human good and a correspondingly distorted set of desires in each citizen. This kind of guidance is, however, essential for most, for most men and women can no longer be guided by these lies about themselves; they no longer see the merits of justice.[42] The philosophic life is open to anyone who is not satisfied with lies, who wishes to ascend from the city's myths about what is desired and what is good for us to what is genuinely desired and genuinely good for us. Most are satisfied with the cities' laws, both the laws' truths and the laws' lies. Some, who are equipped with philosophic natures and who grow up in a fortunate environment, are instead led to question.[43] We question our laws by seeking ways of life different from those praised or mandated by our laws. In order to have the fullest possible array of choices, including those choices that escape the contradictions of the heroic and civic ideals of masculinity, we have to learn to disaggregate our learned gender identities to find those qualities that together make up human excellence. The philosophic life is not a life to be chosen in an ideal choice situation, but is a way of life open to us here and now. It requires any man who would pursue it to question the ideals of the manly life inculcated by his laws and his city.

4.7 IRONY, NATURE, AND POSSIBILITY: THE THREE WAVES AND THE TEACHING OF THE *REPUBLIC*

Some writers contend that the arguments for sexual equality and communism that constitute the first two waves of *Republic* V are not to be

---

[40] As Rutherford writes (1995, 238): "The choices made by the souls in the myth are only the reflection in fabulous terms of a theme which runs through the work."

[41] The myth of Er is not addressed to the multitude (pace Arendt 1961), but to those like Glaucon and Adeimantus who pursue speeches about justice. Indeed, the myth consoles them with the thought that the ultimate reward for justice is reserved for those who aspire to know what virtue is, and is denied to those with merely political support for their virtue (619cd). Yet if Glaucon and Adeimantus can be consoled by a myth, their pride in their own reason (to which the myth appeals) is refuted by their very susceptibility to mythic suasion.

[42] *Republic* 619b–d; also compare the discussion of corruption of moral opinion through dialectic (*Republic* 537e–539c).

[43] On the education of this skeptical few, as described along Platonic lines in medieval Arabic political philosophy, see Kochin 1999b.

taken as practical political proposals or even as serious claims about
what is natural or just. These writers claim that Socrates only argues for
equality and communism to point to the eventual unmanning of the
tyrant and to exalt the life of the philosopher over the life of "manly"
political action.[44] In their view, Socrates' arguments for equality and
communism in the *Republic* are but comic flourishes designed to make
manifest the ironic character of his arguments in the *Republic*, and to
reveal the ultimately unsatisfying nature of political life by describing
a "city laid up in heaven" that transcends the earthly necessities of politics. The Socrates of the *Republic* solves the political problem, they
assert, only by abstracting from the individual attachment to one's own
that makes politics necessary.

   These Straussian scholars claim that Plato's real interest is not in the
questions of gender and politics, but in making the philosophic life
appealing to actual Greek men despite its apparently unmanly character.
The *Republic*, according to them, is a critique of political idealism and
a defense of the antipolitical life of the philosopher.

   Allan Bloom, Mary Nichols, and other Straussian readers rightly
emphasize the importance of Plato's critique of the Greek ideal of masculinity, and I must acknowledge a great debt to their scholarship. Yet
the great weakness of the ironic interpretation is that it renders the
Republic, ostensibly a great work of *political* philosophy, politically irrelevant. If communism of property and the family and the egalitarian treatment of women are both impossible and unnatural, we learn very little
from their description about actual political practice. Strauss and those
who follow him allege that the regime of the *Republic* somehow abstracts
from an essential feature of the human experience, from the body or
from erotic love.[45] Yet if that were so, we would have no reason to think
that when we return from that abstraction and reflect on what we have
read, we will have acquired anything from the *Republic* valuable for
understanding our true situation, apart from confirmation of our sense
that Plato has indeed left out something important.

---

[44] See, e.g., Strauss 1978; Bloom 1968, 1977; Nichols 1983; Saxonhouse 1976, 1985. As
   Leon Craig puts the problem Socrates confronts, "Men who are first of all concerned
   with being men do not take readily to a way of life they believe will emasculate them"
   (1994, 21). Wendy Brown also sees the goal of the *Republic* as a critique of manly politics and an apology for unmanly philosophy, but unlike the ironical school she takes
   Plato's new mode of politics as seriously meant. Brown sees Platonic politics as renounc-
   ing power, and therefore as weak and effeminate (1988b, 612–13). Yet the city-in-speech
   is not purged of all conflict, not least because it is faced with constant external war.
   Because the best city faces up to conflict, its guardians are far from unfamiliar with the
   exercise of public power, as Brown would have it (see *Republic* 473cd, 500d).
[45] Strauss 1978, 110–12, 114–15; Rosen 1988; Bloom 1968, 379–87.

Socrates argues that the egalitarian treatment of women is according to nature (456bc), but he does not make the same claim for communism. This does not mean that communism is unnatural, but rather that the naturalness of the private family is itself questionable. It is one thing to say that nature provides a clear standard for individual human action, as Glaucon does in describing the life of injustice as naturally superior (358e). Nature, in Plato's understanding, provides far more ambiguous guidance in the construction of institutions, for whatever their success in satisfying our natural needs and desires, institutions are human conventions.[46]

The private family allows affection and caring to flourish by establishing legally recognized and enforced bonds between parents and offspring. Yet to maintain these bonds, the family must become patriarchal; it must imprison women in household life to ensure the identity of paternity. This patriarchal family partially meets natural needs and desires because it fosters friendly affection between family members (*philia*), but it is contrary to nature because it binds women to their tasks without regard for their individual natures. The patriarchal family requires the unjust subjugation of women, and this subjugation, like the subjugation of slaves (*Republic* 578b–579a), must be maintained by a patriarchal *political* order.[47] The alternative egalitarian regime meets natural needs and desires because it allows each individual to express his or her natural potential, because it inculcates an undistorted account of human excellence.

Notwithstanding its apparent superiority to a propertarian regime, we cannot simply seek to establish the city-in-speech on the site of some actual regime. The natural force, and, indeed, the goodness, of the family bonds generated under the existing regime constitute a practically insuperable obstacle. Polemarchus conceded too quickly to Socrates that we form friendships only with those who appear useful or good to us. In actuality, we are born into families and wider networks, relations that we cannot simply revise or disregard based on our current opinion, or even knowledge, of what is good for us now. In numerous places, as we have seen, Socrates himself relies on the force of the parental bond. The purge of poetry is partly motivated by the desire to preserve fathers from *just* punishments at the hands of their sons (377e–378b). Even under

---

[46] Compare Strauss 1953, 191ff; and see Yack 1993, 16–17, 90–6.
[47] This point is fundamental to feminist political theory. For formulations helpful in their extremism see Rich 1980; MacKinnon 1989; 1993, 3–8. One must keep in mind that the image of compulsory heterosexuality does not aim to define women's condition in universal terms but to portray the extreme possibilities inherent in that condition in order to show how that extreme colors women's lives.

communism the city is to teach and emphasize the importance of honoring and defending one's father and mother, although this pair could now be any among an entire generation (425b, 463cd, 465ab). Socrates describes the evil character of the tyrant and the tyrannical man by likening him to a parricide (569bc, 574bc). Despite his attack on patriarchy, then, Socrates defends the respect due to father and mother.

Yet when Glaucon asks how the philosophers, should they ever come to power, will establish the just city, Socrates replies in a manner better suited to a tyrannical father- or mother-beater than to his pro-parental sentiments:

Whomever is older than ten [the philosophers] will expel into the fields, and once they've gained control over their children, they will raise [these children] free from their current habits (the very habits which their parents have) in their own manner and custom, which is of the kind we have gone through. And if the city and regime that we were discussing is established thus, which is the swiftest and easiest way, it itself would become happy, and the people in which it is comes about will benefit to the highest degree. (541a)

The crime against father and mother that Socrates here seems to praise is of the very sort that he castigates elsewhere. The slightest observation of actual families will convince us that parents and children love each other too much, and owe too much to each other, to make Socrates' "swiftest and easiest way" more than the barest possibility. Only if we could really convince parents that out of concern for their children they must abandon them to the care of strangers, whose actions and motivations the parents themselves cannot understand, could we bring about the just city in a manner consistent with what Socrates describes as our just obligations to our actual fathers and mothers.[48]

The gulf between the philosopher and the city, however, is so great as to make such persuasion extremely unlikely. Athens regarded Socrates not as the savior but as the corrupter of her youth. Yet even when condemned unjustly to die, Socrates refused to play the father- and mother-beater, refused to do violence against the laws, his parents, by overthrowing their duly determined verdict (*Crito* 50c–51c).

The regime of the *Republic* may well be unrealizable for us; yet it is not unrealizable because it is contrary to nature, in Socrates' view; rather, only this regime allows for the fullest flourishing of the naturally best human type. We cannot bring the best regime into being because we cannot easily or, more importantly, rightly, escape the conventional bonds of actual cities. Only if we could start all over, without any family ties or inherited obligations, could we or should we seek to bring about

---

[48] See Benardete 1989, 146–7; Ober 1999, 237–40.

the regime of the *Republic*. Socrates enables us to see that these actual obligations are conventional, that is to say, they have the force, but only the force, of convention.[49] Political philosophy allows us to see an alternative better than any that can be attained by the tools of political practice, tools that always use rather than transform our prepolitical affective relations with others. The regime of the *Republic* is impossible for us not because it abstracts from some essential aspect of our nature, as many Straussian readers have claimed, for if that were the ground, male domination too would be impossible, because it denies the natural equality of men and women in many aspects of their natures. Yet even if the best regime promised complete satisfaction of our nature, this does not entail that there exists any route to its realization.

An arrangement of relations between men and women could be better only if it is possible. Yet "possible" need not mean "possible for me," but more broadly "possible for other human beings who have the complete set of actual human desires." Plato's best regime is possible in this sense, but given the moral force of actual parental ties, the best regime is possible for us only if we can persuade parents to put the good of their children ahead of maintaining their bonds with their children. Such an orientation of all toward the good would require that all leave behind the images of their own good as proclaimed in their laws for the good as it is in truth. Before parents can be turned out of the city they must, at least in this sense, be brought out of the cave. Such a persuasion is impossible, Plato claims, not because of the nature of individual human beings, for human nature is best expressed by the longing for what is good. It is impossible to persuade all parents to leave their cities and their children to the rule of philosophers because human beings differ by nature in their ability to grasp intellectually the good for which they long. To understand this aspect of human nature, the nature of human beings as a species of varying types,[50] we must understand how the reason that

[49] Gregory Vlastos states that Plato had "the obligation to explain and justify the multitude of bonds which must exist between his new conception of justice and the one embedded in common opinion," because the stability of Platonic justice depends on its citizens' refraining from the ordinary injustices of robbery and perjury (1978, 191). Vlastos thus demands that a purified version of conventional morality be granted a categorical force that cannot be justified for mere convention. Vlastos does not consider that the very superiority of Plato's justice to the conventional account might make these bonds tenuous and few, and, because these bonds are only tenuous, make the philosopher's justice hard to apply (see Shklar 1990, 21–5; Wallach 1997). Platonic justice is not moral (according to the Kantian understanding of morality) because it is not categorical, as we can see already in Socrates' interrogation of Cephalus.

[50] On the variability of natures in the *Republic* see Averroes 22–3. On the fundamental importance of this aspect of nature, as perceived by Leo Strauss, see Kochin 2002. We are most familiar with the notion of human nature as a single and unvarying substrate

directs the city can be expressed in the city's efforts to persuade her citizens of the superior goodness of reformed laws and customs. We must
also understand how the very need to persuade sets limits on the extent
of these reforms.

in all human beings, but the prephilosophic use of *phusis* in Greek denotes what is distinct in each individual or type. In postphilosophic writers who distinguish *nomos* and
phusis according to the distinction between nature and convention, *phusis* usually
denotes what is peculiar or distinctive, not what is general or typical (see, e.g., *Laws*
766a; Demosthenes 25.15; Adkins 1970, 82–3, 158, 171 n. 1; Winkler 1990, 65–9; and
compare our expression "good-natured"). Our view of human nature as essentially
uniform in all individuals also has its classical antecedents: Democritus's "More men
have become good by practice than by nature" (DK B242, cited by Adkins 1970, 94)
is intended to weaken the usual Greek view that natures are diverse in type and rank
by claiming that it is habit that makes gentlemen, rather than nature, as the gentlemen
claim (and contrast B267, B270 for some inegalitarian statements).

5

The Rule of Law and the Goodness of the City

In light of the psychically healthy and truly human ideal of the *Republic*, the manly ills of actual Greek cities and their unphilosophic citizens can be diagnosed. Political and familial obligation will always be in tension: Both obligations will be based on partial but genuine aspects of what is truly good for us. Women will be unjustly excluded from full participation in public life, and the citizens' public self-understanding will incorrectly belittle what the citizens see as the feminine virtues and attributes. Manliness will be seen as the most important or even the whole of virtue; moderation will be ignored or valued only as an instrument for long-run self- and civic aggrandizement. By oppressing women, the regime will make women worse than they could be, so those men with the most refined erotic longings will aim at intercourse with beautiful and virtuous boys instead of ignorant and vicious women. Pederasty will be ennobled, and the city will have to admit its problematic pleasures.[1] The patriarchal city will be excessively warlike, too spirited in the physical and intellectual defense of its own and its rejection of what it sees as other. Because patriarchal families will require private property to sustain them, the city will be perpetually divided between those who have more and those who have less.

To understand how these ills can be mitigated when our obligations to our fathers and mothers will not permit the cure, one must turn to Plato's account of the best propertarian city, the second-best Magnesia of the *Laws*. In speaking with young men, Glaucon and Adeimantus, Socrates allowed himself to suspend actual filial and legal obligations and legislate the best regime. Conversing with the aged Kleinias and Megillus, the Athenian Stranger must pay due respect to the authority of the paternal.

---

[1] See *Laws* 636b–e; Price 1986, 224–5.

5.1 WOMEN AS CITIZENS

In the *Republic*, Socrates attacks the heroic conception of masculinity by appealing to the citizen's ideal of masculinity that includes self-control. In the *Laws*, by contrast, Plato's Athenian Stranger carries out the critique of masculinity by examining and modifying the civic ideal of masculinity as it is expressed in the institutions and mores of the Dorian cities of Crete and Sparta.

Socrates' critique of the heroic conception of manliness in the *Republic* is intended to vindicate the way of life of the philosopher. The Athenian Stranger's critique of the citizen's conception of manliness as exemplified in the Dorian regimes in the *Laws* is intended to vindicate the life of a citizen who rules and is ruled subject always to the overarching sovereignty of a new kind of law. Clearly these two accounts of the good life are not identical; nor can they be reconciled hierarchically, taking the *Republic* to explicate the life of the philosopher-ruler and the *Laws* the life of his or her loyal subject.[2] The life of an auxiliary of the *Republic* and the life of a citizen-warrior of the *Laws* differ too much in detail: Most significantly, men and women participate equally as auxiliaries in the *Republic*, while in the *Laws* female citizens receive a separate and unequal education, shoulder less of the military burden, and are excluded from the most important offices. Nor are the lives of male citizens in the *Laws* equivalent to those of the auxiliaries in the *Republic*: In fundamental respects the men of the second-best city of the *Laws* are excessively spirited and thus suffer, if more mildly than Athenian or Dorian men, from the disease of masculinity.

Greek politics claims to organize the sphere of manly activities, of war and council "where men win honor," as Homer says. Plato's politics of human excellence, by contrast, must make human reproduction, which in actual cities is women's work par excellence, the first object of policy. To begin legislating on marriage and procreation, says the Athenian Stranger, is to proceed according to nature: "Won't it be according to nature that [the legislator], through his ordinances, first arranges the beginning of generation (*genesis*) that concerns cities?"[3]

Reproduction can be political only if women are immediately the subjects and objects of policy. The Athenian Stranger therefore makes the city or regime a city not only of men but also of women (Canto 1986, 343–4). In the *Laws*, women are brought into the official purview of the

---

[2] For a suggestion in this vein see Jaeger 1945, 3:214, 336 n. 6, and compare Saunders' attempt to discover the three classes of the *Republic* in the *Laws* (1962, 43).

[3] *Laws* 720e10–721a9; my translation follows England; see his commentary ad loc. 720e11.

city as legal persons, subject to the ordinary courts and ordinary legal proceedings; as officials or magistrates; and as armed defenders of the city. As Elena Duvergès Blair has put it (1996, 344), Plato's view of women "produces its concrete and prudential application in the *Laws*, where the topic of women is integrated throughout the work."

Just as the city will attempt to regulate reproduction from its beginnings, it will attempt to regulate every aspect of education and child rearing. Indeed, the Athenian Stranger states a compulsory education law, whose effect, he claims, will be to make the children more children of the city than children of their parents (804d5–6; cf. Plutarch, *Life of Lycurgus* 14–15). The aim of the Stranger's education laws is as novel as their reach: Education in a city that aims at human excellence must cultivate in each of its citizens (770cd) the excellences of both men and women as they are conventionally understood, the excellences of both war and peace. The model for the boys and girls shall be Athena, goddess of wisdom and war, female born from male (796bc). Athena can serve as a model only if we can conceive of human excellence as indeed the same for both men and women. Human excellence can be the same for both sexes only if the apparent multiplicity of the virtues, the apparent multiplicity of ways of living a good life, conceals a unity.

Yet Magnesia, the city of the *Laws*, in some sense assigns the excellences separately to the sexes: manliness to men and moderation to women (802e). Every citizen household is separate, and while women in the *Laws* do "men's work" to some extent, they do so in segregated groups. Women in Magnesia are literally second-class citizens in their political rights: They are excluded from the principal offices of the city and, most importantly, from the Nocturnal Council of *Laws* XII. The city described in the *Laws* is a regime ruled by fathers, and its laws express a masculine conception of excellence.[4]

In order to understand the causes and consequences of male domination in the second-best city of Magnesia, the question of women in the *Laws* must be viewed in the context of the aims of the dialogue as a whole. Although the political institutions of Magnesia are not egalitarian, the *Laws* nevertheless carries out a critique of manliness. The Athenian Stranger shows that Dorian institutions are excessively manly: They value supposedly manly excess over moderation, they fail to use women's

---

[4] The regime of Magnesia is, however, far less male-dominated than any Greek city of which we have any knowledge. Women in the *Laws* share some of the military burden, hold certain offices, and participate in the common meals. Only by comparison to the Athenian Stranger's own egalitarian ideals do the laws of Magnesia appear sexist. In the historical context of actual Greek regimes, Magnesia is radically sexually egalitarian.

talents adequately, and by mandating segregation of the sexes they promote ethically maleficent pederastic activity. The Athenian Stranger is, if anything, even harsher than Socrates is in the *Republic* in condemning the deformation of human excellence that results from the differentiation of gender roles.

The Athenian Stranger is thus no friend of Dorian manly prejudice. Yet the institutions proposed in the *Laws* discriminate against women in the allocation of public responsibilities, in the presumption of legal competence, and in the education the laws mandate. These exclusions are consequences of the sovereignty of law in Magnesia, as we shall see – and that sovereignty of law is, in turn, a consequence of the licensing of private families and property. Women are naturally capable of participating in public life, the Athenian Stranger claims, but in the city he describes, the private family structures women's lives so as to make them inferior citizens.

5.2 THE CRITIQUE OF MANLINESS IN THE *LAWS*

The Athenian Stranger conducts an elenchus of the civic ideal of Greek masculinity: He refutes its goodness on its own terms by arguing that it is inconsistent and unstable. The Stranger shows the inconsistencies of the ideal by using this ideal and its rhetoric against itself: He argues that actual cities, both Greek and barbarian, are so exclusively focused on external war and the internal war against fears that they fail ultimately to inculcate their own ideal of manliness in their young men. In a kind of parody of Xenophon's *Cyropaedia*, the Athenian Stranger claims that Cyrus, the mighty king of Persia, was absent for so long while exercising his valor on the field of battle that he left the education of his sons to his wives and eunuchs.[5] Instead of learning from their father's example, Cyrus's sons received a womanly education at women's hands (694e1–4). Cyrus's heirs were thus denied the manly education of a herdsman, the education that had trained Cyrus in virtue. They grew up with eunuchs amid the effeminate luxury of a palace.[6]

---

[5] *Laws* 694c–695b; Tatum 1989, 225–30. Diogenes Laertius relates (III. 34): "It is likely that Xenophon was not well-disposed toward [Plato]. At any rate they have written similar writings as if they were engaged eagerly as rivals. . . . And in the *Laws*, Plato says that the *Education* [of Cyrus] is a phony, for Cyrus was not that sort of man."

[6] In the *Cyropaedia*, this transition is played out in the contrast between the manly dress of the Persians and the luxurious and effeminate dress of the Medes that attracts Cyrus as a youth. It is Medean dress that Cyrus adopts for himself and his courtiers when he consolidates his rule (1.3.2–3, 8.3.1–5, 8.3.13). Xenophon thus points gently to Cyrus's, that is, the Spartans', own want of manliness by showing that their rigorous and moderate life is for them only a contingently valuable means for attaining power and its attendant luxuries.

The Stranger aims to attack not Persia, however, but the Dorian regimes of Sparta and Crete. Like Cyrus, the Dorian regimes are excessively devoted to war (625c–626b) and thoroughly exclude nonwarriors from the body of citizens fully subject to the laws. This exclusive devotion to war and the warrior ideal of masculinity implies that the civic ideal of masculinity that would include self-control is not inculcated with anything like equal force. Yet the Dorians themselves, as represented by Kleinias and Megillus, agree readily that to yield to one's desires for pleasure is at least as bad and unbecoming of a real man as to yield to one's fears (*Laws* 633de). Common meals, gymnastics, hunting, endurance of blows, and the *krypteia*, or "secret service," are all, Megillus asserts, designed to train young Spartan men in overcoming their fears and acting courageously. Nothing trains them in overcoming their desires and acting moderately (633a–d).

The goods won by courage in the Dorian cities' moral economy are goods of reputation, and in the world of reputation, what is is what appears (Arendt 1958, 199).[7] Cretans and Spartans certainly put forward the appearance of lawful habits (625a), and as long as they remain where shame and compulsion can reach them, they continue to act lawfully. When control is absent, Dorians are, however, thoroughly vicious (Redfield 1977–8, 156–8). In consequence, as Megillus admits, good Dorians, unlike good Athenians, are not truly good (642cd). Kleinias, a loyal citizen of Cretan Knossos, thus regards it as shameful to be unjust and hubristic but not bad (661–2). Since the Dorian regimes depend exclusively on shame and constraint, they cannot tolerate the use of wine, which releases men from shame. Spartan colonists, for example, when deprived of the familiar restraints of the mother city, run drunk and riot.[8]

Women in the Dorian cities do not enter the spaces where men's reputations shine forth and so do not submit to the dictates of shame. Women are thus uncontrolled by the city, the magistrates, or the laws. Dorian women do not seriously train for war, nor do they share in the common meals that have their origin in warrior's messes (806a–c, 625e, 781a–d). As a result, the women of Sparta and Crete are sexually loose, fearful, and money-grubbing rather than honor-seeking (637c1–3, 814ab).

---

[7] Dodds famously characterized Homeric society as a shame culture, where the strongest moral force is not piety or moral guilt but "respect for public opinion" (1951, 17–18). In this respect, as Arthur Adkins argues (1960, 154–5), Homeric values survive in classical Greek cities as part of both what I have called the "civic" and "heroic" conceptions of masculinity.

[8] 637ab, 646e–647a, 649ab; v. England ad 637b3–4.

The Dorian valorization of the manly at the expense of and in opposition to the female causes men to exclude women as erotic objects, the Athenian Stranger argues, since Dorian men see women as inferior to men. Moreover, women are in fact rendered inferior in the qualities necessary for public life by the Dorian regimes' failure to regulate their lives. The Dorian regimes lead their citizens to see pederasty as the highest expression of erotic feeling, and provide opportunities for pederasty rather than heterosexual eros by segregating the sexes through all-male gymnasiums and common meals (636bc). In book I the Athenian Stranger condemns those quintessential Dorian institutions on the grounds that they lead to sex between males and sex between females:

And what is more it even seems that this practice has corrupted a law ancient and according to nature, the pleasures concerning sex not only of humans but also of beasts.[9] And someone could accuse your cities first of these things and however many other cities embrace naked exercise [or gymnastics]. And whether it is necessary to consider these sorts of things in jest or in seriousness, it must be considered that the pleasure concerning [sex] seems to be produced according to nature for the female nature and for the nature of males coming into partnership of procreation, but [the partnership] of males with males and females with females seems to be contrary to nature and the daring of those who did it first seems to be explained by weakness before pleasure. (636b–e)

The core of Plato's argument against homosexual intercourse is an appeal to *human* nature simply.[10] In particular, the normative form of sexual

---

[9] The text of this sentence is translated from Burnet 636b4–6, following the original reading of the principal manuscripts. As Martha Nussbaum notes, to accept this reading we must understand what the Athenian means when he says that the heterosexual pleasures are a law according to nature (1994, 1625–6). The Athenian claims somewhat further on that the law itself is a calculation in regard to pleasures and pains (*Laws* 644cd). Just as the law prescribes and proscribes pleasures, so too the pleasures themselves serve as laws for us in regulating our conduct (and see Section 2.1). Compare also Euripides fragment 388 (cited by Claus 1981, 84), where the speaker says of the eros of a just, moderate, and good soul for the pious and moderate that "this must be a law for mortals." Given these parallels, Burnet's text is preferable to the emendation by Böckh adopted by England and Des Places and endorsed by Nussbaum, which renders the sentence "And what is more it even seems that this practice, an ancient custom, has corrupted the natural pleasures concerning sex not only of humans but also of beasts." John Rist endorses Burnet's text, if without great confidence (1997, 74 n. 15).

[10] Dover claims that the argument against homosexual intercourse rests on an appeal to animal rather than human nature (1989, 167). The appeal to animals (836c), however, is brought in a fortiori: Homosexual acts are not merely inhuman, they are even unbeastly. Note that the appeal to the beasts, in contrast with the appeal to human nature, is described as "unpersuasive" (836c7). Simon Goldhill (1995, 50–66) gives an account of the subsequent career of the appeal to the example of the beasts in Greek erotic literature. The argument, Goldhill shows, is repeatedly seized by the defenders of pederasty to argue that male–male sexual relations are superior to heterosexual

relations between males, pederasty, a man's love for a boy, is unnatural for human beings because it undermines the virtues of moderation and manliness (836de). In valorizing the sexual success of the pederast, the elder in a pederastic relationship, Dorian customs undermine moderation by encouraging the pederast to satisfy his unnecessary, homosexual, desire (Nussbaum 1994, 1632). In licensing the pederast to seek to feminize the *eromenos*, his beloved boy, by making him submit sexually, the Dorian regimes allow the manliness publicly inculcated in the boy to be privately subverted.

Discussing pederasty in book VIII before giving the sexual laws of his own regime, the Athenian Stranger asserts that "everyone" reproves as softness the conduct of the seduced and regards as shameful his undertaking the imitation of the female. But for his part he asks, "Will the habit of manliness be implanted and come to be in the soul of the seduced, or some kind of moderate form (*idea*) in the soul of the seducer?" (836de; see England 1921, ad loc.). Pederasty, which the Dorian gymnastics and common meals encourage, undermines the virtue of moderation that Dorian regimes generally devalue. Pederasty also undermines, in the seduced, the virtue of manliness at which these regimes profess to aim.

In general, the Athenian Stranger's diagnosis is that the Dorians suffer from an excess of spiritedness. Their preoccupation with maintaining and increasing their domination over other men, with maintaining their manliness at the expense of other men, causes them to devalue the goods that can come from peace and moderation. In their spirited quest for respect they possess an excessive degree of self-respect, or of self-love. They are excessively admiring of what is their own: Of their own laws and institutions they will brook no public criticism, nor will they seek publicly to learn from foreigners.[11] To an extent that undermines the political reproduction of manliness, Dorian men pursue the love of beautiful boys to minimize erotic confrontations with those inferior, unmanly, un-Dorian women.

5.3 SENTIMENTAL EQUALITY, LEGAL DISCRIMINATION: THE PUZZLE OF WOMEN'S STATUS IN PLATO'S *LAWS*

The Athenian Stranger appears to critique Dorian manliness in the light of women's natural equality. The Athenian Stranger argues for the

---

relation because the former transcend the limited natures of nonhuman animals (see, e.g., [Lucian] *Erotēs* 36). See also Lewis 1994, 6; Nussbaum 1994, 1631; Rist 1997, 72–6.

[11] The "finely made" Cretan and Spartan law regulating criticism of the laws turns out not to be so finely made when compared with the law that the Athenian Stranger legislates for Magnesia (cf. 634de with 950ab). The Athenian Stranger does not, however, explicitly retract the praise of this law that he offers in book I.

participation of women in riding and gymnastics, citing not only ancient myths but also the example of the Sarmatian women, "to whom an equally assigned sharing with the men is exercised equally, a sharing not of horses alone but also of bows and arrows and the rest of weapons" (804e–805a). Spartan women make these Sarmatian women look like men (806bc).

Immediately after explicitly raising the question of the military education of both girls and boys, the Athenian Stranger argues for their equal employment under the cover of a discussion of the training of the right and left hands, Pythagorean symbols for male and female:

The nature of our right and left hands are nearly equal, but we, on account of our habits, have made them different by not employing them rightly. (794e2–4)

If women in actual cities are the moral inferiors of men to the extent that Greek and especially Dorian men believe that they are, the Stranger's solution is to change the customs and laws that reproduce this inferiority in each generation of young women. The Athenian Stranger claims that the Dorian oppositional construction of the female as fearful, lustful, useless in war, fit only to be ruled – in every sense unworthy of full citizenship – reflects not the nature of women but the failings of Dorian laws.

In particular, the claim of men to rule women, of husbands to rule wives, is not among the claims that any city must reconcile. The rule of men over women is not among the seven titles or claims to rule listed at 690a–c, and in contrast to the practice of actual Greek cities, it is parents, both mother and father, not fathers alone, who have a claim to rule over their children.[12]

In his own legislation the Athenian Stranger does indeed demand equal treatment of men and women in some areas. Both newborn boys and newborn girls are to have their names written on the wall belonging to each phratry; both are therefore counted on the roster of the citizens.[13] The laws regulating assaults, and those bestowing encomia,

---

[12] *Laws* 690a3–5; Wender 1973, 77. Aristotle, by contrast, states that "the male is more leaderly (*hegemonikōteron*) by nature than the female, unless they are together contrary to nature, just as the elder and more grown up [is more leaderly] than the younger and more immature" (*Politics* 1259b). For Aristotle, in contradiction to the view of the Athenian Stranger, the authority of the male over the female is on a natural par with that of the elder over the younger, which latter *is* one of the seven claims to rule that the Athenian Stranger admits.

[13] *Laws* 785a, 814c; Morrow 1993, 127–8. On the peculiarly civic significance of the phratry in the *Laws* see Jones 1990, 486.

to pick only the clearest examples, treat men and women precisely equally.[14]

Despite these egalitarian provisions, the Athenian Stranger draws our attention in his legislation concerning music to the difference between "the songs fitting for females from those fitting for males." Just as the laws of the Dorian cities (which he himself criticized) separate the excellence surrounding the control of fears and assign it to men, the Athenian Stranger, also, in discussing the allocation of songs, assigns separate excellences to men and women:

What befits greatness and what inclines toward manliness ought to be said to be masculine-looking, but what rather falls away toward order and moderation ought to be handed down in law and speech as more feminine. (802e)

The laws themselves, in regulating music, seemingly ought to confirm, not challenge, the separation of the virtues of manliness and moderation in the division between male and female.

And yet, at the same time "in whatever way someone should become a good *man* (*anēr*), and have the excellence of soul fitting for a human being . . . whether their nature among the coinhabitants is masculine or feminine . . . every serious straining will be made throughout the whole of life" (770cd). The laws that the Athenian Stranger would legislate, like the laws of the Dorian cities, seem to hold up the male character as the ideal for all citizens, as the character possessed of "the excellence of soul fitting for a human being." Simultaneously, these very remodeled Magnesian laws work to confirm women in their womanliness. The laws command that women be inferior and teach them to acknowledge their inferiority.

As the Athenian Stranger's proclamation of separate songs for men and women shows, Magnesia fails to promulgate *human* excellence, at least among its women. Magnesia is second best, as we shall see in chapter 6, because she fails not only to realize the single human excellence but also fails to aspire to it.[15] It is no surprise that the city of the *Laws* fails in some way: The Athenian Stranger states clearly that the city of the *Laws* is a second-best city (*Laws* 739b–e), second-best when compared to the city of the *Republic* that this passage describes.

These second-best laws and preludes themselves seem to be generally directed toward men, even when their application ought to be broader.

---

[14] *Laws* 882c, 802a. The laws regulating priests and priestesses also treat men and women equally (759cd).

[15] Wersinger's comments on this passage (2001, 7–9) must therefore be supplemented with a recognition of the gap between the policies and the aspirations of Magnesia and the Athenian Stranger's own teaching regarding the unity of human excellence.

The first law the Athenian Stranger gives is the law on marriage, which commands men, but only men, to marry (774a). Women, it appears, are commanded to marry by their relatives.[16] In book I the Athenian Stranger includes both males having intercourse with males and females with females as seeming against nature and as having arisen from a lack of self-restraint in respect to pleasure (636c). Yet when he lays down the sexual code itself in book VIII, he restricts sex between males (841d), but makes no reference to sex between females.

As inferiors, women are excluded from the principal offices of the city. The Superintendent of Education must be a father of sons and daughters (765cd). Ten men from among the Guardians of the Laws, from whom the Superintendent of Education is chosen, meet in the case of divorce with the women officers concerned with marriage (930a), which suggests that the Guardians of the Laws are all men; otherwise, this ad hoc tribunal on divorce could be formed entirely out of the Guardians themselves. The Auditors are repeatedly referred to as men (946–7). "The one who lacks a share in judging," says the Athenian Stranger, "believes himself altogether not to be a partner in the city" (768b2–4). Whether women, despite their exclusion from the most important offices, participate in any way in judicial deliberation so as to be in this sense partners in the city the Athenian Stranger never makes clear.

The most peculiar but somehow most important office, the office called the "salvation of the city" (965a), is the Nocturnal Council described in book XII. This council is composed of men over the age of fifty selected from among other high magistracies, each barred to women, together with their young male companions. Its membership includes the Auditors, the ten oldest Guardians of the Laws, and the present and all former Supervisors of Education. "Each of these is not to attend alone, but with a young man between the ages of thirty and forty, having chosen the man that pleases him" (951e).

There are some sorts of women's offices appointed over marriage and childbearing (784); but although the Athenian Stranger chides the legislators of Sparta and Crete for neglecting women's affairs, and claims that "a lawgiver must be complete, and not half a lawgiver" (781ab,

[16] *Laws* 771e; Okin 1992, 45. A man, it seems, picks not so much a wife as a set of in-laws (*Laws* 774). *Laws* 772 describes the choral dancing that allows both boys and girls to see and be seen nude as far as "moderate shame" allows. It is unclear, however, whether the seeing and being seen extend to both sexes simultaneously, or whether the women of the groom's family are to pass judgment on the bride (and perhaps the bride on *them*), and the men of the bride's family are to pass judgment on the groom. The discussion of military gymnastics (813b) suggests that in general women's bodies are to be protected from men's gaze, which would imply that the choruses of 772 are *not* festivals of mutual inspection of prospective partners.

806c), he neglects the details of these offices – whereas he specifies the terms, eligibility, and mode of election for every named office, all of which appear to be reserved for men.[17] Female officers are largely relegated to supervising women's work,[18] and even that not to an exalted degree. *Female* officers of education watch over the games and nurses, while *male* officers watch over the studies.[19]

Women seem to be partly exempted from the burdens of public life so that they can concentrate on women's peculiar duty of childbearing. Women of childbearing age do not march in the Auditors' funeral processions, nor do they participate in choral competitions.[20] Married women do not appear on their own behalf in court, and they are not competent to indict (937a). Such women as are selected to serve as officers have as their domain marriage difficulties and fertility problems (930a,c).

Women in the *Laws* are prepared for their exclusion from the most important aspects of political life by a separate and unequal education from the age of six (794cd). Nothing better represents this separate education and its concessions to the ordinary Greek understanding of women's place than its new mode of gymnastics, literally, of "naked

---

[17] Women's status in the assembly is obscure. The enumeration of those eligible to vote in the election of a guardian of the laws gives the best clue to the assembly's composition: "All are to have a share in the election of new guardians of the law, who bear cavalry or infantry arms and those who have shared in war in the capacity of their age-cohort" (753b). Presumably these electors also constitute the assembly, which is described as seated by the type of military service each citizen has performed (755e; Morrow 1993, 157 and n. 5). Since women also will perform some sort of military service (785b5–9), Morrow suggests, and Stalley and Cohen assert, that they are members of the assembly according to the provision at 753b (Morrow 1993, 157; Stalley 1983, 105–6; Cohen 1987). The inclusion of all who do or have done military service at 753b is most simply understood, however, as aiming to ensure that aged veterans retain their political rights. Strauss's suggestion that it refers to the lightly armed troops is also plausible and, as the late Trevor Saunders pointed out to me, fits with the concern that forms the principal theme of Aristotle's *Politics*: the determination to ensure that political participation is balanced by class (Strauss 1975, 84; v. *Laws* 755e7–8; *Politics* 1283a18, 1290a24–9, 1291b, etc.). Morrow's claim that women are eligible for the *boulē* or council (1993, 167–8) seems, in all events, unduly speculative. Note that the actual duties of the council and the assembly are at best underspecified – perhaps evidence that they can be filled by women – and at worst minimal.

[18] For example, in the case of offspring born from intercourse between a slave and a free man or woman, the female officers deal with the offspring of free women, while their male collaborators in these most important matters of reproductive politics deal with the offspring from free men (930de).

[19] *Laws* 795cd; Morrow 1993, 327. Note, however, that these female officers are presumably part of the college of "all the officials except the *boulē* and the *prytanes*" (766b2–3) that elects the Superintendent of Education (Cohen 1987, 34).

[20] *Laws* 947c, 764e; Okin [1979] 1992, 48.

exercise": In the *Republic* "the women of the Guardians must strip, since they will be clothed with virtue as their garment, and must take their part with the men in war and the other duties of civic guardianship" (*Republic* 457a). In the *Laws*, the girls strip for exercise, but they do so only before female dancing teachers or at the festivals for inspection of prospective marriage partners.[21] Women in the *Laws* are burdened in their public activities by the clothing of private family life.

Ostensibly, women and men are to be trained in gymnastics and riding equally, without regard for sex, and "the business of war is to be a concern to all male and female citizens."[22] Yet women's participation in military training appears optional or voluntary: They are to study the use of weapons "if in some way they will agree" (794d1). This note of the voluntary jars with the Stranger's later description of military life as ideally a life of rigid hierarchy and complete obedience, without room for discretion.[23]

The Stranger's martial gymnastics, in keeping with the Greek love of competition, motivates students, both male and female, through frequent and varied athletic contests. Women are subject to different laws governing their gymnastic competitions, however. Contests for young girls and virgins (*parthenoi*) in horsemanship, javelin throwing, and archery are optional, but the same contests are mandatory for males, and adult women are excluded from the contests entirely (833–4). Boys and young males compete naked, but girls over the age of puberty compete clothed.[24] In general, then, the military and gymnastic education is systematically discriminatory: "[T]he men and boys in the city must be students (*mathētas*), and the girls and women knowers (*epistēmonas*)," of military matters.[25]

---

[21] *Laws* 813b, 772a.
[22] *Laws* 814c. As Morrow points out, Plato's gymnastics is exclusively and rigorously military, more so even than that of the Spartans (Morrow 1993, 333–4).
[23] *Laws* 942; Okin 1992, 48–9. On the scope of this passage see Silverthorne 1973.
[24] *Laws* 833d. Spartan women, whom the Athenian Stranger stigmatizes as failing to share properly in the city's military gymnastics, were not known for the modesty of their dress (Cartledge 1981, 91–2).
[25] *Laws* 813e5–7. With Pangle and Libes, and against the definite opinions of Bury, Taylor, and Diès (and the "probably masculine" of England ad loc.) I take the *toutōn* of 813e5 to be neuter and to refer to the military matters to which the other uses of *toutōn* in this passage (e4 and e7) also refer. The Athenian Stranger does not expand on his distinction between male students and female knowers. In Homer the verb *manthanō* means to learn as a habit (*Iliad* 6.444; *Odyssey* 17.226, 18.362), whereas the verb *epistamai* frequently means to know how as a capacity (see, e.g., *Iliad* 2.611, 5.60; *Odyssey* 2.117; but see *Iliad* 14.92, undertranslated in LSJ). If the distinction were certain (either in reference or in sense!), one could say that the Athenian demands that the women of Magnesia acquire a capacity for war that the city's men are to exercise constantly. Even if the masculine construal at 813e5 is preferred, the strange reference to young girls and women as "knowers of military things" still requires explanation.

Given this inferior military education, women's participation in the actual business of war is similarly partial. On the one hand, it is by virtue of this participation in war that the women of Magnesia are called *politides*, female citizens (814c).[26] When the whole city is led out on military maneuvers, women and children are to take part (829b). The Stranger, also stresses that women should learn to use the characteristic arms of fourth-century Greek infantry, the heavy shield and spear of the hoplite (813e7–814a1; cf. 795b3–4). In the military festivals and in the celebration of military valor through the licensing of free speech in poetry, men and women are to be treated equally (829e). Yet women's military obligations are significantly limited: Women are called up for service during a much shorter period of their lives than are men (785b4–9), and they take up arms only as the last reserve, when the whole mass of the army is called for foreign service, or when the enemy attempts to conquer the city itself (814a).

While women are excluded from much of public life, it is unclear what they are engaged in instead. Marriage and family life somehow seem to prevent women in the second-best city from assuming as large a share of public burdens as they do in the *Republic*. Yet the laws of Magnesia appear to limit the effects of marriage on women's education and training, given, first, that the number of children and the time of childbearing are restricted by the city's population control laws and, second, that the children are largely cared for by servants or by the city. Before the age of three, children seem mostly to be taken care of by nurses; from ages three to six they are watched over at the district temple by nurses and female officials; and from the age of six, both boys and girls begin their (segregated) public martial education at dawn every day.[27] All the while, mothers are relieved of the greatest part of household duties by the public provision of common meals for women as well as men (780b). Thus, it cannot be owing to the great burdens of rearing children or keeping house that women, even young wives, are excluded from most of the offices and partially excused from the military burden.

In legislating for Magnesia, the Athenian Stranger commits many of the same errors that he himself found in the Dorian regimes. The

[26] Benardete's translation "citizenesses" brings out the oddity of the term (2000, 184). Women are hardly ever called citizens in actual Greek cities, because they are excluded from the principal activity of the *polis*: making war (Gould 1980, 40). Aristotle uses the word *politis* in discussing the rule that a male Athenian citizen had to be born from an Athenian father and an Athenian mother (*Politics* 1275b33, 1278a28), but the word does not appear in the much more complex rules of endogamy in the *Laws*.

[27] *Laws* 789, 794a, 808d. Susan Moller Okin argues that women in the *Laws* are burdened by the obligations of infant-rearing, unlike the female guardians of the *Republic* (Okin 1982, 48). This is correct, but of uncertain significance, since the baseline of the comparison, the "easy childbirth" of the female guardians of the *Republic*, is very low.

Athenian Stranger criticized the Dorian cities for excluding women from public life and for failing to make use of them to meet the military needs of the city. Yet despite his egalitarian principles, his own city of Magnesia fails to give women equal treatment in the allocation of public office or an equal military education. He faults the Dorian regimes for admitting pederasty, but his own preferred sexual law would allow pederastic relationships, as long as they do not lead to "the sowing of sterile seed" (*Laws* 841d). His description of the Nocturnal Council, whose members are older male magistrates, each together with "the young man that pleases him," suggests that this institution even encourages some sort of eros between older lover and younger beloved. Magnesia thus shares the failings of the Dorian regimes: It too is excessively manly; it too sets up the good *man* (*ho agathos anēr*) as the model of *human* excellence to be imitated by the citizens in speech, song, and action.

5.4 PRIVATE FAMILIES, LAW, AND INEQUALITY

The law code of Magnesia described in the *Laws* is addressed to men, as we have seen, and it discriminates against women in public life, education, military training and obligations, and the legal presumption of competence. This exclusion is especially surprising since the Athenian Stranger personally is at least as egalitarian in his view of women's capacities as the Socrates of the *Republic*. Whereas Socrates allows that the class of women is inferior in everything to the class of men (*Republic* 455bc), the Athenian Stranger says that the right and left hands, Pythagorean symbols for man and woman, are of nearly equally balanced natures (*Laws* 794e2–4).

Yet while the city of the *Laws* will have private families, the law also seeks to remove as much as possible of the burden of child care and housekeeping from married women through the institution of public education of children and common meals. That women are relegated to the home does not, in itself, seem sufficient explanation for their exclusion from the most important public duties.[28]

Gregory Vlastos has proposed that the discriminatory treatment of women in the *Laws* results from a change in the definition of justice. In the *Republic*, the guardians, at least, are to have only and as much as

---

[28] Okin argues that because the women of Magnesia are private wives, they are effectively the private property of their husbands, and these women suffer numerous discriminations because they are property rather than persons (Okin 1992, 44–50). Okin thus sees Magnesia's fundamental concession to the private as the granting of private property. Private property requires legitimate heirs, and legitimate heirs, she rightly claims, imply restriction of women. Yet the women of Magnesia are not, as Okin would have it, owned objects, but citizens (*Laws* 785a).

they need to do their own work as well as they can (*Republic* 420–1). Vlastos calls this justice "functional reciprocity": Each person receives goods and honors not in proportion to his or her own contribution, but as much and as good as is necessary to maximize that contribution (1977, 23; 1978, 178). In the *Laws*, the principle of justice is simple proportional equality (757c). Each person is to receive according to his or her contribution, but women contribute less to the city, and so "legally, politically, and vocationally they are virtually back in their traditional inferior Athenian status" (Vlastos 1978, 186).[29]

Vlastos's explanation is, however, radically incomplete. If proportional equality warrants discrimination against women, it can only be because women's civic contribution is inferior to that of men. We then need to understand why women manage to accomplish so much less in the city of the *Laws* than in the city of the *Republic*. If indeed women do accomplish less, it would seem to be mainly a consequence of their exclusion from the most important political activities and from a central military role. Justice as proportional equality can then explain why women ought to receive less honor and status in a patriarchal regime, but it cannot justify the regime itself.

Nonetheless, considering the difference between the two definitions of justice in the *Republic* and the *Laws* can guide us toward the correct explanation of women's low status in Magnesia. If these two principles of justice are not simply postulated but in fact have to be explicated and defended, justice as functional reciprocity would be more reasonable insofar as each citizen's individual happiness consists in mutual enjoyment of goods produced by their cooperative activities. In that case, as under the communist superfamily in the *Republic*, each individual would want to maximize the contribution of everyone to the collective product, and would do well to agree to distribute resources to each so as to maximize the recipient's contribution.

In Magnesia, however, each citizen's happiness is more a private matter, since each family provides for itself, at least partially, out of its own resources. Collective production is thus restricted when compared with the perfect communism described in the *Republic*. In Magnesia's case, the principle of functional reciprocity is generally inferior to the principle of reciprocal equality, since her citizens would not wish to maximize the production of the now restricted set of collective goods, but

[29] A similar view is expressed by Ste. Croix 1981, 557–8 n. 30. This is, of course, an overstatement of women's inferior position in Magnesia, but it is correct in describing the movement from the *Republic* to the *Laws*. Vlastos admits that women's status in Magnesia is greatly reformed from the practices of actual Greek cities in a subsequent discussion (1989).

rather the production of all goods both public and private. The change in the principle of justice from the *Republic* to the *Laws* itself thus seems to be a consequence of the *Laws'* licensing of separate family life, which allows the citizens to develop their affective ties more firmly with the members of their own family than with the citizens at large. To understand why women have a lower status in the *Laws*, I will look to the licensing of private families, as the Athenian Stranger himself suggests when he calls the regime he is describing "second best," and not, as Vlastos urges, to the principle of distributive justice to which that licensing gives rise.

Whereas in the *Republic* Socrates portrays the city as a coming together of nonautarkic, ungendered *individuals* (see section 3.2), in the *Laws* the Athenian Stranger describes the city as a coming together of *families* (*Laws* 680e–681a). Families are understood as pre-political units, regimes in themselves "ruled by the eldest on account of the rule having come to them from father and mother" (680e). These families originally have no written laws, but "they live following habits and the laws called paternal" (680a). The diversity of such paternal or, one might say, patriarchal laws and customs must be reconciled so that the different clans can live together in a single city; thus the city requires legislation (681cd).

The origin of cities in the archaeology of the third book of the *Laws* prefigures the founding of the colony in the fourth book of the *Laws*. Just as the founding of cities in general in book III assumed the prepolitical existence of the family, so too Magnesia, which takes its circumstances from those of the soon-to-be-founded Cretan colony, is to have private families and private property. As a result, the Athenian Stranger concedes, the city founded in the *Laws* necessarily becomes second best:

A city is first, and a regime and set of laws are best, where the ancient saying comes into being throughout the whole city in what way it is so most of all. For it is said that the things of friends are really in common. This then, whether, I suppose, it now exists or whether it ever will exist – women are common, children are common, entirely all goods are common; and by every device the thing called private has been entirely removed from all places . . . no one will ever go beyond these in excellence if one puts down another mark as more correct, nor even will one legislate better. . . . On this very account, it is not necessary to examine another city for the model of a regime, but it is necessary for us to hold to the regime of this city that is most of this sort as far as is in our power when we inquire. What city we have put our hand to, however, would somehow be nearest in immortality and is one only secondarily. (739b8–e4)[30]

---

[30] The text translated is that of England 1921.

The legislator for the second-best city must look to the best city, where private families and private property are abolished, as the model of the city that is truly one. He must strive to unify the city for which he legislates as far as possible, given the presence within the city of the private families and property that cause it to be second best (*Laws* 807b).

What compels the Athenian Stranger to "abandon the sacred line" of perfect communism and allow private families? Any answer must be speculative, since the Athenian Stranger does not articulate his reasons for making "these concessions to prejudices which he has come to regard as ineradicable" (Brunt 1993, 245). For any reader of Plato, such a concession demands that one strive to understand the relevant prejudices in relation to the human soul. I will therefore argue, on the basis of the significance that "ordinary Greek morality" assigned to reproduction, that private families are necessary in order to satisfy the male desire to ensure the paternity of one's offspring, a desire for which nature provides but uncertain support.

In the prelude to the marriage laws the Stranger appeals to our desire for immortality, for continued existence through the rest of time. The continued existence of *this* soul with *this* body is beyond our reach, but we can hope to attain a kind of immortality through procreation (721c). Yet the present man looks on his progeny as continuing his existence, and continuing *his* existence in the measure in which they resemble him. Justly, he thinks, his sons should look exactly like him.[31] "Who is good for me?" he asks himself. "He who is most like me." In seeking to procreate *himself*, man indulges his spirit in an exercise of self-love, of love of the same, which is not necessarily warranted by the goodness of his object.[32]

This desire is different in kind from the simple desire for sexual pleasure: The desire to reproduce oneself is obviously self-regarding and proceeds from a certain aspect of self-respect. A man wants to be a father because he wants his children to be like him, and because he wants to be known as man enough to father his own children and to keep anyone else from fathering children on his women. Nature does not cooperate fully in the satisfaction of man's desire to reproduce himself, for biological fathers cannot identify their own offspring with the certainty that biological mothers naturally possess. Fatherhood is conventional because

---

[31] Even as the mare in Pharsalus that bore colts that looked exactly like their sires was named "Just" (Aristotle, *Politics* 1262a24). Randall Clark gives a very helpful discussion of the Greek understanding of this male drive for self-reproduction (2000, 25–6), though in that article he moves beyond the evidence in seeing Plato's critique of pederasty as coming out of a concern with narcissistic male self-admiration.

[32] Cf. Plutarch, *Life of Lycurgus* 15.

the father can ensure his paternity only by keeping "his" women from
having intercourse with other men. Such patriarchal restrictions must be
imposed by laws, whether written or unwritten, and must be enforced
with the cooperation, in the first instance, of other fathers but secondarily of mothers as well.[33]

To ensure his self-reproduction, a man must ensure the paternity of
the children he brings up. To ensure his paternity, he must acquire control
over sexual access to a woman; he must make her *his* and none other's.
A man's *gunē*, his woman or wife, must be kept separate from other men
and from the public space where men act. If she is to enter that public
space, it can only be in a closely watched and segregated group. Under
no circumstances can she work with other men in a sexually integrated
group; under no circumstances can she share in the tasks of men (*Laws*
835dff.; cf. *Republic* 458d). Adulterers, says the speaker in Lysias' *On
the Murder of Eratosthenes*, are worse than rapists because, by seduc-
ing other men's wives, "They corrupt their souls, so as to make the wives
of others relate more to themselves than to their husbands, and so as for
all the household to be in their power, and so as for the children to be
unclear (*adēlous*) as to which of the two's children they happen to be,
the husbands' or the adulterers'."[34]

The Athenian Stranger founds a city with fathers and mothers, who
by definition are brought up to see their offspring as continuations of
themselves, and who desire to reproduce themselves in children as similar
to themselves as possible. In such a city, the father's right over the
sexuality of his wife and daughters is an inheritance from the first fathers,
who brought their wives and children with them when they founded the
city. The legal reinforcement of the father's assertion of paternity – what

---

[33] This cooperation of mothers in their own subordination is what feminists influenced by
Marx call "false consciousness."

[34] Lysias 1.33; see Cohen 1984, 150 n. 9; O'Brien 1981, 56. I should add that the point
is not that the children themselves are unclear on their parentage; rather, it is their public
or visible status as legitimate heirs of their mother's husband that adultery threatens. It
is an objective rather than a subjective unclarity. In Greek, as Heidegger famously
pointed out (1998), truth and clarity are properties of objects rather than of statements
or perceptions. Harris 1990 shows that this passage from Lysias cannot be considered
evidence that the Athenians in fact punished adultery more severely than rape, as many
scholars have thought. Yet he provides no evidence that the laws of Athens or any other
Greek city recognized the issue of consent that distinguishes rape from seduction as being
of fundamental legal importance (Foxhall 1998, 132). In Gortyn, as Harris himself
notes, the law prescribes the same penalty for rape of a free woman as for her seduction in the house of her father, brother, or husband (1990, 375). Katharine Philippakis
and I are trying to elucidate the structural and institutional preconditions for rape as a
distinctive category of sexual relations in a series of papers on the myth of Lucretia
(Kochin 1999c, Kochin and Philippakis 2000).

writers on politics and the family since Bachofen have called "the law of the father" – is the one law on which, despite their other legal differences (681bc), all of the fathers must agree to maintain their paternal claims.[35] The law of the father could be abolished only if fathers themselves were to be banished from the newly founded city (cf. *Republic* 541a). Yet the Athenian Stranger must legislate for a city of Dorian fathers and mothers, not for children voluntarily handed over by their parents to the rule of philosophers.

   To maintain the sexual purity of wives and daughters, the Greek ideology of paternity insists, women and men must be segregated in education and in occupation in the second-best city. This patriarchal system of sexual regulation does not yet explain why this separation cannot allow woman full "separate development" within their female-only sphere. To answer this question, we must explore further the consequences of the separation of men's public and women's private spheres.

   A private family requires private space, a household or *oikos* that partitions space between familial and nonfamilial. To make a space for themselves, when a young couple marries, they are to take over one of the two households allotted to the bridegroom's family (*Laws* 775e–776b). To maintain itself as separate, the household requires a separate economic base. In the context of the founding of Magnesia, this would mean that each household would need a separate plot of land, its own land to ensure its own support.[36]

---

[35] In contrast with the contemporary anthropological use of "the law of the father" to describe the law that institutes patriarchal lineage, the law concerning fathers (*nomos peri pateras*) that Socrates mentions at *Republic* 463d2 is the law that constitutes paternity as a respectable estate, in abstraction from the particular laws that define within each city who is called "father."

[36] The movement from private families through private houses to private property in land is not as logically immediate as some writers on the *Laws* have claimed, since families could live in private households while holding and working land in common. (see, e.g., Rankin 1964, 85; Lange 1979, 13; Okin runs the argument the other way, claiming that because Magnesia allots land to several possessors, its laws must license private families (1992, 44). Doyne Dawson claims that "The Greek concept of the household embraced both property and family to such an extent that it seemed entirely natural for theoretical communism to embrace both" (1992, 8). Yet the Greeks were aware of the alternative of common property and separate households between the full-scale communism of the *Republic* and the complete privatization of property found in cities such as Athens, and Aristotle discusses its disadvantages at some length (*Politics* 1262b37–1263b14). To look for a moment at modern agricultural organizations, the classical Soviet state and collective farms, as well as the Israeli voluntary collective type referred to as a "cooperative settlement" (*moshav shitufi*), combine joint ownership and working of the land with separate households (see Humphrey 1983; Kochin 1996).

   The Athenian Stranger, however, dismisses the possibly of joint tillage with separate households quickly and enigmatically: "let them first divide land and dwellings, and let

With the admission of the private – private families, private space, and private property – the problem faced by the legislator thus becomes the right regulation of the private through the sovereignty of law for the sake of the public.[37] The authority of the law over the private is mediated: If some members of the household live their entire lives in private space, the law's authority over them will be mediated also. In order to limit the authority of the head of the household over the women within the private domain he rules, women must be brought into public space and public life. Only insofar as all are subject to public norms and participate in public life will the public and the common regulate the private. Only insofar as the household is broken open by the law, and its inhabitants dragged into public spaces, will the city rule the household for the

them not farm in common, since this sort of arrangement has been said to be greater than accords with their actual begetting and nurture and education" (739e8–740a2). Here too in regard to the tilling of land, just as on the question of patriarchy simply, the problem appears to be connected with the circumstances of Magnesia's founding. The colonists come as separate families from separate regions seeking land in order to continue the family line (707e–708d). They do not have the common bonds with another, or the desire to form such a commonality, that would make joint farming possible. These families will interact mainly because the live on neighboring farms, and in order to regulate these interactions so as to maintain amity between neighbors, the Athenian expounds the agricultural laws at relative length (842eff.). The allotment gives each citizen a stake in the security of the city: In order to ensure that all of the citizens respond similarly to possible foreign threats, each family is to have two allotments of land, one near the city and the other near the borders (*Laws* 745c–e; cf. Aristophanes, *Acharnians* 204–36; Aristotle, *Politics* 1330a; Pritchett 1971–91, part V, 357–8).

From the legislator's point of view, the allotments' role in mediating the relationship between the families and the city as a whole is so important as to make the family seem almost an appendage of the plot. The allotment, says the Athenian Stranger, must always have an heir, and an only daughter who is orphaned should marry the young man whom she would have as the heir to her father's allotment (923ff.). In this political or rhetorical sense the property allotment indeed precedes the family, though in the founding of the city the family comes first in time. "Not one household of the 5040 belongs to its inhabitant or to his entire family as much as it belongs to the city as a public and as a private matter" (877d; on the translation see England 1921 ad 877d7). Not only are the household and its lands subject to the political authority of city, they are also liable to be treated as though they were the private property of the city, which implies that the city can employ them in its service with great discretion and flexibility, at the expense of the private rights of the householders.

[37] *Laws* 779–80, 790b; see Lange 1979, 13. As André Laks writes, "the substitution of a regime of private property for communism . . . is less a piece of legislation than a precondition of legislation in general" (2000, 272). In the *Republic*, *nomos* is generally used to refer to the laws that Socrates and Glaucon lay down for the city-in-speech, but only rarely for a code, whether fixed or flexible, that the citizens are to follow. In that sense the rule of law – as opposed to the rule of the wise in accord with the founding laws "legislated" by Socrates and his interlocutors – is not present in the best city of the *Republic*.

sake of the common goods of political life, rather than the private goods of life within the household.[38]

The Athenian Stranger weakens the family to the advantage of the city by subordinating all familial relations to the laws. The first law to be given, the law governing marriage, not only commands men to marry but also regulates wedding feasts and prohibits dowries (720–1; Pangle 1980, 471). Officers, male and female, have jurisdiction over these laws, and over divorce and remarriage (930a–c).[39] Property in the second-best city of Magnesia indeed belongs to the family, but the family and its property, even its allegedly exclusive space, the household, belong first and foremost to the city.[40]

In his most radical attempt to regulate the private by the public for the sake of the common, the Athenian Stranger institutes common meals for women. The law will command both men and women to participate in segregated common meals after marriage, just as before (780b, 806d–807b). Since, as the Athenian Stranger asserts, segregated common meals produce homosexual attractions (636b–e), the purpose of common meals would seem to be the erosion of the bonds between husband and wife, and especially of the husband's power over his wife.[41] In Sparta, if we may trust Plutarch, family sacrifices excused

---

[38] *Laws* 923ab; cf. Averroes 45.1–8, 84.3–6.

[39] Trevor Saunders (1995, 599–600) points out the strikingly sexually egalitarian character of the Magnesian law of divorce as contrasted with the Athenian.

[40] *Laws* 877d6–e1, 923ab. The indivisibility of the allotment also serves to hasten the breakup of the family (Gouldner 1965, 211). Under partible inheritance, the norm in both Athens and Sparta, adult brothers even after the father's death would frequently work the land together. In Magnesia, one brother alone can inherit an allotment of land. The other brother must either leave his biological family and be adopted as heir by another; marry an heiress (*epiklēros*) and in effect be adopted after the death of his adopted father; or leave the city entirely (923).

[41] Were it not for the segregation by sex that the Athenian Stranger institutes for Magnesia's common meals, we might think that these meals would serve to maintain the ideal degree of separation to maintain affection at its peak, such as the Athenian prescribes between parents and married offspring (*Laws* 776a–b). Yet segregated common meals effect not only the separation of husband and wife but also homoerotic bondings that compete with the spousal tie, as the Athenian himself admits. Contrast Morrow (1993, 397), who recognizes that common meals and private families are contraries, but claims that Plato "found it difficult to set up other groups so as not to undermine marriage." Rather, the Athenian Stranger wishes to set up groups so as to undermine marriage. Closer to the mark is W. K. Lacey: In the *Laws*, Lacey writes, the existence of common meals for women "is proof that the family was only very partially reinstated; the *syssition* under whatever title and the family are incompatible" (1968, 314 n. 14). Note also (with Saunders 1995; and pace Okin 1992, 46) that the penalties for adultery in the second-best city are extremely light in comparison to Greek norms. According to the legislation of the Athenian Stranger, men and women are punished equally for adultery, which he broadens to include unfaithfulness by the wife and by the husband, and

participating men from common meals; the Athenian Stranger instead abolishes private shrines and private sacrifices.[42]

The political unity of Magnesia, and the subordination of the households to that unity, are symbolized in the Stranger's urban plan:

But if indeed a wall is in some way useful for human beings, it is necessary to plat the house-buildings of the private households from the beginning in such a way that all the city be one wall, and that all the houses are easily defended because they present a similar even front to the roads. Then the city would not itself be unpleasant to look upon, having the appearance of a single house, and on the whole and in every way it would be superior in ease of guarding and in security. (779a7–b7)

Magnesia is not a single house – it is propertarian rather than communist – but for the sake of unity and defense it imitates the appearance of communism.

Magnesia's civic cult also strives to give the city the appearance of a single house by consecrating a symbolic single hearth. In actual Greek cities the hearth was the religious focus of the *oikos*, the altar of the family cult. These cities had a "civic hearth" as a religious symbol of the unity of the city, but replaced Hestia, deified hearth, with Dionysus in the Olympian pantheon.[43] Magnesia, where private rituals and family cults are forbidden, will have a temple to Hestia as one of the three temples on its acropolis and a shrine to Hestia as one of the three shrines in each village.[44] In banishing Hestia from the home and returning her to the acropolis, the Athenian Stranger intends to elevate the cult of the unity of the city at the expense of the sacredness of the family.

Even the father's desire to reproduce himself in his offspring is limited in Magnesia. The compulsory education law, already mentioned, makes children more children of the city than children of their fathers: It is the legislator's, not the father's, preferences that determine how children are to be educated (804d5–6, 810a).[45] Marriages of similar men and women,

the punishment for both is merely exclusion from feasts and festivals (*Laws* 784de). There is no formal penalty or prosecution for seduction of a married or unmarried woman, even if the seducer is caught in the act, when under Athenian law he could be killed (Cohen 1984, 157–8 n. 17; Sealey 1990, 28–9; Saunders 1991, 247). Nor does the adulterer in Magnesia have to pay statutory fines, as the laws of the Cretan city of Gortyn commanded (Sealey 1990, 70).

[42] Plutarch *Life of Lycurgus* 12.2, cited by Morrow 1993, 390; *Laws* 909d–910d.
[43] Morrow 1993, 436; Pangle 1980, 527 n. 21; Vernant 1983, 146, 151; Arendt 1958, 24–5 n.6; Graves 1958, 106.
[44] 909d–910d, 745b, 848d5; Morrow 1993, 435.
[45] Magnesia is Dorian because only in Sparta and in Crete did the laws "impose compulsory public education; elsewhere it probably would have been regarded as an insupportable interference with the father's right over his own children"; Brunt 1993, 254; see Xenophon *Cyropaedia* I.ii.2, cited by Morrow 1993, 298; *Constitution of the Lacedaimonians* II.1.

in character traits such as hastiness or orderliness, or in wealth, are discouraged (773). A father, the law teaches, should seek to procreate not children like himself, but children who are as even-tempered or balanced as possible (Fortenbaugh 1975b). Moreover, the bond between father and son is thus further weakened by making it subject to legal revision: Fathers are permitted to disown their sons completely (928d–929d) or to give them to other men to adopt as heirs (923d).

The most important measure, however, for the subordination of the private to the public is subjugation of the rulers to written law. Self-love, says the Stranger, leads to preferring one's own above the truth and the just (731d7–732b4). First, because "it is difficult to know that in the true political art it is necessary to be concerned not with the private but with the common" (875a), law's commands must substitute for knowledge about the common. Second, even one who has knowledge of the common tends to subordinate the common to his own private interest:

> Even if one sufficiently grasps in art the knowing of how these things have grown, but besides this rules a city as an autocrat and one not liable to give an account, one would not ever be able to cleave to this opinion and to spend one's life nourishing the common governance in the city, and the private pursuit only following the common; but one's mortal nature will always urge one toward a disposition to take more than one's share and [toward] private matters, fleeing pain unreasonably and pursuing pleasure, and one will set both of these over the juster and better [action]. . . .[46]

Until we find someone who both has sufficient knowledge to rule and is of such a good nature as to rule according to the knowledge of the common, we must subordinate the rulers to the law, the Athenian Stranger proclaims. In following the law, the rulers are forced to uphold the common even at the expense of their private interests.[47]

Law, however, "sees and looks towards as much as possible, but is unable to look toward everything" (875d). All laws have limitations, but some of these limitations are not peculiar to this law or that law but are concomitants of law as such.[48] The law is often stupid in its generality: The Athenian Stranger gives a striking example of the irrationality of law when he describes the law on inheritance that the legislator enjoined, although "completely unknowing" (926a). This law on inheritance

---

[46] *Laws* 875b. The late Arthur Adkins assisted me in the translation of this passage.

[47] Note that this ethical argument for the rule of law is quite distinct from the cognitive argument present in the *Statesman* 294a–301e, where law is said to be necessary only in the absence of the scientific ruler possessed of the true art of statesmanship (see Vlastos 1981, 214–15 n. 25). The *Laws* and the *Statesman* are often considered together as "Plato's later political thought" (as in Saunders 1992), but this striking difference in the arguments for the rule of law calls this conjunction into question (Kochin 1999a).

[48] These concomitants are explored very thoroughly in Benardete 2000; see esp. 143–52.

marries couples without attention to their particular character, holding
the most particular of human affairs to a general rule.[49]

Because law is incapable of seeing everything, it does not necessarily
command the good for each individual in each case. In the *Statesman*
the Eleatic Stranger compares the political situation to the situation of a
patient who believes that his or her doctors are not interested in healing
but are malevolently disposed (*Statesman* 298aff.). Certainly in the case
of medicine this condition of malevolent healers is a paranoid fantasy,
but for the citizen confronted by a harsh, unfeeling, and perhaps unjust
demand made by the law, this sense of the law's malevolence or at best its
indifference to his or her individual well-being may indeed be justified.[50]

To care for the common, law must address the common in general
terms; to subjugate the private interest of the rulers, these general principles must be applied in every case even where they seem unsuitable.
Even one who possesses knowledge of how to rule for the sake of the
common cannot reliably subjugate his or her private good to the
common good. No mortal nature can fully control its passions and
appetites without the assistance of the common law of the city
(644d–645b). Thus everyone, whether citizen or ruler, whether knowing
or ignorant concerning the most important things, must always and in
every case be subject to the law without exception.

Women, even in the second-best city, remain subordinate to their
husbands and fathers. Women are thus subordinated to the public and
common law only through law's domain over the behavior of their husbands, through an extra layer of personal rather than legal authority.
Because women remain under the rule of their men in the darkness of
private space, they are incompletely disciplined by the concern for
reputation and appearance that characterizes public life. No one subordinated to an individual human sovereign, a *kurios*, can truly be a slave

---

[49] Of course, in acting so unjustly, the law on inheritance also serves to weaken the ties of
marriage, ties that threaten allegiance to the private.

[50] When the Athenian Stranger appeals to the analogy of medicine to justify adding persuasive preludes to the law (719eff.), he glosses over a very disturbing difference between
doctors and lawgivers. The physician persuades the individual patient for his or her own
good; the laws aim to persuade the individual citizen for the good of the city as a whole.
This gap between city and individual can only be remedied by a doctrine of particular
divine providence like the one the Athenian Stranger puts forth in *Laws* X. If such a
doctrine is untenable, then the only alternative is to console the exceptional citizen, who
rightly denies that the general providence of the laws is adequate in his or her case, with
an explanation of the inadequacy and a defense of its inevitability. In place of a political theodicy, the city and its ruler must supply the questioner with a political philosophy – but this is precisely the business of the Nocturnal Council, as described in *Laws*
X and XII. I say more about this false analogy between legislator and physician,
especially with reference to the *Statesman*, in Kochin 1999a.

to the laws; but in Magnesia, where law is sovereign, the most power-ful and honored citizens must be the most enslaved.

In the second-best city, women, confined within women's space and to women's work, to a greater degree prefer the goods of the private to the goods of the public, *to idion* to *to koinon*. Women, generally speak-ing, will participate in public life only if and as far as they are dragged out of their private concerns.[51] To a greater degree than men, they resist the yoke of the law that always upholds the common over the private. The Athenian Stranger's language is extremely harsh: Women, who are by nature more secretive and cunning because of their weakness, will prefer the shadows of private consumption and resist forcefully the institution of common meals for them throughout their lives (781).

A male-dominated regime makes women weak in private life because it subjects them to the personal authority of their several *kurioi*, and makes women unable to call upon the city or the public for aid against them. Yet, paradoxically, under male domination, women are weaker still in public life, where the city neither recognizes them as full citizens nor can their *kurioi* protect them.[52] Women therefore flee the public space, where they are not welcomed, for the very marginal additional safety of the private household (cf. Song of Songs 5:7). Women must therefore be dragged out of their homes and compelled to eat together, whereas men have to be dragged into private homes by a law that imposes penalties for failure to marry.[53]

The law can no longer assign political tasks on the basis of individ-ual capacities, as does the regime of the *Republic*, but must rely on gen-eralizations to decide who shall be assigned to what office or occupation. Because law must rule, the rule for women must conform to their gen-erality. Individual natures cannot, as they do in the *Republic*, require exceptions. The participation of *every* woman in public life must be restricted in the second-best city where law rules, because, according to the Athenian Stranger, women on average are unsuited for it. Since the city of the *Laws* allows private families, and women in general are more drawn to the private, where families exist, the laws must exclude even the few competent women from high public office because of the general weakness and secretiveness of women as a class.

---

[51] Nor can their attachment to the private be faulted as irrational: The rule of law itself substitutes the rule of written unreason for the rule of unwritten reason (*Laws* 875d; cf. *Statesman* 299d).

[52] In English, "public men" are politicians and "public women" are whores.

[53] *Laws* 721b–e, 781c. The Athenian Stranger never provides us with the promised final law on common meals for women, however. (Morrow 1993, 394; and compare *Laws* 783bc.) In that sense, he himself is, by his own criterion, half a legislator at best (see 781ab, 805ab, 806c).

6

Patriarchy and Philosophy

He [Plato], first in philosophy, coined antipodes, element, dialectic, quantity, the oblong number, the plane surface among the boundaries, and divine providence.

        – Diogenes Laertius III.24

The Athenian Stranger characterizes Magnesia as second best, as inferior to the city that realizes perfect communism and sexual equality. Plato's intention in ranking these cities is, however, obscure. To many modern readers, the *Laws* descends from the ideal of philosopher-rulership because men and women with sufficient knowledge to be philosopher-rulers cannot be found. Yet Magnesia does not, in fact, lack for philosophers, since she institutionalizes philosophy in the Nocturnal Council of book XII.

I will argue that Magnesia's failure, the failure that makes it only a second-best regime in the understanding of the Athenian Stranger, is not cognitive but moral, not the lack of philosophers but the failure to realize perfect communism and to unify the virtues in a single human excellence. This moral failure leads the regime to substitute manliness for justice, law for wisdom, and friendship for goodness and piety. Magnesia fails to be the best city, according to the Athenian Stranger, because she fails to realize a single concept of human virtue that transcends the allegedly separate virtues of men and women.

Magnesia's Nocturnal Council studies foreign customs and foreign philosophy in order to mitigate Magnesia's overspiritedness and her overspirited self-admiration. The Council explores the unity of virtue to overcome Magnesia's failure to completely reconcile manliness and moderation in a single human excellence. Magnesia thus shows us how philosophy can guide reform, including reform of the condition of women in actual cities. In Magnesia the laws' reverence for the paternal limits the possibilities for reform of women's status. Plato claims that those limits on the improvement of women's status are limits on the goodness of political life.

6.1 RIGHT PEDERASTY

In criticizing the Dorians and in legislating his own sexual law, we have seen that the Athenian Stranger claimed that pederasty corrupts both lover and beloved (see Section 5.2). The pederast, by indulging his love of boys, undermines his own resistance to pleasures, while the *eromenos*, by submitting sexually to the pederast, defines himself as a sexual subordinate and therefore as effeminate rather than manly. In a city where the ideal of human excellence is the ideal of the good *man*, for a boy to choose to be less than manly is to choose to be less than virtuous.

A young male Magnesian might deny the law's claim that to be an *eromenos*, a young male beloved, is vicious. Yet in general, his choice to submit sexually to his *erastēs*, his older male lover, is a choice to submit to a sexual subordination that part of him, namely, the beliefs and desires implanted by the law, regards as vicious. The boy's choice to submit is, when seen from his perspective, a preference for vice over virtue.

Moreover, Magnesia has no small ground for labeling anything effeminate as vicious, since Magnesian women *are* inferior in the excellence of manliness and in the love of honor to Magnesian men. Magnesian men are correct in seeing women as inferior to themselves in the virtues they see as most important: It is a measure of men's own failings that they devalue the virtue of moderation that Magnesian women may exemplify more perfectly than Magnesian men. In the *Republic*, where men and women are treated equally by the city, the only problem posed by pederasty is the problem of moderation of vehement desires in the active partner (402d–403c). In the *Laws*, where the sexes are unequal in virtue and made so by the laws and customs of the city, the sexual submission of the passive partner is gendered as unmanly and is thus ignoble. Yet the Athenian Stranger legislates sex-segregated exercises and common meals in his city, although both of these produce homosexual attractions and, inevitably, the consummations he affects to despise as unnatural (636b–e). The Stranger's first and preferred sexual law permits male homoeroticism and passes over female homoeroticism in silence (838e–839b).[1]

---

[1] The hunting laws seem to discuss the pursuit of beautiful boys euphemistically, since they regulate "hunting through friendship" and assert that "manliness is divine to those who hunt" (823b6–7, 824a9; cf. *Protagoras* 309a). As Harvey Yunis notes, the Athenian Stranger's rhetoric is comically elaborate given the ostensible subject (1996, 285). Yunis sees a violation of logographic propriety where I see double entendres. On hunting as an image of pederasty see Dover 1989, 87–8.

Most strikingly, the capstone or anchor of the Magnesian regime, the Nocturnal Council, is somehow pederastic. As was shown in Section 5.3, the older members of the Council appear to be all male, and each older member is to attend the meetings with the young man between thirty and forty "who pleases him."[2] Although the "young man" is well beyond the usual age for a Greek beloved, the law nonetheless orders the senior member to choose according to his homoerotic affections, or perhaps according to his past affections.

Pederasty remains in Magnesia, despite its unnaturalness, because the laws of the city idealize men at women's expense. Men in Magnesia must be compelled by law to marry (721b–e), to turn to the erotic love of women, who in Magnesia are inferior in those excellences the city most values to beautiful boys. Women, it seems, must be dragged out of the home, while men must be dragged in. While the age of marriage for men has both a legal ceiling at thirty-five and a legal floor at thirty or twenty-five, there are fines and punishments for men who fail to marry before thirty-five but no punishment at all for marrying too early. The legislator does not fear that a man would desire to marry too early.[3]

A. W. Price charges Plato with viewing women as aggregations of qualities and strictly from a homoerotic standpoint (1986, 227). Women possess human worth, Price's Plato claims, only to the great but not complete extent that they can acquire the excellences that are naturally better instantiated in men. The *Republic*, says Price, is a coercive fantasy that turns women into men; the *Laws*, less perfectly coercive, makes women less good because it makes them less manly.[4]

Price's analysis is subject to two different objections. First, Socrates and the Athenian Stranger are radical critics of Greek men as they are, and of the Greek ideal of masculinity. Women ought to be more like men, but men too ought to acquire the excellence of moderation (which the heroic conception of masculinity sees as effeminate); and even manliness must be transformed from heroic self-assertion into spirited confidence in the goodness of the practices and beliefs inculcated by the city.[5] Second, Price's idealized concept of pederasty glosses over the Greek anxiety over sexual submission by the young men who were supposed to become self-controlled male citizens. As Michel Foucault argues at

---

[2] See Section 5.3; 951e, 961ab.
[3] *Laws* 781, 770cd, 785, 772e; England ad loc. 721b1; see Strauss 1975, 63–4.
[4] Price 1986, 167; cf. Rousseau 1997, 104–5; 1979, 362.
[5] Plato, then, indeed endorses what Price calls the "androgynous solution" to the problem of sexual difference (1986, 168–9).

length in the second volume of his *History of Sexuality*, the pederast also wishes to manifest his dominance over his boy by rendering him effeminate through active anal intercourse (Foucault 1985; cf. Gouldner 1965, 62). This feminization of the *eromenos* was the basis of the Athenian ambivalence about pederasty.[6] True, an *erastēs* gains honor by feminizing the *eromenos* (Cohen 1991), but the boy suffers a loss of honor, even a great loss of honor, for submitting.[7] What is of the greatest importance is that the Athenians were more comfortable with the double standard in heterosexuality than in pederasty, because the male subordinated partner, the boy or *pais*, is expected to grow up to dominate women and boys as a mature *erastēs*.[8]

It is thus partly this feminization of the *eromenos* that makes pederasty problematic for Plato as well.[9] Yet for Plato, unlike the ordinary Athenian, the pederast himself was also in danger of psychic harm. In indulging his desires by seeking pleasures that are unnecessary and therefore not according to nature, the pederast weakens his hold over his desires and weakens his adherence to the laws that command moderation. The Athenian Stranger describes pederastic sex as immoderate and political immoderation as in itself sexually charged and even phallic: The third savior of Sparta acted to moderate its regime by instituting the ephorate when he saw the magistracy still "swollen (*spargōsan*) and thumotic," erect and manly, and seeking to dominate, tyrannize, and thereby feminize the ruled.[10]

For Plato, the proper kind of eros seeks to transform the beloved for the good. The Dorian pederasty that keeps its young in a flock, like colts in a herd, is not to be encouraged in Magnesia. Rather, the Athenian substitutes the right pederasty that is "the most beautiful song," in which the pederast draws his own youngster away from the flock and "educates him by currying and soothing him, giving him all that is necessary for child rearing" (666e). This proper "Attic" pederasty, which focuses on the cultivation of the good in the beloved and abstains from the phallic, consummated pederasty that

---

[6] This ambivalence is manipulated in an illuminating way by the nonlover in the speech attributed to Lysias in the *Phaedrus* (230e–234c; Ferrari 1987, 51).

[7] Dover himself described the double standard in Athenian pederasty (1964; 1989, 88–91), though in the earlier article he interpreted the double standard as a strictly lower-class view, a reservation he later abandoned. Later writers such as Foucault 1985 and Cohen 1991 rightly emphasize that the relationship of every pederast and *eromenos* was structured by the conflict of norms that created the double standard.

[8] For example, it is striking that the most explicit representations found on vases are only of heterosexual couplings (Shapiro 1992, 56–8).

[9] See *Laws* 836de, 669c4.   [10] *Laws* 692a; cf. *Phaedrus* 256a.

would subjugate him, is the erotic foundation of a philosophic education, and as such it is to be encouraged in Magnesia (838e–839b, 837d).

6.2 MANLY SPIRIT VERSUS HUMAN EXCELLENCE

The second-best city not only restricts women unnaturally and unjustly, but also taints with overmanliness the city's pursuit of human excellence. Magnesia needs the sovereignty of law because she admits private families to satisfy the fathers' desire to reproduce themselves in their offspring. Although the rule of law does serve to mitigate the attachment to the private, it does not mitigate the excessive attachment to one's own that makes private families and property necessary. Law, by implanting itself as "a golden cord" within the souls of its subjects, encourages an attachment to one's own law in place of the good. Legislation is manly in a way that ruling is not: Kleinias, says the Athenian Stranger, will seem most manly in taking up the art of legislation (969a9). The rulers of the regime in the *Republic* are never, by contrast, described as ipso facto manly, or as manly more than moderate. The regime of philosopher-kings and philosopher-queens, in which those elected to rule are to be *forced* back inside, into the cave, would hardly praise manliness or self-assertion in its rulers.

The laws license private families, which weaken women to ensure that they remain subordinate to the rule of the father; to compensate, the laws themselves must attempt to make women more responsive to spirit (*thumos*). The laws of Magnesia therefore mandate a spirited education for both males and females. To foster greater spiritedness in the citizens, the education in the *Laws* begins with gymnastics, conducive to spiritedness (*Republic* 410: *Laws* 791bc). In the *Laws* the earliest period of life is seen as the time when the infants are most plastic in body, so the law commands pregnant mothers to exercise and tells nurses how to swaddle the infants in their charge (789ff.). In the *Republic*, by contrast, the earliest period of life, beginning after birth, is seen as the time when the infants are most plastic in soul, so their education is to begin with music, which is conducive to gentleness (*Republic* 377, 411).

The purpose of this spirited education, as we have seen, is to make everyone, whether male or female, into a good man (*anēr*). Indeed, the women in the *Laws* are to be more manly than the Spartan women, that is to say, more dedicated to the preservation of the city through action (814bc). The Athenian Stranger even legislates proper sleep habits so as to promote manliness in both men and women (807–8). In the second-best city the women will at least in the utmost emergency, when the enemy comes to capture the city itself, take up arms and stand against the enemy, not run wailing to shrines (814b).[11]

Nevertheless, the radical separation between the genders in courage or manliness remains, because even in the second-best city of the *Laws*, women remain much less manly than the men. In the *Republic*, the punishment for a guardian who throws away his weapons is reduction to the class of farmers and craftsmen, but in the *Laws* the punishment of a male citizen for cowardice ought to be transformation into a woman (*Republic* 468a; *Laws* 944d).

Because it goes to such lengths to foster spiritedness, the regime of the *Laws* is so spirited that it lacks any place for justice, the truest human excellence. The Athenian Stranger legislates manly songs, moderate songs, but no just songs.[12] The distinction between songs calls into question the applicability of any single standard of human excellence to both men and women (Strauss 1975, 105). If justice is human excellence, as Socrates states in the *Republic* (335c4), Magnesia and its choruses know nothing about it.

Instead of true justice Magnesia has manliness:

If the opinion of the best, however a city or private individuals believe [the best] will be, rules in souls and orders every man (*anēr*), even if [this opinion] fails in some way, it is necessary to say that everything done in this manner [viz., following the opinion of the best], and the part of each [city or private individual] that becomes subject to this kind of rule, is just, and is best in regard to the whole life of human beings. (864a1–6)[13]

Justice, according to the laws of Magnesia, consists in perfect obedience to the opinion of the best, whether that opinion is perfectly right or "fails in some way." Yet in the *Republic*, Socrates calls this obedience to the opinion of the best manliness:

The power of this sort and preservation through everything of right and lawful opinion concerning fearful things and things which are not [to be feared] I call and posit as manliness. (*Republic* 430b2–4)

---

[11] The Athenian Stranger is referring to the conduct of the women of Sparta in 369 B.C.E., when Epaminondas invaded at the head of the Theban army (Aristotle *Politics* 1269b). Xenophon apologetically excuses the women's helplessness on the grounds that they had never before seen an enemy attacking Sparta itself (*Hellenica* 6.5.28). The Spartans had often compelled other cities to defend themselves on their lands, he implies, but had never been forced to defend their own.

[12] *Laws* 802e, 814e–815a; Anderson 1966, 80.

[13] The text is very difficult and almost certainly corrupt, and I have translated following England 1921. Diès 1956 accepts two additional emendations by Bury that do not affect my point.

Socratic manliness even requires that the opinion of the best be right opinion; Magnesian justice, or manliness masquerading as justice, does not require even that.

6.3 WOMEN, MANLINESS, PIETY, AND PHILOSOPHY

Because the city is only second best it can always be improved, and so the Athenian Stranger legislates the Nocturnal Council as the institutionalized organ for correction of the laws toward the pursuit of the truly unified human excellence. Yet the Nocturnal Council is itself compromised by overmanliness. Its membership is all male, old men and young men linked as couples by male homosexual eros.

Philosophy in other cities is a private matter, which the laws of those cities do nothing to encourage, to say the least (*Laws* 951bc; cf. 821a). In actual cities, philosophy is carried on inside the house or outside the city; indeed, citizens are wont to accuse philosophers of effeminacy, because philosophers remove themselves from the areas of public space set aside for manly activity (*Gorgias* 485d). Because it is such a private, indoor matter, philosophy in actual cities is at least in principle open to women.[14] Yet in Magnesia, where philosophy structures the education of the city and is legally mandated for certain citizens, those citizens, the members of the Nocturnal Council, are exclusively male. In the second-best city, women are excluded from the highest human possibility in a way they are not in actual inferior cities.

Why ought women to be denied philosophy? Why, even if women must be excluded from the other important offices because of their general preference for the private, must they also be excluded from the Nocturnal Council, and thus from a share in the quest for the unified human excellence? What is the general truth about women's lot in the second-best city that would cause them to lose their philosophic capacity?

In the course of the dialogue, the Athenian Stranger repeatedly opposes piety to manliness, both manliness as courage and manliness as against womanliness (Strauss 1975, 110). The atheistic youth – necessarily a youth, says the Athenian Stranger, for no one abides in atheistic opinions when old – is addressed as "most manly."[15] Unmanly thieves cheat in business; manly thieves rob temples (831e4–832a3). The sexual

---

[14] Diogenes Laertius (III. 46) numbers among the disciples of Plato two women, "Lastheneia the Mantinikean; and Axiothea the Phleiasian, who used to wear men's things, as Dikaiarchus says." He also states that Aristippus, another follower of Socrates, had as a pupil his daughter Aretē, who herself taught philosophy to her son, also named Aristippus (II. 86).

[15] *Laws* 888bc, 905c; Strauss 1975, 154.

laws, which alone among the particular laws, the Athenian Stranger says, must be hallowed and said to be of divine origin, are defied by a "young man full of sperm."[16]

The young atheist asserts his manliness by rejecting the authority of the paternal, and of the gods of the father and his mother and nurses (themselves subject to the father) – gods his paternal laws raised him to revere (887de; cf. 681ab). Impiety is the principal root of irreverence toward the laws: The atheist denies the particular providence of the laws and the lawgiver when he denies the particular providence of the gods (886cd). To realize that your own laws are less than perfectly good is to realize that you are not truly born a child of the laws, that you are *illegitimate*, and that the laws' claim of paternal authority over you is false (*Republic* 537e1–539a4). If the laws' authority is only pretense, then the authority of the father, whose father-right can exist only if it is guaranteed by the laws, must also be less substantial than the father has claimed (and see *Odyssey* 1.215–20).

Whereas impiety in Magnesia is a manly vice, the women of the second-best city are pious to a fault. Women in Dorian cities, the Athenian Stranger asserts, tend to run to shrines rather than take up arms to defend the city (814b). Even in second-best Magnesia, women are more drawn to private shrines than are men (909e). The first legislation addressed to women is that regarding priestesses (759cd), and the only female magistrates whose number and duties are specified have their station in the twelve tribal temples, whereas no male magistrate who is not also specifically named as a priest is stationed at a temple.[17]

The men of Magnesia are overspirited in defense of their autonomy, their freedom, overspirited lovers of their own souls. Since soul is self-motion (895e–896a), men's potential for impiety springs from their spirited desire to let loose this self-motion in opposition to the stately and ordered motions of the city in honor of the gods (see Pangle 1980, 500). Magnesia's propertarian, patriarchal law constrains women's potential for self-motion. Any law that enforces the father's desire for paternity, any patriarchal law, must segregate women from men spatially and occupationally. In a propertarian regime, women are taught to be weak, they

---

[16] *Laws* 838d, 835c, 839b.

[17] In actual Greek cities, women's role outside of the *oikos* was exclusively religious. In Athens the religious life of the city, unlike its political life, used women in public spaces as priestesses and celebrants (Just 1989, 23), and women acquired status independent of their husbands only through religious functions (Gould 1980, 46; Zeitlin 1982). In the *Lysistrata*, for example, the chorus of women claims to be fitted to advise Athens because the women had played their proper parts in Athenian ceremonies, as if this could constitute a substitute for the initiation rituals that made young men into citizens (*Lysistrata* 639–48; Bowie 1993, 180; Vidal-Naquet 1986, 184–5).

learn how to be victims, and they learn to prefer being the victims of their own men and their own gods rather than those of strange men and strange ideas. Women learn not to be autonomous; in the language of *Laws* X, they learn not to be autokinetic, not to be "self-movers," but to accept the spatial restrictions on their motion imposed by their patriarchal law.

The laws of Magnesia thus restrict women in their mobility or self-motion by limiting their role in the public and military practices of the city. As a result, women are less spirited in defense of their less complete freedom, more willing and even overwilling to move in the direction they believe mandated by the divine. In their avidity for private worship, women are linked together with the sick and endangered (909e); they are sick and endangered, more in soul than in body, by their confinement within women's space (cf. *Republic* 549–50; Rosenstock 1994).

Women are pious because the laws make them weak, but in Magnesia, philosophy has its origins in the spirited rejection of the law and in manly atheism. The materialistic, atheistic philosophies are unknown to the Dorians who will colonize Magnesia, yet the Athenian mentions them anyway. The Athenian Stranger himself plants the seed of Athenian or Ionian atheism in his reconstructed Dorian city so as to make explicit the need for the speeches in defense of the gods and the law.[18]

The Nocturnal Council must converse with the young man who realizes the questionability of the city's teaching on the gods and its failure to achieve true human excellence, and must persuade him no longer to deny the existence and providence of the gods.[19] If the young man continues to question, to engage in dialogue, the conversation with him will rise to the highest things. These arguments on the unity of virtue and the existence of the gods form the principal business of the Nocturnal Council (964–6); this council is therefore entirely male.

Since in the second-best city women are moderate rather than manly, they are overly pious; they do not have within them the psychological root of impiety and thus of the philosophic education. Plato must believe that women in the second-best city do not lack this root by nature – the women among philosopher-rulers of the best city of the *Republic*

[18] *Laws* 886ab, 891b; and see Strauss 1975, 146. As Benardete point out, atheism would seem be the theological upshot of the endless strife between cities that Kleinias posits at the beginning of the *Laws* (*Laws* 626ab; Benardete 2000, 287–8). The difficulty that Kleinias's opinion poses for justice can only be answered, it would seem, by following his opinion to its atheistic consequences, consequences he personally would never have reached on his own had his Dorian bellicism not encountered Athenian or Ionian philosophy.
[19] *Laws* 888a; and compare *Sophist* 265d.

must have natures suited for philosophy – but rather because of their separate education and their restriction to women's work and women's space.

In one sense, we now understand why the laws of Magnesia exclude women from the institutional practice of philosophy: Their separate education cultivates traits in women opposed to those of the philosophic individual. Philosophy is, however, the most private of pursuits (*Apology* 31c–32a), and the philosophic education is the most private, most particular, of educations. A private philosophic education ought to make allowance for individual variation, for the exceptional woman who, despite all barriers both natural and legal, has emerged with a soul suitable for philosophy. Nonetheless, no woman can be seated on the Nocturnal Council, the official philosophic institution of the second-best city. Yet if the relationship between the elder and his beloved is to be private, why can it not encompass as beloved that rare young woman, who, despite the sexist education of the second-best city, emerges with a suitable soul?

Herein lies precisely the female tragedy of the second-best city. In a democracy, where the laws are in no way conducive to goodness (642cd), but rather where each person becomes excellent or not because of wholly private actions, philosophers and young potential philosophers come about spontaneously (951bc), and some of them may very well be women. In the best city, where not law but intelligence is sovereign, the possibility of philosophy is available to all whose individual natures are suitable, including, of course, women.

Law, however, "sees and looks toward as much as possible, but is unable to look toward everything" (*Laws* 875d). In the second-best city, where law is sovereign even over those who possess intelligence, even over the philosophic members of the Nocturnal Council, women's *general* philosophic incapacity, fostered by the laws themselves, must be presumed in law *without exception*. Because philosophy is licensed, it is regulated; philosophy becomes a concern for the second-best city, presumably an improvement over Athenian official neglect and Dorian ignorance. Yet the sovereignty of law over philosophy, just as in all other areas, distorts that over which it is sovereign (875cd), for the rule of law unjustly denies the possibility of philosophy to those women suited for it by nature.

6.4 THE STATUS OF WOMEN AND THE LIMITS OF MAGNESIA

Many writers have argued that Magnesia's fundamental lack is not to be found in the ethical character of her citizens, or in her laws and institutions, but rather in her lack of a philosophic element. All of Magnesia's concessions to possibility and practicability, they claim, are made because of the difficulty of finding men (or women) with sufficient knowledge to be philosopher-rulers.[20] I will argue, by contrast, that Magnesia's second-best status is a consequence of ethical rather than cognitive insufficiency.[21]

When we ask why Magnesia is second best, we are asking two different questions: First, what are the qualities of the regime that mark it out as inferior to other, better regimes? Second, why does Magnesia have these inferior qualities?

The second question has the shorter answer. Magnesia has inferior qualities, the Athenian Stranger states, because it admits private families and property, because it is not thoroughly communistic (*Laws* 739c–e, 807b). If Magnesia is a second-best regime in virtue of lacking communism, a regime lacking both communism and philosophers would be not second but third best.[22]

Magnesia's true flaws follow from this concession to the private or particular.[23] A city with private families and private property needs detailed legislation simply to counteract its rulers' inevitable preference for the private over the public, whether or not they have knowledge of how to rule.

Magnesia's ethical failures are thus consequences rather then causes of the rule of law. Law, not wisdom, is sovereign in the city of the *Laws*; *nomos* takes the place that ought to belong to *nous* (cf. 957c). The Athenian Stranger admits that knowledge ought to be sovereign, if it

---

[20] See inter alia Arendt 1958, 227 n. 69; Stalley 1983, 14–19. Cohen 1987, 31. Christopher Bruell (1994, 276) appears to suggest that Magnesia lacks a philosophic element because she does not implement communism.

[21] All are agreed, however, that if a philosophic element is to be found in Magnesia, it can be found only in the Nocturnal Council (see, e.g., Klosko 1988). Trevor Saunders claims that the Nocturnal Council is, however, no philosophic element, but a mere assemblage of gentleman-farmers (1992, 465). Martin Ostwald (1977, 59) rightly points out that while legislation is subordinate to the truth reached by the royal or political science in the *Statesman*, in the *Laws* the legislator is said to have an art that gives him "a truth he can hold on to" (*Laws* 709c8).

[22] This is true in the technical sense of third best introduced by Yew-Kwang Ng (1977), where a second-best solution is one adopted because of some policy constraint (e.g., in our case, no communism) and a third-best solution is one adopted because the second-best solution cannot be implemented without an unrealistic quantity of information (in our case, no philosophers).

[23] The contrast between the best and the second-best regimes in the *Laws* is in accord with the account of the emergence of the timocratic regime out of the best regime in the *Republic*. The best regime is transformed into a timocratic regime when some but not all members of the ruling class begin to covet private property (*Republic* 547bc). Thus in the *Republic*, as well as in the *Laws*, the private family and private property are the main instruments by which the timocratic man and the timocratic city are shaped (Andersson 1971, 165).

could come about in a human being together with the desire to give priority to the common (875) – that is, if knowledge could be joined with an ethical preference for the public or common over the private. Yet this coincidence of knowledge of how to rule rightly and of the desire to rule rightly has not yet occurred anywhere, it would appear, to such an extent as to enable any city to be ruled well by men rather than by laws. As Martin Ostwald writes, Plato recognizes in the *Laws* that the application of the true science of politics "is more safely left to laws rooted in a transcendental knowable nature than to frail human beings" (1977, 63). Nature is knowable by human beings, but we cannot be trusted to apply this knowledge against the pull of our desires without institutional restraints that pull us from without and persuasive preambles that move us from within.[24]

The laws of Magnesia maintain utter ignorance of justice as the following of the *logos* (cf. *Republic* 607a), and these laws deny that

---

[24] This point may be better understood through an examination of the work of a philosophic, if not always reliable, historian, Titus Livy. Livy's subject is the history of Rome "from the founding of the city," but his thesis is that political power is constituted by the voluntary transformation of natural necessities into political necessities. Livy conveys this thesis by narrating episodes in which the Roman people are managed within the city and when in arms against her enemies. Within the city, natural necessities become political necessities through law when a legislator imposes visible sanctions to keep the Romans away from distant harms. Outside the city, Rome's successful war leaders, whether patrician or plebeian, move her citizens to achieve previously unimagined glories by manipulating the circumstances that these citizens face. They are not afraid to manipulate the symbols and ceremonies of religion, to alter auguries, interpret oracles, and forge prophecies, so that Roman piety redounds to the glory of the Roman fatherland. More typically, however, commanders and statesmen, both Roman and foreign, conquer when they can arrange matters so that the path of glory before their troops is also the only path of safety.

Yet, since such an understanding is available only to the most exceptional individuals, what guides these individuals in their manipulation of public necessities can never be publicly revealed. That, one may say, is the tragedy of the greatest Roman, Scipio Africanus, who for all his achievements dies exiled, if not disgraced.

Livy presents these individuals within a larger tragic framework, the tragedy of Rome as a whole. These great Romans were so successful at spurring Romans through the manipulation of public necessities that they utterly destroyed the enemies who were the necessary instruments of this manipulation. Once the Romans no longer faced these political necessities, the necessities imposed by their laws were by themselves insufficient to prevent them from living according to their individual understandings of the needs and promptings of human nature. Yet, for those who are ignorant of the nature of human happiness, including the wealthy and powerful who aspired to tyrannize over Roman citizens and the foreigners subject to them, this freedom from political necessity meant a descent into luxury and corruption. In that sense, Livy ended his history on an optimistic note: The summary of book 142 concludes with the defeat of Varus by the Germans. This disastrous destruction of three legions heralds a mighty enemy, in the face of whom the manipulation or political necessities, and thus the revival of Roman virtue, might again be possible.

moral virtue requires any kind of intellectual virtue or theoretical achievement. In Magnesia, truth is subordinate to expedience[25] and manliness masquerades as justice. The laws claim that wisdom has nothing essentially to do with knowledge but is simply to live with a consonance between opinion and action (689d). In Magnesia, one need not know anything to be wise, nor does one need to possess right opinion! These ignorant laws are Magnesia's models for excellence: Poets must seek to imitate them, and teachers are required to praise them (811c–e).

As law replaces wisdom, old age replaces youth or maturity as the idealized period of human life, and friendship among citizens rather than the good of the city becomes the preeminent goal of political life. When the Stranger endorses the sovereignty of law, Kleinias the Cretan praises him with the remarkable words "you see with the sharpness of age" (715d; Strauss 1975, 59). As the Athenian will point out, the old are not known for their sharpness of vision, whether actual or intellectual (964e). Yet the stability of old age is necessary for maintaining adherence to an already existing law code; as a result, the Athenian Stranger stresses that old age must be overcome in order to legislate (752a8). To change the laws requires a youthful suspension of shame (Strauss 1975, 21).

The pursuit of human excellence in Magnesia is further constrained by the city's spirited elevation of friendship to become the highest principle of politics. Magnesia's laws insist that there is no greater good for a city than to have citizens familiar to one another.[26] Friendship is problematic as the goal of the city because, while friendship is love of one's own, the good is not simply possessed by human beings.[27] Whereas one ought to love or desire the good without limit, friendship always requires measure, similitude, and thus an upper bound to the goodness of the friend, since we do not want our friend to become too good to remain friendly toward us.[28] We turn toward the familiar when we are ignorant of the good, as little children turn toward their parents, for our actual friends are not necessarily those we think good or even good for us.[29]

---

[25] As when the laws teach that the life of justice is more pleasant than the life of injustice because such a belief is simply useful or expedient, without any regard for its truth or even its plausibility (663b).

[26] *Laws* 738e1–2. Magnesia, like Kleinias, thus considers the third-best judge, who reconciles the wicked to the good "by putting laws for them for the remaining time, so that he would be able to watch them so as for them to be friends," to be first best (v. 627e–628a; Strauss 1975, 5; Benardete 2000, 14–18).

[27] Indeed, we would seem to belong among the bad souls that oppose the good soul that is the source and cause of all good (*Laws* 896eff.).

[28] *Laws* 716c, Aristotle *Nicomachean Ethics* 1165b23–32; cf. *Phaedrus* 239e–240a.

[29] *Laws* 754b; cf. Cross and Woozley 1966, 19.

Even Kleinias can see that the identification of friendship and virtue that the city of the *Laws* presumes is questionable (693bc). If the gravest fault in a soul is to care for itself and its belongings rather than for justice (726a–728c), Magnesia, whose justice is but manliness with pretensions and who encourages friendship at the expense of piety and goodness, educates her citizens to have souls flawed by design.

Magnesia, then, is collectively guilty of excessive self-love. The city remedies excessive self-love in individuals by teaching them to love themselves as Magnesians and to love their own laws more than the goodness of the city or its laws warrants. The public legal teaching of the city is that its laws are superior to any foreign laws (950e–951a); the law is ignorant but claims to be wise.[30] Magnesia's excessive friendship for itself, like any excessive friendship for oneself, is a *spirited* error (Pangle 1976, 1073–4). Such friendship must be spirited rather than appetitive because friendship for oneself is an affect linked with a self-image, and spirited desires, unlike appetitive desires, are precisely those desires connected to a self-image.[31] Because Magnesia institutionalizes this spirited error, her ideal human being is excessively manly, is an ideal *man* (770cd).

The law of Magnesia itself, then, limits the goodness of its citizens. Good laws do not, therefore, make the best men. The best Athenians are better than any Dorians, and philosophers, "divine natures," do not by nature grow more frequently in cities with good laws than in cities with bad laws (642cd, 951bc). The rule of law thwarts the fullest possible human development by inculcating an inferior, overspirited, conception of human excellence. A city with a better system of laws is more effective at inculcating the laws' (compromised) version of human excellence. Since human excellence as constrained by the rule of law is necessarily overspirited, the highest human types will indeed be less fully developed in a regime governed more effectively by law.

The second-best city possesses second-best features inasmuch as it shares in the faults of the Dorian cities that the Athenian Stranger himself criticizes. The laws of Magnesia despise women as inferior: The punishment for cowardice, as we have seen, ought to be for a man to turn into a woman (944d)! Men, in turn, are excessively manly and look to manliness as their ideal instead of justice. Magnesia, like Sparta and Crete,

---

[30] The law of Magnesia may thus not be able to tolerate the public pursuit of any science that demonstrates our ignorance. Mathematics, the Athenian Stranger claims, is the teaching or science that makes us truly human because it teaches us, through the proof of the existence of incommensurables, that there are limits on our understanding (819c–820c). Nonetheless, the study of mathematics can be detached from the laws of Magnesia if it is not dear or friendly to the lawgivers (820e2–7).

[31] See Section 2.2.

fails, then, to prosecute fully the war against pleasures. In particular, the city of the *Laws* fails to eliminate pederastic indulgence, although the Athenian Stranger stigmatized the pleasures of homosexual inter-course as unnatural and, more importantly, ethically corrupting in his critique of the Dorian regimes.

6.5 THE PROBLEM OF REFORM UNDER PATRIARCHY

A law that assigns moderation to women and manliness to men distorts the true human excellence, which demands both moderation and man-liness of every human being. Since the laws of the *Laws* fail to promul-gate properly the unity of human excellence in a single individual, they contain within themselves a permanent tension. The philosopher cannot simply legislate and then abandon Magnesia if her regime is to remain second-best – the best possible regime among the regimes that allow for private families and property.

The preservation of the laws requires a knowledge of the unity of human excellence (962bff.), so the regime that professes to be ruled by law cannot dispense with the scientifically trained ruler.[32] Without a continual infusion of Athenian philosophy, the overmanliness of the second-best regime may make it into just another Sparta. As long as the contradictions of manliness and gentleness in the soul remain unmodi-fied, the inadequate unity of virtue will continue to demand philosophic reconciliation. Yet since law must be sovereign in the second-best city, philosophy itself, in striving to reform law, must unjustly be subject to law.

The Nocturnal Council, the Athenian Stranger says, is introduced in order to make the laws of the city irreversible (960–1). Yet irreversible is not the same as unchanging: Because the regime of the *Laws* fails to instill complete human excellence, it is always susceptible to improve-ment. In book VI (769–70) the Athenian Stranger compares the city they are founding to an incomplete painting, an outline unfinished in detail.

---

[32] George Klosko (1988) claims that while the Nocturnal Council described in Book XII of the *Laws* does indeed aim for a true philosophy, the detailed nature of the legislation in Books I–XI is not compatible with a state that has a philosophic element. Klosko therefore postulates that this contradiction is merely the result of Plato's having failed to revise the text of the laws before his death. Yet the Nocturnal Council has an inte-gral place in the *drama* of the *Laws*: The Council plays a crucial role in the problem of the unity of human excellence, a problem thematic throughout the dialogue. Klosko is in some sense correct in arguing that the Nocturnal Council lacks an integral place in the *regime* described there: As André Laks writes, "the Nocturnal Council cannot but be 'external' to the other institutions, since it is the instrument of their preservation" (Laks 2000, 283). Bradley Lewis (1998) provides a thorough and helpful discussion of the place of the Nocturnal Council, and of Klosko's thesis, which Lewis rejects.

To finish the details, he says, "it is necessary for us at the same time to legislate, and to try as far as possible to make these [men] both legislators and Guardians of the Law" (770a). These Guardians, the members of the Nocturnal Council, whom the Athenian Stranger describes as "perfected guardians" (969c), are the Guardians of the Law in the truest sense, those who will continue to improve the painting.[33]

Innovation in Magnesia thus ought to occur, but it must be continually concealed to preserve the lie that the laws are forever fixed.[34] While the laws claim that they are forever fixed and unchanging, their unalterability turns out to be a myth. The laws inculcate this myth in order to conceal from ordinary Magnesians that the Nocturnal Council is continually legislating. As Anton Powell puts it, "a technique of control allied with gerontocracy in the *Laws* is deceit"; part of the deceit lies in the fact that the elders of the Nocturnal Council are philosophers in disguise.[35] Crucial to the deceit is that the authority of the aged and of the law that favors them is not quite as complete as the laws themselves profess: The Nocturnal Council where changes are mooted is itself composed of both older and younger men, so that the old will learn to appreciate the youthful critique of the paternal even as the critical vehemence of the young is moderated by the experience – or at least the stolidity – of the aged.[36] Yet in Magnesia, the young ought always to address the same things as dear (797b5–6), and the city must accept the admittedly strange dogma that songs should become laws (799e10), that music itself, where novelty and youth are most delightful and necessary, be held forever to canons with Egyptian rigidity. It is this conflict between fixity and innovation, father and son, aged, fearful theist and youthful, brash atheist, that is ineradicable even in the second-best city. This conflict drives the permanent politics of Magnesia.[37]

Magnesia is to effect this steady improvement by being partly open, despite its excessive self-admiration, to foreign things: to philosophy and

---

[33] The best city, by contrast, is described in the *Republic* as a painting of a perfect man, which can only degenerate (*Republic* 470d).

[34] See *Laws* 798b; Farabi, *Plato's Laws*, 7.12–13.

[35] Powell 1994, 284; Vidal-Naquet 1986, 298.

[36] See on this point Benardete 2000, 68: "The problem, then, is not how to ram the choice of the old down the throats of the young, but how to induce the old to accept with understanding the pleasure of the young."

[37] Sheldon Wolin misses this conflict between Youth and Age when he claims that Plato's political science seeks to stamp out politics (1960, 42), though this conflict played an important role in Athenian political debates in the classical period. Alcibiades symbolized hubristic youth (Strauss 1993), while democrats emphasized the authority of the aged and paternal. Frequently the partisans of the few adopted the democratic lexicon wherein older is always better by speaking of the "ancestral constitution" (Finley 1990).

to possibly superior foreign customs. The first mention of the Nocturnal Council as such occurs in the discussion of foreign missions:

For there are always among the many some divine human beings, not many, worth any price to have intercourse with – and they do not grow more in well-legislated cities (*en eunomenais polesin*) than in not at all [well-legislated cities].[38] It is always useful for the inhabitant of the well-legislated cities to search for them, if [that inhabitant] is incorruptible, and to travel through land and sea, in order to make fast some of the lawful things, as many as are finely legislated among them, but correcting others, if they are in any way neglected. For without this very observation (*tautēs tēs theōrias*) and search a city will not remain perfect, nor [will it] if they conduct this observation poorly. (951bc)

Because the second-best city fails to actualize true human excellence, it always has something to learn from the laws and inhabitants of other cities, and especially from those divine human beings, philosophers (see *Sophist* 216b), who themselves know and practice privately the truest human excellence. The observers sent out on this most important observation are to report to the Nocturnal Council, and if these observers return with some wisdom of use in improving the laws, they are to be honored and seated on the council (*Laws* 952, 961a).

The Nocturnal Council is to study not merely philosophy but also foreign customs in their particularity, to the extent that this study is helpful in improving Magnesia's own legislation (952a).[39] Thus the second-best regime will always be on guard against the excess of spirit that would lead its citizens to scorn all foreign laws and influences (compare *Laws* 950). This excess is especially dangerous precisely because the regime's imperfect conception of human excellence, which separates the excellences of men and women and substitutes manliness for justice, makes the citizens whom it has educated unworthy of such pride.

The Nocturnal Council explores the problem of the unity of the virtues precisely to ameliorate the failures of Magnesia's gendered conception of virtue. The problem of the unity of the virtues is posed most seriously by the apparent opposition between manliness and the other virtues of justice, moderation, and wisdom. Manliness seems irrational in a way that justice and wisdom are not: Manliness is present in very young children (963e) and even in animals that fight to protect their young (814b).

If the kinds of human excellence cannot be brought into harmony, then the city cannot have a single aim (963a). Since manliness both in

---

[38] On the spontaneous growths that are potential philosophers see Kochin 1999b.
[39] Magnesian court procedure, for example, will be set up on foreign models (957ab).

the ordinary Greek understanding and in the self-understanding of Magnesia is peculiarly the excellence of men, while moderation is the excellence of women, the inability to unify the virtues implies an inability to give any kind of account of a single human excellence equally available and applicable to both men and women.

The only hope for such a single human excellence is to show that the human excellences are led by mind or truth (631b–d). For the philosopher, who is indeed led by truth, the apparent irreconcilability of the virtues, as evidenced by the separation of the virtues into male and female, calls into question the seriousness of human things. Immediately after legislating that Magnesia will distinguish between the songs fitting for women and those fitting for men, thereby "attempting to separate the forms of lives according to the habits of souls" (803a6–8), the Athenian Stranger adds that "the affairs of human beings are not worthy of great seriousness, but it is necessary nonetheless to be serious about them" (803b3–5).[40] The Athenian Stranger raises this issue of the seriousness of human affairs only to drop it when challenged by Megillus, saying, "let our species not be unimportant, if it is dear to you" (804b9–c1).

We, unfortunately, must be serious about the human things, understood as the separate, perhaps irreconcilable things of men and things of women, because they are dear to us, because all of our laws, customs, family relationships, and erotic strivings have already been founded on this difference as it exists in our regime.

The difference between the sexes becomes a political problem only when the best regime is abandoned, when the philosopher's justice that consists in obedience to the logos is abandoned. If we remain below the level of the logos, below the level of complete submission of the human things to intelligence and truth, we are confronted, Plato shows us in the *Laws*, by an irreconcilable difference between the sexes. It is a difference that a second-best city, which admits the private and is governed by law, can only hope to mitigate.

We learn from the Athenian Stranger's account of the Nocturnal Council that a proper institutionalization of permanent reform allows each improvement to provide an opportunity for further improvement, and we learn from his account of economic redistribution that reform *can* come through the generosity of the powerful (736d4–737a6). We may hope to accomplish reform of women's condition in actual cities

---

[40] One should keep in mind Angela Hobbs's observation that if the human things do not matter much, "the perception that this is so does not matter much either" (2000, 217). As I have argued elsewhere, this is in a most pristine version the political teaching of Plato's Eleatic Stranger (Kochin 1999a).

through persuasion of men, who seem to benefit from women's oppression. But as the Athenian Stranger's discussion of the concealment of innovation shows, such reform through persuasion would seem to require that the partisans of the improvement of women's condition couch their arguments in terms of the existing ideals. To do that, they must, as the Athenian Stranger does, portray manliness itself, however it is understood in their regime, as an incomplete ideal of human excellence. If their city proclaims manliness to be the sum or peak of human excellence, they must instead show that their city's concept of manliness is problematic and even self-undermining.

We can achieve full reconciliation of the so-called excellences of women and the so-called excellences of men, says Plato, only through rule of philosophers, that is to say, through the complete rationalization of political life. The city, however, exists for the sake of philosophy, for the sake of the pursuit of wisdom, since the uncivilized herdsmen were more moderate, more manly, and more just (679e; Pangle 1980, 426–7). The city looks toward the wisdom of the goddess Athena (796bc; Pangle 1980, 486); that is, Magnesia looks toward the armed goddess as a model of the true *human* excellence that combines manliness and moderation with justice and philosophic wisdom. Athena embodies the reconciliation of male and female excellences at which Magnesia aims but cannot by its very construction ever attain.

Magnesia will send out only men as ambassadors to study foreign laws and sit at the knees of foreign philosophers, but it will receive both men and women as ambassadors (*presbutai*, respected elders) from other cities.[41] A female ambassador would have to have been sent by a city where women shared more fully in public life. A female ambassador would appear to the Magnesian, or at least to the (entirely male) philosophic element of Magnesia that constitutes the Nocturnal Council, as a representative of a city more successful in attaining human excellence than their own – not merely an envoy, but an inspiration.

---

[41] *Laws* 951cd, 953e1; England ad loc. 953e1. Pace Monoson (2000, 228), there is no suggestion that Magnesia will send out female ambassadors or observers for any purpose, whether legislative, diplomatic, or religious.

Conclusion

From Plato Back to Politics

For Plato the defense of justice, and thus of the philosophic life, required the appropriation and deployment of the commonplaces furnished by the civic and heroic conceptions of masculinity. Even if we took Plato as our model, we could hardly hope to persuade by repeating his speeches or even by the arguments and motifs he composed. What we must learn from Plato, however, is that any serious attempt to address questions of gender with speeches that ought to persuade must address human beings in the actual complexity of their desires.

Plato, we have seen, gives three arguments for the thesis that the unequal treatment of women is bad for men. In the *Laws* the Athenian Stranger decries the waste of women's talents and resources that results from the restrictions that actual Greek cities impose on women's activities.[1] Such an argument based on political efficiency is subordinate, however, to an account of the ends to be attained. The end of the regime ought to be human excellence, Plato claims, that is to say, the excellence of the individual citizens who compose the city.[2] Through his psychology of human excellence and its corruptions, Plato develops two more fundamental arguments against sexual inequality.

I will begin with the more peculiar of what Plato alleges are the corruptions of human excellence due to sexual inequality. A regime that treats women and men equally grants greater possibilities to the love of men and women, Plato claims. Insofar as a regime treats men and women unequally, it discourages the love of men for women and encourages the love of men for men (*Laws* 839b). Plato thought that the love of men

---

[1] *Laws* 806c. Pace Annas, this argument is present only in the *Laws* and plays no role in the *Republic* (Annas 1976, 315–16; 1981, 183; cf. Osborne 1978, 89).

[2] See, e.g., *Republic* 456de, *Laws* 630e, 963a. The claim that Plato subordinates the good of individuals to the good of the city as a superordinate individual is refuted by Vlastos (1977, 13–17).

for men was problematic in a sexually inegalitarian community because, when consummated, it tended to foster manly vice in the lover and effeminate vice in the beloved.[3]

No doubt it is difficult for us to accept Plato's argument that sex between males is wrong because it undermines the virtues of manliness and moderation necessary for citizenship. If we wished to challenge the logic of this argument directly, we could imitate Phaedrus and Pausanius in Plato's own *Symposium* and point out that a discourse of pederasty reemerges as part of the revival of civic life and its virtues, both in republican Florence and in Elizabethan England.[4]

Yet it is not so much Plato's inference from pederasty to the ethical corruption of citizens as his appraisal of the civic virtues that we reject. Modern civil society demands that its members be productive workers rather than active patriots, and to that end places different moral burdens on its members than did the ancient city. In particular we assume that sexual relations ought to be companionate and long-lasting, whether they are relations between men, between women, or between men and women. Our debate over the morality of sex between men becomes a debate over the distinction between moral and immoral forms of sexuality generally speaking: To avoid probing the ontological and therefore ethical implications of sex between men, we assimilate gay and lesbian couplings to male–female couples and turn to ponder gay marriage. In our reflections on the question of gay marriage, we articulate bourgeois concerns about health and "family values" rather than civic concerns about freedom and independence. Plato's political case against pederasty cannot claim our attention not because of our opinions about sex and nature, but because we do not share the classical sense of the primacy of the political.[5] In that sense, few today believe that "the personal is political."

Plato's third argument that men suffer from the political exclusion of the female does not rely on any claim that sexual love between men is

---

[3] See Section 6.1.

[4] See *Symposium* 178d–179a, 182a–185c, parodied notoriously by Aristophanes at 192a; and on the integral place of pederasty within free political life see Rahe 1992, 128–33. On pederasty and politics in Florence see Rocke 1996, Masters 1998. For Elizabethan England, one should consider the dedications of Shakespeare's *Venus and Adonis* and *Rape of Lucrece* to Southampton in the light of Southampton's role in Sir Philip Sidney's literary circle and subsequently in the rising of his friend Essex against Elizabeth – a matter I am exploring jointly with Katherine Philippakis.

[5] Reading carefully Rocke 1996, one discovers that male–male sexual relations were more strictly governed in those periods of the fifteenth and sixteenth centuries when republican institutions were strong, and that their regulation was dissolved during periods of Medici domination.

bad or unnatural. Plato argues, I have shown, that the conceptions of masculinity held by the citizens of patriarchal regimes teach these citizens to devalue the virtue of moderation. The civic conception of masculinity teaches that moderation is only an instrumental good; the heroic conception teaches that only excess is suitable for real men, whereas women should abstain from the greatest possible engorgement of their appetites. By treating women more equally, men, Plato claims, would learn to revalue in themselves the traits that the laws of actual cities have taught them to see as effeminate. Only then could men seek moderation wholeheartedly as part of their own excellence, whether as moderate citizens or as citizens of a more moderate city.

Modern pluralism has seemingly rendered outdated the Platonic quest for a unified account of human goods and thus of human virtues: "The progress of civilization," Benjamin Constant writes, "the commercial tendency of the age, the communication among peoples, have infinitely multiplied and varied the means of individual happiness."[6] Yet our demand, as citizens, for public accountability and responsibility from some members of the state apparatus is in large part a demand for officials to act in constant accord with unified norms of character (Kochin n.d.). The unity of the virtues remains fundamental to our ideal of political virtue in itself or of political life as a life worth living among the multiplicity of life choices available in modern society. John Casey has written that we take the "pagan" virtues "more seriously than we are usually prepared to recognize" (1990, viii). It is in what we possess of political life, if anywhere, that the life of virtue still appears to us as a life worthy of choice. To the extent that the problems of gender are problems for men and women not merely as members of society but as citizens with political duties and ambitions, Plato's aspiration for a political unification of the virtues still speaks to our own aspirations. The most that can be said for Plato's aspiration is that it takes seriously the problem of the relation between the needs of the community and the happiness of the individual. The most that can be said against our view is that, notwithstanding Constant's claim about the *means* of happiness, we seem to deny that the *achievement* of happiness is possible or even meaningful.[7]

---

[6] Part II of *The Spirit of Conquest and Usurpation and Their Relation to European Civilization*, chap. 6; translation slightly modified from Constant 1988, 104.

[7] A more gentle version of this critique of our society as closed to happiness is offered by Milan Kundera (1997); a harsher one is offered by Michel Houellebecq (1998, 2000). For the philosophical roots of our predicament see Thomas Hobbes, *Leviathan*, Book 1, Chapter 11; John Locke, *An Essay Concerning Human Understanding*, Book 2, Chapter 21.

Plato's fundamental arguments for sexual egalitarianism are grounded in an appeal to the conditions of male moral development. Such an appeal would have to be reformulated for the contemporary political community, which includes both men and women, as an appeal to the conditions of moral development of both sexes. To be rhetorically successful, however, such arguments must address the distinctive moral understandings and concerns of women and men, as well as the differentiated understandings of men's and women's roles that still structure our prejudices.

The contemporary feminist movement, like most other supposedly political movements of the last fifty years, too often understands itself to stand before the administrative and judicial apparatus of the state for recognition and redress of grievances. What we, male and female citizens, are to do about these matters besides demand action from others, and how we can use the state machinery – or, one should say, how we can work *our* state machinery – to achieve feminist ends are questions that require us to shoulder the burdens of citizenship forthrightly. Among the rights of citizenship is the right to government by consent; the corresponding duty of citizenship is the duty to secure the consent of others to the political acts that we undertake in the name of all. Consent is achieved through rhetoric, but too often contemporary political and intellectual elites shirk the burden of persuasion by moving immediately from arguments that they think ought to persuade all rational men and women to the forcible imposition of their conclusions on men and women who vocally and sincerely dissent. They simply respond with additional violence when they realize that they have not actually persuaded those who are ruled.

It may seem unjust that those who know better must condescend to moderate the power of their knowledge by enforcing their rule only to the extent that they can persuade. Plato's Eleatic Stranger, the principal interlocutor of the *Statesman*, claims that the rightness of any form of government depends on the possession of the true art of governing by the rulers and not on the consent or dissent of the ruled (293). Yet in the *Laws* the Athenian Stranger is no less certain that human beings cannot fully control their passions and appetites so as to rule without law and without account to their fellow citizens (644d–645b, 875b). It is thus a paradoxical fact that Plato bequeathed upon us both the most forceful rejection of the duty to achieve consent in the arguments of the Eleatic Stranger in the *Statesman* and the most profound exploration of the rhetoric of gender in the *Republic* and the *Laws*. Because we think that gender relations are amenable to transformation through political action, the question is not whether we want to be Platonists, but which kind of Platonist we want to be. Plato's return to rhetoric and persuasion in his last work, the *Laws*, makes his own choice manifest, but we are more faithful to the intentions of Plato the philosopher if in pondering his writings we force ourselves to answer afresh both Plato's questions and our own.

Modern Works Cited

Adam, James, ed. [1902] 1963. *The Republic of Plato*. 2 vols. Second edition, with an introduction by D. A. Rees. Cambridge: Cambridge University Press.

Adams, William. 1988. "History, Interpretation, and the Politics of Theory." *Polity* 21:46–66.

Adkins, A. W. H. 1960. *Merit and Responsibility*. Oxford: Oxford University Press.

1970. *From the Many to the One: A Study of Personality and Views of Human Nature in the Context of Ancient Greek Society, Values, and Beliefs*. Ithaca: Cornell University Press.

1976. "*Polupragmosune* and 'Minding One's Own Business': A Study in Greek Social and Political Values." *Classical Philology* 71:301–27.

Alford, C. Fred. 1991. *The Self in Social Theory: A Psychoanalytic Account of Its Construction in Plato, Hobbes, Locke, Rawls, and Rousseau*. New Haven: Yale University Press.

Allen, Danielle S. 2000. *The World of Prometheus: The Politics of Punishing in Democratic Athens*. Princeton: Princeton University Press.

Allen, R. E. 1987a. "The Speech of Glaucon in Plato's *Republic*." *Journal of the History of Philosophy* 25:3–11.

1987b. "The Speech of Glaucon: On Contract and the Common Good." In *Justice, Law, and Method in Plato and Aristotle*, ed. Spiro Panagiotou. Edmonton, Alberta, Canada: Academic Printing and Publishing.

Anderson, Warren D. 1966. *Ethos and Education in Greek Music: The Evidence of Poetry and Philosophy*. Cambridge, Massachusetts: Harvard University Press.

Andersson, Torsten J. 1971. *Polis and Psyche: A Motif in Plato's Republic. Studia Graeca et Latina Gothoburgensia* 30.

Andrew, Edward. 1989. "Equality of Opportunity as the Noble Lie." *History of Political Thought* 10:577–95.

Annas, Julia. 1976. "Plato's *Republic* and Feminism." *Philosophy* 51:307–21.

1981. *Introduction to Plato's Republic*. Oxford: Oxford University Press.

Arendt, Hannah. 1958. *The Human Condition*. Chicago: University of Chicago Press.

1959. "Reflections on Little Rock." *Dissent* 6:45–56.

1965. *On Revolution*. New York: Viking.

1968. "What Is Authority?" In *Between Past and Future: Eight Essays in Political Thought*. New York: Viking.

Averroes. 1966. *Averroes' Commentary on Plato's Republic*, ed. and tr. E. I. J. Rosenthal. Cambridge: Cambridge University Press.

1974. *Averroes on Plato's Republic*, tr. Ralph Lerner. Ithaca: Cornell University Press.

Barker, Ernest. 1947. *Greek Political Theory: Plato and His Predecessors*. London: Methuen.

Benardete, Seth. 1989. *Socrates' Second Sailing: On Plato's Republic*. Chicago: University of Chicago Press.

2000. *Plato's "Laws": The Discovery of Being*. Chicago: University of Chicago Press.

Berent, Moshe. 1998. "*Stasis*, or the Greek Invention of Politics." *History of Political Thought* 19:331–62.

2000. "Sovereignty: Ancient and Modern." *Polis* 17:2–34.

Black, Edwin. 1965. *Rhetorical Criticism: A Study in Method*. New York: Macmillan.

Blair, Elena Duvergès. 1996. "Women: The Unrecognized Teachers of the Platonic Socrates." *Ancient Philosophy* 16:333–50.

Blitz, Mark. 1991. "Strauss's Laws." *Political Science Reviewer* 20(1):186–222.

Bloom, Allan, tr. 1968. *The Republic of Plato*. New York: Basic Books.

1977. "Response to Hall." *Political Theory* 5:315–30.

Bluestone, Natalie Harris. 1987. *Women and the Ideal Society: Plato's Republic and Modern Myths of Gender*. Amherst: University of Massachusetts Press.

Bobonich, Christopher. 1994. "Akrasia and Agency in Plato's *Laws* and *Republic*." *Archiv für Geschichte der Philosophie* 76:3–36.

Bowden, Hugh. 1993. "Hoplites and Homer: Warfare, Hero Cult, and the Ideology of the Polis." In *War and Society in the Greek World*, ed. John Rich and Graham Shipley. London: Routledge.

Bowie, A. M. 1993. *Aristophanes: Myth, Ritual and Comedy*. Cambridge: Cambridge University Press.

Brown, Wendy. 1988a. *Manhood and Politics*. Totowa, New Jersey: Rowman and Littlefield.

1988b. "Supposing Truth Were a Woman: Plato's Subversion of Masculine Discourse." *Political Theory* 16:594–616.

Bruell, Christopher. 1994. "On Plato's Political Philosophy." *Review of Politics* 56:261–82.

Brunt, P. A. 1993. "The Model City of Plato's *Laws*." In *Studies in Greek History and Thought*. Oxford: Oxford University Press.

Buchan, Morag. 1999. *Women in Plato's Political Theory*. New York: Routledge.

Burnet, John, ed. 1900–2. *Platonis Opera*. 5 vols. Oxford: Oxford University Press.

Burns, Steven. 1984. "Women in Bloom." *Dialogue* 23:135–40.

Bury, R. G. 1926. *Plato: Laws*. 2 vols. London: Heinemann.

Calvert, Brian. 1975. "Plato and the Equality of Women." *Phoenix* 29:231–43.

Canto, Monique. 1986. "The Politics of Women's Bodies: Reflections on Plato," tr. Arthur Goldhammer. In *The Female Body in Western Culture: Contemporary Perspectives*. Cambridge, Massachusetts: Harvard University Press, 339–53.

Cartledge, Paul. 1981. "Spartan Wives: Liberation or License." *Classical Quarterly* 31:84–105.

Casey, John. 1990. *Pagan Virtues: An Essay in Ethics*. Oxford: Oxford University Press.

Clark, Randall Baldwin. 2000. "Platonic Love in a Colorado Courtroom: Martha Nussbaum, John Finnis, and Plato's *Laws* in *Evans v. Romer*." *Yale Journal of Law and the Humanities* 12:1–38.

Claus, David. 1981. *Toward the Soul: An Inquiry into the Meaning of Psuchē before Plato*. New Haven: Yale University Press.

Cocks, Joan. 1989. *The Oppositional Imagination*. London and New York: Routledge.

Cohen, David. 1984. "The Athenian Law of Adultery." *Revue International Des Droits de L'Antiquité* 3rd ser. 31:147–65.

1987. "The Legal Status and Political Role of Women in Plato's Laws." *Revue International Des Droits de L'Antiquité* 3rd ser. 34:27–40.

1991. *Law, Sexuality, and Society: The Enforcement of Morals in Classical Athens*. Cambridge: Cambridge University Press.

1993. "Law, Autonomy, and Political Community in Plato's *Laws*." *Classical Philology* 88:301–17.

1995. *Law, Violence and Community in Classical Athens*. Cambridge: Cambridge University Press.

Cole, Thomas. 1991. *The Origins of Rhetoric in Ancient Greece*. Baltimore: Johns Hopkins University Press.

Constant, Benjamin. 1988. *Political Writings*, tr. and ed. Biancamaria Fontana. Cambridge: Cambridge University Press.

Cooper, John M. 1984. "Plato's Theory of Human Motivation." *History of Philosophy Quarterly* 1:3–21.

Cornford, F. M. 1912. "Psychology and Social Structure in the *Republic* of Plato." *Classical Quarterly* 6:246–65.

1929–30. "The Division of the Soul." *Hibbert Journal* 27:206–19.

Craig, Leon Harold. 1994. *The War Lover: A Study of Plato's Republic*. Toronto: University of Toronto Press.

Cross, R. C. and A. D. Woozley. 1966. *Plato's Republic: A Philosophical Commentary*. London: Macmillan.

Crossman, R. H. S. 1959. *Plato To-Day*. Revised Edition. London: George Allen & Unwin.

Davidson, James. 1998. *Courtesans and Fishcakes: The Consuming Passions of Classical Athens*. New York: St. Martin's Press.

Dawson, Doyne. 1992. *Cities of the Gods: Communist Utopias in Greek Thought*. Oxford: Oxford University Press.

Defoe, Daniel. 1971. *The Fortunes and Misfortunes of the Famous Moll Flanders*, ed. G. A. Starr. London: Oxford University Press.

Derrida, Jacques. 1981. "Plato's Pharmacy." In *Dissemination*, tr. Barbara Johnson. Chicago: University of Chicago Press.

Des Places, Édouard, ed. and trans. 1951. *Les Lois Livres I–VI*. In *Platon: Oeuvres Complètes*, vol. XI, pts. 1–2. Paris: Société D'Édition "Les Belles Lettres."

Despland, Michel. 1985. *The Education of Desire: Plato and the Philosophy of Religion*. Toronto: University of Toronto Press.

Diès, A., ed. and trans. 1956. *Les Lois Livres VII–XII*. In *Platon: Oeuvres Complètes*, vol. XII, pts. 1–2. Paris: Société D'Édition "Les Belles Lettres."

Dobbs, Darrell. 1985. "Aristotle's Anticommunism." *American Journal of Political Science* 29:29–46.

———. 1994. "Choosing Justice: Socrates' Model City and the Practice of Dialectic." *American Political Science Review* 88:263–77

Dodds, E. R. 1951. *The Greeks and the Irrational*. Berkeley: University of California Press.

Dover, K. J. 1964. "Eros and Nomos (Plato, *Symposium* 182a–185c)." *Institute of Classical Studies Bulletin* 11:31–42.

———. 1974. *Greek Popular Morality in the Time of Plato and Aristotle*. Oxford: Basil Blackwell.

———. 1989. *Greek Homosexuality*. Second Edition. Cambridge, Massachusetts: Harvard University Press.

duBois, Page. 1982. *Centaurs and Amazons: Women and the Pre-History of the Great Chain of Being*. Ann Arbor: University of Michigan Press.

Dworkin, Andrea. 1987. *Intercourse*. New York: Free Press.

Edmonds, J. M., ed. and tr. 1931. *Greek Elegy and Iambus*, vol. I. Cambridge, Massachusetts: Harvard University Press.

Elshtain, Jean Bethke. 1981. *Public Man, Private Woman: Women in Social and Political Thought*. Princeton: Princeton University Press.

———. 1987. *Women and War*. New York: Basic Books.

England, E. B., ed. 1921. *The Laws of Plato*. 2 vols. Manchester: The University Press.

al-Farabi, Abu Nasr Muhammad. n.d. "*Plato's Laws*," tr. Muhsin Mahdi. Unpublished manuscript.

Ferrari, G. R. F. 1987. *Listening to the Cicadas: A Study of Plato's* Phaedrus. Cambridge: Cambridge University Press.

Finley, M. I. 1990. "The Ancestral Constitution." In *The Use and Abuse of History*. London: Penguin.

Forde, Steven. 1997. "Gender and Justice in Plato." *American Political Science Review* 91:657–70.

Fortenbaugh, William W. 1975a. "On Plato's Feminism in *Republic* V." *Apeiron* 9:1–4.

———. 1975b. "Plato: Temperament and Eugenic Policy." *Arethusa* 8:283–305.

Foucault, Michel. 1985. *The Uses of Pleasure*, tr. Robert Hurley. Vol. 2 of *The History of Sexuality*. New York: Vintage Books.

Foxhall, Lin. 1998. "Pandora Unbound: A Feminist Critique of Foucault's *History of Sexuality*." In *Rethinking Sexuality: Foucault and Classical*

Antiquity, ed. David H. J. Larmour, Paul Allen Miller, and Charles Plattner. Princeton: Princeton University Press.

Frankfurt, Harry G. 1971. "Freedom of the Will and the Concept of a Person." *Journal of Philosophy* 68:5–20.

Freud, Sigmund. 1963. "The Unconscious," tr. Cecil M. Baines. In *General Psychological Theory: Papers on Metapsychology*, ed. Philip Reiss. New York: Macmillan. [German original first published 1915.]

Friedländer, Paul. 1964–9. *Plato.* 3 vols. New York: Bollingen.

Goldhill, Simon. 1995. *Foucault's Virginity: Ancient Erotic Fiction and the History of Sexuality.* Cambridge: Cambridge University Press.

Gould, John. 1980. "Law, Custom and Myth: Aspects of the Social Position of Women in Classical Athens." *Journal of Hellenic Studies* 100:38–59.

Gouldner, Alvin W. 1965. *Enter Plato: Classical Greece and the Origins of Social Theory.* New York: Basic Books.

Graves, Robert. 1958. *Greek Mythology.* London: Cassell and Company.

Gray, J. Glenn. 1967. *The Warriors: Reflections on Men in Battle.* With an Introduction by Hannah Arendt. New York: Harper and Row.

Grube, G. M. A. 1927. "The Marriage Laws in Plato's *Republic.*" *Classical Quarterly* 21:95–9.

    1935. *Plato's Thought.* Boston: Beacon Press.

Guthrie, W. K. C. 1975. *A History of Greek Philosophy.* Vol. IV, *Plato, the Man and His Dialogues: Earlier Period.* Cambridge: Cambridge University Press.

Gutzwiller, Kathryn J. and Ann Norris Michelini. 1991. "Women and Other Strangers: Feminist Perspectives in Classical Literature." In *(En)Gendering Knowledge: Feminists in Academe*, ed. Joan E. Hartman and Ellen Messer-Davidow. Knoxville: University of Tennessee Press.

Halliwell, S., ed. and tr. 1993. *Plato: Republic 5.* Warminister, England: Aris & Phillips.

Halperin, David M. 1989. "Sex Before Sexuality: Pederasty, Politics and Power in Classical Athens." In *One Hundred Years of Homosexuality and Other Essays on Greek Love.* New York: Routledge.

Hanson, Victor Davis. 1989. *The Western Way of War: Infantry Battle in Classical Greece.* New York: Alfred A. Knopf.

Haraway, Donna J. 1997. *Modest–Witness@Second–Millennium.FemaleMan©–Meets–OncoMouse^{TM}: Feminism and Technoscience.* New York: Routledge.

Harris, Edward M. 1990. "Did the Athenians Regard Seduction as a Worse Crime Than Rape?" *Classical Quarterly* 40:370–7.

Heidegger, Martin. 1998. "Plato's Doctrine of Truth," tr. Thomas Sheehan. In *Pathmarks*, ed. William McNeill. Cambridge: Cambridge UniversityPress.

Hobbs, Angela. 2000. *Plato and the Hero: Courage, Manliness, and the Impersonal Good.* Cambridge: Cambridge University Press.

Holmes, Stephen. 1979. "Aristippus in and out of Athens." *American Political Science Review* 73:113–28.

hooks, bell. 1984. *Feminist Theory: From Margin to Center.* Boston: South End Press.

Houllebecq, Michel. 1998. *Whatever*, tr. Paul Hammond. London: Serpent's Tail. 2000. *Atomised*, tr. Frank Wynne. London: Heinemann.

Howland, Jacob. 1993. *The Republic: The Odyssey of Philosophy. Twayne's Masterwork Studies* 122. New York: Twayne Publishers.

Humphrey, Catherine. 1983. *Karl Marx Collective: Economy, Society, and Religion in a Siberian Collective Farm*. Cambridge: Cambridge University Press.

Hyland, Drew A. 1990. "Plato's Three Waves and the Question of Utopia." *Intepretation* 18:91–109.

Irigaray, Luce. 1985. *Speculum of the Other Woman*, tr. Gillian Gill. Ithaca: Cornell University Press.

Irwin, Terence. 1995. *Plato's Ethics*. Oxford: Oxford University Press.

Jacobs, William. 1978. "Plato on Female Emancipation and the Traditional Family." *Apeiron* 12:29–31.

Jaeger, Werner. 1945. *Paideia: The Ideals of Greek Culture*, tr. Gilbert Highet, second edition. 3 vols. New York and Oxford: Oxford University Press.

Jang, In Ha. 1996. "The Problematic Character of Socrates' Defense of Justice in Plato's *Republic*." *Interpretation* 24:85–107.

Johnson, Pauline. 1994. *Feminism as Radical Humanism*. Boulder and San Francisco: Westview.

Jones, Nicholas F. 1990. "The Organization of the Kretan City in Plato's *Laws*." *Classical World* 83:473–92.

Joseph, Horace W. B. 1935. *Essays in Ancient and Modern Philosophy*. Reprint, Freeport, New York: Books for Libraries Press, 1971.

Just, Roger. 1989. *Women in Athenian Law and Life*. London and New York: Routledge.

Kenny, A. S. P. 1969. "Mental Health in Plato's *Republic*." *Proceedings of the British Academy* 40:231–53.

Kelly, John Clardy. 1989. "Virtue and Inwardness in Plato's *Republic*." *Ancient Philosophy* 9:189–205.

Klosko, George. 1986. *The Development of Plato's Political Theory*. New York and London: Methuen.

1988. "The Nocturnal Council in Plato's *Laws*." *Political Studies* 36:74–88.

Kochin, Michael S. 1996. "Decollectivization of Agriculture and the Planned Economy." *American Journal of Political Science* 40:717–39.

1999a. "Plato's Eleatic and Athenian Sciences of Politics." *Review of Politics* 61:57–84.

1999b. "Weeds: Cultivating the Imagination in Medieval Arabic Political Philosophy." *Journal of the History of Ideas* 60:399–416.

1999c. "The Death of Tragedy: Genre, Politics, and the Myth of Lucretia." Available at http://www.geocities.com/mskochin

2002. "Morality, Nature, and Esotericism in Leo Strauss's *Persecution and the Art of Writing*." *Review of Politics* 64.

n.d. "Individual Narrative and Political Character." *Review of Metaphysics*.

Kochin, Michael S. and Philippakis, Katherine A. 2000. "The Richardsonian Republic." Delivered at the annual meeting of the American Political Science Association. Available at http://www.geocities.com/mskochin

Kraut, Richard. 1973. "Egoism, Love, and Political Office in Plato." *Philosophical Review* 82:330–44.

Kundera, Milan. 1997. *Slowness*, tr. Linda Asher. New York: HarperCollins.

Lacey, W. K. 1968. *The Family in Classical Greece*. Ithaca: Cornell University Press.

Laks, André. 2000. "The *Laws*." In *The Cambridge History of Greek and Roman Political Thought*, ed. Christopher Rowe and Malcom Schofield. Cambridge: Cambridge University Press.

Lange, Lynda. 1979. "The Function of Equal Education in Plato's *Republic* and *Laws*." In *The Sexism of Social and Political Theory: Women and Reproduction from Plato to Nietzsche*, ed. Lorenne M. G. Clark and Lynda Lange. Toronto: University of Toronto Press.

Latour, Bruno. 1999. *Pandora's Hope: Essays on the Reality of Science Studies*. Cambridge: Harvard University Press.

Le Dœuff, Michèle. 1989. "Long Hair, Short Ideas." In *The Philosophical Imaginary*, tr. Colin Gordon. London: Athlone Press.

—— 1991. *Hipparchia's Choice*, tr. Trista Selous. Oxford: Basil Blackwell.

Lear, Jonathan. 1992. "Inside and Outside the Republic." *Phronesis* 37:184–215.

—— 1994. "Plato's Politics of Narcissism." In *Virtue, Love and the Dialogue Form: Essays in Memory of Gregory Vlastos*, ed. Terence Irwin and Martha C. Nussbaum. Edmonton; Alberta, Canada: Academic Printing and Publishing.

Lesser, Harry. 1979. "Plato's Feminism." *Philosophy* 54:113–17.

Levin, Susan B. 1996. "Women's Nature and Role in the Ideal *Polis*." In *Feminism and Ancient Philosophy*, ed. Julie K. Ward. New York and London: Routledge.

Lewis, V. Bradley. 1994. "The Archaeology of the Theological-Political Problem in Plato's *Laws*." Delivered at the annual meeting of the Midwest Political Science Association.

—— 1998. "The Nocturnal Council and Platonic Political Philosophy." *History of Political Thought* 19:1–20.

Libes, Yosef G., tr. 1974. *The Writings of Plato* [in Hebrew]. 5 vols. Tel Aviv: Schocken.

Lloyd-Jones, Hugh. 1983. *The Justice of Zeus*, Second Edition. Berkeley and Los Angeles: University of California Press.

Long, A. A. 1970. "Morals and Values in Homer." *Journal of the Hellenic Society* 90:121–39.

Loraux, Nicole. 1986. *The Invention of Athens: The Funeral Oration in the Classical City*, tr. Alan Sheridan. Cambridge, Massachusetts: Harvard University Press.

—— 1987. *Tragic Ways of Killing a Woman*, tr. Anthony Forster. Cambridge, Massachusetts: Harvard University Press.

—— 1993. *The Children of Athena: Athenian Ideas about Citizenship and the Division between the Sexes*, tr. Caroline Levine. Princeton: Princeton University Press.

—— 1998. *Mothers in Mourning*, tr. Corinne Pache. Ithaca: Cornell University Press.

Lucas, John. 1990. "Plato's Philosophy of Sex." In *'Owls to Athens': Essays on Classical Subjects Presented to Sir Kenneth Dover*, ed. E. M. Craik. Oxford: Oxford University Press.

MacKinnon, Catherine A. 1989. *Toward a Feminist Theory of the State.* Cambridge, Massachusetts: Harvard University Press.

——— 1993. *Only Words.* Cambridge, Massachusetts: Harvard University Press.

Masters, Roger D. 1998. "Machiavelli's Sexuality: 'Love Be My Guide, My Leader'." Presented at the annual meeting of the American Political Science Association.

Mayhew, Robert. 1996. "Aristotle's Criticism of Plato's Communism of Women and Children." *Apeiron* 29:231–48.

——— 1997. *Aristotle's Criticism of Plato's* Republic. Lanham, Maryland: Rowman and Littlefield.

McGlew, James F. 1993. *Tyranny and Political Culture in Ancient Greece.* Ithaca: Cornell University Press.

Meier, Christian. 1990. *The Greek Discovery of Politics.* Cambridge, Massachusetts: Harvard University Press.

Mill, John Stuart. 1988. *The Subjection of Women*, ed. Susan Moller Okin. Indianapolis: Hackett.

Moline, Jon. 1978. "Plato on the Complexity of the Psyche." *Archive für Geschichte der Philosophie* 60:1–26.

——— 1981. *Plato's Theory of Understanding.* Madison: University of Wisconsin Press.

Monoson, S. Sarah. 2000. *Plato's Democratic Entanglements: Athenian Politics and the Practice of Philosophy.* Princeton: Princeton University Press.

Moore, Barrington, Jr. 1984. *Privacy: Studies in Social and Cultural History.* Armonk, New York: M. E. Sharpe.

Morgan, Michael L. 1990. *Platonic Piety: Philosophy and Ritual in Fourth-Century Athens.* New Haven: Yale University Press.

Morrow, Glen R. [1960] 1993. *Plato's Cretan City: A Historical Interpretation of the Laws.* With a New Foreword by Charles H. Kahn. Princeton: Princeton University Press.

Mouffe, Chantal. 1993. *The Return of the Political.* London: Verso.

Murphy, N. R. 1967. *The Intepretation of Plato's Republic.* Oxford: Oxford University Press.

Ng, Yew-Kwang. 1977. "Towards a Theory of Third-Best." *Public Finance/ Finances Publiques* 32:1–15.

Nichols, Mary P. 1983. Review of Okin, *Women in Western Political Thought. Political Science Reviewer* 13:241–60.

——— 1987. *Socrates and the Political Community: An Ancient Debate.* Albany: SUNY Press.

Nightingale, Andrea. 1993. "Writing/Reading a Sacred Text: A Literary Interpretation of Plato's *Laws*." *Classical Philology* 88:279–300.

——— 1995. *Genres in Dialogue: Plato and the Construct of Philosophy.* Cambridge: Cambridge University Press.

North, Helen. 1966. *Sophrosyne: Self Knowledge and Self-Restraint in Greek Literature. Cornell Studies in Classical Philology* 35. Ithaca: Cornell University Press.

Nussbaum, Martha Craven. 1980. "Shame, Separateness, and Political Unity: Aristotle's Criticism of Plato." In *Essays in Aristotle's Ethics*, ed. A. Oksenberg-Rorty. Berkeley: University of California Press.

1986. *The Fragility of Goodness: Luck and Ethics in Greek Tragedy and Philosophy*. Cambridge: Cambridge University Press.

1994. "Platonic Love and Colorado Law: The Relevance of Ancient Greek Norms to Modern Sexual Controversies." *Virginia Law Review* 80:1515–1651.

Ober, Josiah. 1989. *Mass and Elite in Democratic Athens: Rhetoric, Ideology and the Power of the People*. Princeton: Princeton University Press.

1996. *The Athenian Revolution: Essays on Ancient Greek Democracy and Political Theory*. Princeton: Princeton University Press.

1999. *Political Dissent in Democratic Athens: Intellectual Critics of Popular Rule*. Princeton: Princeton University Press.

O'Brien, Mary. 1981. *The Politics of Reproduction*. Boston, London, and Henley: Routledge & Kegan Paul.

O'Donnell, J. J. 1991. Review of Thomas Cole, *The Origins of Rhetoric in Ancient Greece*. *Bryn Mawr Classical Review* 2.2.5. Available at http://ccat.sas.upenn.edu/bmcr/1991/02.02.05.html

Okin, Susan Moller. 1982. "Philosopher Queens and Private Wives: Plato on Women and the Family." In *The Family in Political Thought*, ed. Jean Bethke Elshtain. Amherst: University of Massachusetts Press.

1989. *Justice, Gender and the Family*. New York: Basic Books.

[1979] 1992. *Women in Western Political Thought*. With a new Afterword. Princeton: Princeton University Press.

Ophir, Adi. 1991. *Plato's Invisible Cities: Discourse and Power in The Republic*. Savage, Maryland: Barnes & Noble.

Osborne, Martha Lee. 1975. "Plato's Unchanging View of Women: A Denial That Anatomy Spells Destiny." *Philosophical Forum* 6:447–52.

1978. "Plato's Feminism." Unpublished Ph.D. dissertation, University of Tennessee, Knoxville.

Ostwald, Martin. 1977. "Plato on Law and Nature." In *Interpretations of Plato: A Swarthmore Symposium*, ed. Helen North. *Memnosyne Supplementum* 50:41–63.

Pangle, Thomas L. 1976. "The Political Psychology of Religion in Plato's *Laws*." *American Political Science Review* 70:1059–77.

tr. 1980. *The Laws of Plato*. New York: Basic Books.

1998. "Justice Among Nations in Platonic and Aristotelian Political Philosophy." *American Journal of Political Science* 42:377–97.

Pangle, Thomas L., and Peter Ahrensdorf. 1999. *Justice Among Nations: On the Moral Basis of Power and Peace*. Lawrence: University Press of Kansas.

Pateman, Carole. 1989. "Feminism and Democracy." In *The Disorder of Women: Democracy, Feminism, and Political Theory*. Cambridge: Polity Press.

Patterson, Cynthia. 1986. "*Hai Attikai*: The Other Athenians." *Helios* 13:49–67.

Perelman, C. and L. Olbrechts-Tyteca. 1969. *The New Rhetoric: A Treatise on Argumentation*, tr. John Wilkinson and Purcell Weaver. Notre Dame: University of Notre Dame Press.

Peters, James Robert. 1989. "Reason and Passion in Plato's *Republic.*" *Ancient Philosophy* 9:173–87.

Pierce, Christine. 1973. "Equality: Republic V." *Monist* 57:1–11.

Pitkin, Hanna Fenichel. 1981. "Justice: On Relating Private and Public." *Political Theory* 9:327–52.

    1998. *The Attack of the Blob: Hannah Arendt's Concept of the Social.* Chicago: University of Chicago Press.

Planinc, Zdravko. 1991. *Plato's Political Philosophy: Prudence in the Republic and the Laws.* Columbia and London: University of Missouri Press.

Pomeroy, Sarah. 1974. "Feminism in Book V of Plato's *Republic.*" *Apeiron* 8:33–5.

    1978. "Plato and the Female Physician (*Republic* 454d2)." *American Journal of Philology* 99:496–500.

Popper, Karl. 1963. *The Open Society and Its Enemies,* fourth edition. 2 vols. New York: Harper and Row.

Powell, Anton. 1994. "Plato and Sparta: Modes of Rule and of Non-rational Persuasion in Plato's *Laws.*" In *The Shadow of Sparta,* ed. Anton Powell and Stephen Hodkinson. London: Routledge.

Price, A. W. 1986. *Love and Friendship in Plato and Aristotle.* Oxford: Clarendon Press.

Pringle, Rosemary and Sophie Watson. 1992. "Women's Interests and the Post-Structuralist State." In *Destabilizing Theory: Contemporary Feminist Debates,* ed. Michèle Barrett and Anne Phillips. Cambridge: Polity Press.

Pritchett, W. Kendrick. 1971–91. *The Greek State at War.* Parts I–V. Berkeley and Los Angeles: University of California Press.

Przeworski, Adam. 1990. "Transitions and Reforms: East and South." Chapter 3, "Capitalism and Socialism." Unpublished manuscript.

Raaflaub, Kurt. 1994. "Democracy, Power, and Imperialism in Fifth-Century Athens." In *Athenian Political Thought and the Reconstruction of American Democracy,* ed. J. Peter Euben, John R. Wallach, and Josiah Ober. Ithaca: Cornell University Press.

Rahe, Paul A. 1992. *Republics Ancient and Modern: Classical Republicanism and the American Revolution.* Chapel Hill: University of North Carolina Press.

Rankin, H. D. 1964. *Plato and the Individual.* New York: Barnes & Noble.

Rawls, John. 1971. *A Theory of Justice.* Cambridge: Harvard University Press.

    1993. *Political Liberalism.* New York: Columbia University Press.

Redfield, James. 1977–8. "The Women of Sparta." *Classical Journal* 73:146–61.

Reeve, C. D. C. 1988. *Philosopher-Kings: The Argument of Plato's Republic.* Princeton: Princeton University Press.

Rich, Adrienne. 1980. "Compulsory Heterosexuality and Lesbian Existence." *Signs* 5:631–60.

Rist, John. 1982. *Human Value: A Study in Ancient Philosophical Ethics.* Leiden: E. J. Brill.

    1997. "Plato and Professor Nussbaum on Acts 'Contrary to Nature.'" In *Studies in Plato and the Platonic Tradition,* ed. Mark Joyal. Aldershot: Ashgate.

Robinson, T. M. 1970. *Plato's Psychology*. Toronto: University of Toronto Press.

Rocke, Michael. 1996 *Forbidden Friendships*. Oxford: Oxford University Press.

Rogers, Joseph Michael. 1991. "The Coherence of Ethical and Political Thought in the *Laws* and the *Republic*." Unpublished Ph.D. dissertation, University of Texas at Austin.

Rosen, Stanley. 1988. "The Role of Eros in Plato's *Republic*." In *The Quarrel Between Philosophy and Poetry: Studies in Ancient Thought*. New York and London: Routledge.

Rosenstock, Bruce. 1994. "Athena's Cloak: Plato's Critique of the Democratic City in the *Republic*." *Political Theory* 22:363–90.

Rousseau, Jean Jacques. 1979. *Emile*, tr. Allan Bloom. New York: Basic Books.
    1997. *Julie, or the New Heloise*, tr. Philip Stewart and Jean Vaché. Hanover, New Hampshire: University Press of New England.

Rutherford, R. B. 1995. *The Art of Plato*. London: Duckworth.

Sachs, David. 1963. "A Fallacy in Plato's *Republic*." *Philosophical Review* 72:141–58.

Salkever, Stephen. 1986. "Women, Soldiers, Citizens: Plato and Aristotle on the Politics of Virility." *Polity* 19:232–53.
    1990. *Finding the Mean: Theory and Practice in Aristotelian Political Philosophy*. Princeton: Princeton University Press.

Sartre, Jean-Paul. 1956. *Being and Nothingness*, tr. Hazel E. Barnes. New York: Philosophical Library.

Saunders, Trevor J. 1962. "The Structure of the Soul and the State in Plato's *Laws*." *Eranos* 60:37–55.
    1991. *Plato's Penal Code: Tradition, Controversy, and Reform in Greek Penology*. Oxford: Oxford University Press.
    1992. "Plato's Later Political Thought." In *The Cambridge Companion to Plato*, ed. Richard Kraut. Cambridge: Cambridge University Press.
    1995. "Plato on Women in the *Laws*." In *The Greek World*, ed. A. Powell. London: Routledge.

Saxonhouse, Arlene W. 1976. "The Philosopher and the Female in the Political Thought of Plato." *Political Theory* 4:195–212.
    1985. *Women in the History of Political Thought: Ancient Greece to Machiavelli*. New York: Praeger.
    1992. *Fear of Diversity: The Birth of Political Science in Ancient Greek Thought*. Chicago and London: University of Chicago Press.
    1996. "Diversity and Ancient Democracy: A Response to Schwartz." *Political Theory* 24:321–5

Schaps, David. 1977. "The Woman Least Mentioned: Etiquette and Women's Names." *Classical Quarterly*, n.s., 27:323–30.

Schmid, Walter T. 1992. *On Manly Courage: A Study of Plato's Laches*. Carbondale and Edwardsville: Southern Illinois University Press.

Schofield, Malcom. 2000. "Approaching the *Republic*." In *The Cambridge History of Greek and Roman Political Thought*, ed. Christopher Rowe and Malcom Schofield. Cambridge: Cambridge University Press.

Schreiber, Scott G. 1996. Review of Tuana, ed., *Feminist Interpretations of Plato*. *Ancient Philosophy* 16:492–5.

Scolnicov, Samuel. 1988. *Plato's Metaphysics of Education*. London and New York: Routledge.

Sealey, Raphael. 1990. *Women and Law in Classical Greece*. Chapel Hill: University of North Carolina Press.

Segal, Charles. 1978. "The Myth Was Saved: Reflections on Homer and the Mythology of Plato's *Republic*." *Hermes* 108:315–36.

Shapiro, H. A. 1992. "Eros in Love: Pederasty and Pornography in Greece." In *Pornography and Representation in Greece and Rome*, ed. Amy Richlin. Oxford: Oxford University Press.

Shklar, Judith. 1990. *The Faces of Injustice*. New Haven and London: Yale University Press.

Silverthorne, M. J. 1973. "Militarism in the *Laws*? (*Laws* 942a5–943a3)." *Symbolae Osloenses* 49:29–38.

Smith, Janet Farrell. 1983. "Plato, Irony, and Equality." *Women's Studies International Forum* 6:597–607.

Spelman, Elizabeth V. 1988. *Inessential Woman: Problems of Exclusion in Feminist Thought*. Boston: Beacon Press.

——— 1997. "Good Grief, It's Plato." In *Feminists Rethink the Self*, ed. Diana Tietjens Meyers. Boulder: Westview.

Stalley, R. F. 1983. *An Introduction to Plato's Laws*. Oxford: Basil Blackwell.

Ste. Croix, G. E. M. 1981. *The Class Struggle in the Ancient Greek World from the Archaic Age to the Arab Conquests*. Ithaca: Cornell University Press.

Steinberger, Peter J. 1989. "Ruling: Guardians and Philosopher Kings." *American Political Science Review* 83:1207–25.

——— 1996. "Who Is Cephalus?" *Political Theory* 24:172–99.

Strauss, Barry. 1993. *Fathers and Sons in Athens: Ideology and Society in the Era of the Peloponnesian War*. Princeton: Princeton University Press.

——— 1994. "The Melting Pot, the Mosaic, and the Agora." In *Athenian Political Thought and the Reconstruction of American Democracy*, ed. J. Peter Euben, John R. Wallach, and Josiah Ober. Ithaca: Cornell University Press.

Strauss, Leo. 1953. *Natural Right and History*. Chicago: University of Chicago Press.

——— 1975. *The Argument and the Action of Plato's Laws*. Chicago: University of Chicago Press.

——— 1978. *The City and Man*. Chicago: Rand McNally, 1964. Reprint, Chicago: University of Chicago Press.

Sullivan, Andrew. 1995. *Virtually Normal: An Argument About Homosexuality*. New York: Random House.

——— ed. 1997. *Same-Sex Marriage: Pro and Con: A Reader*. New York: Random House.

——— 1999. *Love Undetectable: Note on Friendship, Sex, and Survival*. New York: Vintage Books.

Tarcov, Nathan. 1985. "American Constitutionalism and Individual Rights." In *How Does the Constitution Secure Rights?*, ed. Robert A. Goldwin and William A. Schambra. Washington, D.C.: American Enterprise Institute for Public Policy Research.

Tatum, James. 1989. *Xenophon's Imperial Fiction: On the Education of Cyrus.* Princeton: Princeton University Press.

Taylor, A. E., tr. 1960. *Plato: The Laws.* London: J. M. Dent.

Thornton, Merle. 1986. "Sex Equality Is Not Enough for Feminism." In *Feminist Challenges: Social and Political Theory*, ed. Carole Pateman and Elizabeth Gross. Boston: Northeastern University Press.

Tovey, Barbara and George Tovey. 1974. "Women's Philosophical Friends and Enemies." *Social Science Quarterly* 55:586–604.

Trebilcot, Joyce. 1975. "Sex Roles: The Argument from Nature." *Ethics* 85:249–55.

Tuana, Nancy. 1992. *Woman and the History of Philosophy.* New York: Paragon.

    ed. 1994. *Feminist Interpretations of Plato.* University Park: Pennsylvania State University Press.

Vernant, Jean Pierre. 1983. *Myth and Thought among the Greeks.* London: Routledge and Kegan Paul.

Vickers, Brian. 1988. *In Defence of Rhetoric.* Oxford: Oxford University Press.

Vidal-Naquet, Pierre. 1986. *The Black Hunter: Forms of Thought and Forms of Society in the Greek World*, tr. Andrew Szegedy-Maszak. Baltimore and London: Johns Hopkins University Press.

Vlastos, Gregory. 1977. "The Theory of Social Justice in the *Polis* in Plato's *Republic*." In *Interpretations of Plato: A Swarthmore Symposium*, ed. Helen North (*Memnosyne Supplementum* 50:1–40). Also in Gregory Vlastos, *Studies in Greek Philosophy*, vol. II, ed. Daniel W. Graham (Princeton: Princeton University Press, 1995), 69–103.

    1978. "The Rights of Persons in Plato's Conception of the Foundations of Justice." In *The Foundations of Ethics and Its Relationship to Science*, vol. III, *Morals, Science, and Society*, ed. H. Tristram Engelhardt and Daniel Callahan. Hastings on Hudson, New York: Hastings Center. Also in Gregory Vlastos, *Studies in Greek Philosophy*, vol. II, ed. Daniel W. Graham (Princeton: Princeton University Press, 1995), 104–25.

    1981. *Platonic Studies.* Second Edition. Princeton: Princeton University Press.

    1989. "Was Plato a Feminist?" *Times Literary Supplement* 4485 (March 17–23):276, 288–9. Also in Gregory Vlastos, *Studies in Greek Philosophy*, vol. II, ed. Daniel W. Graham (Princeton: Princeton University Press, 1995), 133–43.

Voegelin, Eric. 1957. *Order and History.* Vol. III, *Plato and Aristotle.* Baton Rouge: Louisiana State University Press.

Wallach, John R. 1997. "Plato's Socratic Problem, and Ours." *History of Political Thought* 18:377–98.

Wardy, Robert. 1996. *The Birth of Rhetoric: Gorgias, Plato, and their Successors.* London and New York: Routledge.

Wender, Dorothy. 1973. "Plato: Misogynist, Paedophile, Feminist." *Arethusa* 6:75–90.

Wersinger, Anne Gabrièle. 2001. "Musique et philosophie dans les *Lois* de Platon." Paper presented at the Sixth Symposium Platonicum, "Plato's *Laws*," Jerusalem, Israel.

Wheeler, Everett L. 1991. "The General as Hoplite." In *Hoplites: The Classical Greek Battle Experience*, ed. Victor Davis Hanson. London: Routledge.

Williams, Bernard. 1973. "The Analogy of City and Soul in Plato's *Republic*." In *Exegesis and Argument: Studies in Greek Philosophy Presented to Gregory Vlastos*, ed. E. N. Lee, A. P. D. Mourelatos, and R. M. Rorty. Assen, the Netherlands: Van Gorcum.

———. 1993. *Shame and Necessity*. Berkeley and Los Angeles: University of California Press.

Winkler, John J. 1990. *The Constraints of Desire: The Anthropology of Sex and Gender in Ancient Greece*. New York and London: Routledge.

Wolin, Sheldon. 1960. *Politics and Vision: Continuity and Innovation in Western Political Thought*. Boston: Little, Brown.

Yack, Bernard. 1993. *The Problems of a Political Animal: Community, Justice, and Conflict in Aristotelian Political Thought*. Berkeley and Los Angeles: University of California Press.

Young-Bruehl, Elisabeth. 1982. *Hannah Arendt: For Love of the World*. New Haven: Yale University Press.

Yunis, Harvey. 1996. *Taming Democracy: Models of Political Rhetoric in Classical Athens*. Ithaca: Cornell University Press.

Zeitlin, Froma I. 1982. "Cultic Models of the Female: Rites of Dionysus and Demeter." *Arethusa* 15:129–57.

Index

Achilles, 39, 41, 51–2, 57, 70

Adeimantus, 27, 37n2, 41, 46–7, 49, 87; realism of, 55–7; and spirited desires, 50n31

Adkins, Arthur, 6, 21n33, 91n7

adultery, 104, 104n34, 107–8n41

age (*see also* youth), 87, 124, 127

akrasia (lack of self-control), 33

Alcibiades, 127n37

andreia (manliness), 3, 19, 24, 27, 117–18; in music for men, 95; and pederasty, 93, 113; and right opinion, 52, 117–18; as standard for women in Magnesia, 95, 116–17; *see also aretē*

Annas, Julia, 61

appearance, 53, 79, 91n7

appetites; appetitive part of the soul, 32–4, 33–4n20; in city of sows, 48; rule of, in oligarchy, 78

Arendt, Hannah, 13, 13n11

aretē (virtue), 19; *anthropinē aretē* (human excellence), 24, 117, 130

aristocracy, 20; as name for best city, 76; and noble lie, 54

assembly, women in Magnesian, 97n17

Athena, 89, 130

auditors, 96

autocthony, 54, 54n46

Bachofen, Johann Jakob, 105

Bacon, Francis, 17

barbarians, 70n24

Benardete, Seth, 63n9, 109n48

Bloom, Allan, 37n1, 40n9, 63n9, 81–2

Bobonich, Christopher, 30n10

body, 71; and self, 72, 74

Brown, Wendy, 37n2, 82n44

Callicles, 23–4, 57, 58

cave, image of the, 27–8

Cephalus, 41, 42–3, 85n49

character, 14, 133

civil society, 37n1; virtues in, 133

Clark, Randall, 103n31

class (*see also* aristocracy, democracy, oligarchy), 20, 48, 97n17; in *Laws*, 87; and noble lie, 54; and plurality, 56, 71, 87

Cocks, Joan, 62n7

Cole, Thomas, 16n19

common meals, 107–8, 107n41, 111

communism, 37, 101–3; and economic classes, 65n15; and equality, 62–4; of the family, 62–6, 83; and justice, 101; and law, 106n37; Magnesia imitates, 108; and nature, 83; justified by the noble lie, 54; and philosophy, 122n20; of property, 54, 74–6, 105–6n36; and self, 72–6; Soviet, 105n36; and soul–city analogy, 75–6; and unity, 64–6

consent, 110, 129–30, 134–5

151

Constant, Benjamin, 133
council, women in Magnesian, 97n17
Craig, Leon, 34n20, 70n24, 82n44
Crete, 88, 91; *see also* Dorian cities, Sparta
Cronus, 51; age of, 67n20
Crossman, Richard, 31n12

Davidson, James, 50n30
Dawson, Doyne, 105n36
death, 43
democracy, 54, 78, 121; equality of desires in, 78; freedom to be virtuous in, 91, 125; and tyranny, 79, 79n37
Derrida, Jacques, 30n11
desires (*epithumiai*), 39, 41, 42; division of the soul as partition of the desires, 31–4; equality of in democracy, 78; second-order, 34n20; *see also* appetites, pleasure, reason, soul, *thumos*
dikaiosunē, *see* justice
divorce, *see* marriage
Dodds, E. R., 91n7
Dorian cities, 91–5, 96; education in, 108n45; masculinity in, 88–90; *sōphrosunē* neglected in, 89, 91; spiritedness of, 93; women in, 91; *see also* Crete, pederasty, Sparta
Dworkin, Andrea, 28

education, control by city, 108; gymnastics, 51, 97–8, 116; honors as, 69, 69n22–3; military, 66–7, 68–9, 98–9; music, 51, 83, 116, 117; poets, as teachers of injustice and vice, 46, 51–2; war as, 69–71; *see also* law, myth, opinion
Elshtain, Jean Bethke, 40n9
epithumia (desires), *see* desires
equality, 60–4, 83, 93, 102; and communism, 62–4; and democracy, 78; and justice, 62; in *Laws*, 94–5; and masculinity, 93–5; and nature, 85; and noble lie, 54

Er, myth of, 80–1
eros, 42–3, 63, 82; and common meals, 107–8n41; and compulsory heterosexuality, 83n47; and paternity, 104–5; regulation of, 52–3, 53n42, 68–9, 92–3, 96, 97n18, 99n26, 113; and war, 68–9; *see also* family, homoeroticism, marriage, pederasty

family, 73–4, 87; communism of, 62–6, 74, 75, 84–6; and inheritance, 109–10; justice within, 73n30; and nature, 83–6; at origins of city in *Laws*, 102; and property, 105, 105–6n36; weakened in Magnesia, 107–9; *see also* communism, friendship, *kurios*, *oikos*, property
fatherhood, *see* paternity
femininity, 21
feminism, 17–18n21, 37n1; compulsory heterosexuality, 83n47; "femocrats" (Australian feminist bureaucrats), 10n5; and self-government, 134
Ferrari, G. R. F., 32n16
Filmer, Robert, 4n3
Fish, Stanley, 11n6
Forde, Steven, 60n2
Foucault, Michel, 114–15
Frankfurt, Harry, 34n20
Freud, Sigmund, 33n20
friendship (*philia*); contrasted with justice and virtue, 43–4, 47–8, 51, 51n35, 71–2, 73–4, 83–6; in Magnesia, 124–6, 124n26; *see also* family

gender difference, 62n7; denial by Plato, 114; in Magnesia, 95–100; in music, 95; Socrates' appeal to, 40
gender-inclusive language, 18, 18n22; *see also* "we"

gender roles, 89; in Magnesia, 99–100, 118–21

Glaucon, 87; his attack on justice, 15, 27, 31, 35, 39, 41, 58; and city of sows, 49–50; and Gyges, 45–6; and life of Guardians as described in *Republic* II–IV, 50, 59, 62; purge of, 59, 59n56

gods, see *hosiotēs*

Goldhill, Simon, 92–3n10

grief, as effeminate, 39n8; to be purged from education of guardians, 51–2

Grube, G. M. A., 53n42

Guardians of the Laws, 96

Gyges, ring of, 45–6, 79

gymnastics, *see* education

Habermas, Jürgen, 12

happiness, 15n16, 45n25, 55, 133

Harris, Edward, 104n34

Hegel, G. W. F., 25n1

Heidegger, Martin, 104n34

Hobbes, Thomas, 35n23, 133n7

Hobbs, Angela, 37n2, 39n6

homoeroticism (*see also* pederasty); female, 113; and marriage, 132; and nature, 92–3, 92n9, 92–3n10

hooks, bell, 11n7

hoplites, 20n32

hosiotēs (piety), 29n9, 42–3, 49n29; as feminine, 119–21; and justice, 46; and providence, 119; Socratic, 51n34, 51n35; and war, 71

Houellebecq, Michel, 133n7

hunting, *see* pederasty

impiety; as denial of providence, 119; and masculinity, 118–20

inheritance, *see* family, marriage, property

intention (*boulēsis*), 33n20

Irigaray, Luce, 25n1, 40n9

Israel, collective settlements in, 105n36

justice (*dikaiosunē*), 10n4, 34–6, 100–2, 117–18; defense of, 131–3; just speech, 15; masculinity and, 35–6, 46; not present in city of sows, 49, 49n27; public-private distinction and, 101–2; self-interest and, 34–6; Socratic, vs. ordinary, 56, 85n49; in the soul, 75; unjust speech, 14, 15; war and, 55–7, 71–2; *see also* Sachs fallacy

Kant, Immanuel, 8–11, 25n1, 85n49

Kleinias, 87, 124n26

Klosko, George, 126n32

Kraut, Richard, 73–4

Kundera, Milan, 133n7

kurios, 4, 110–11

Laks, André, 106n37, 126n32

law, 4–5, 6, 27–31, 109–11; and communism, 106n37; legislation analogized to medicine, 110; and philosophy, 121; preludes to laws, 15–16, 95–6; and public-private distinction, 106–11, 116, 122–3; as second-best rule of general principles, 109–11, 121, 123–5; and spiritedness, 93, 112, 116, 124–6; as teacher of vice, 35, 80, 113, 116–18, 130; as teacher of virtue, 89; *see also* education, opinion, property, public-private distinction

Lear, Jonathan, 29n8

legislation, *see* law

Leontius, 33; *see also thumos*

Levin, Susan, 41n13

Lewis, V. Bradley, 126n32

Livy, 123n24

Lucretia, 104n34

Locke, John, 4n3, 133n7

Loraux, Nicole, 24n46

MacKinnon, Catherine, 17–18n21, 83n47

Index Locorum